SHOW ME
........YOUR WORDS........

Connie Haham grew up in Texas, lived and studied in Spain and then made her home in France, where she began teaching English as a foreign language. She revelled in Paris' rich film culture, saw films from around the world and eventually researched Hindi cinema. Her first book, *Enchantment of the Mind: Manmohan Desai's Films*, was published in 2006. She now divides her time between Paris and Austin, where she has studied Urdu, Hindi and sociolinguistics at The University of Texas.

SHOW ME YOUR WORDS
THE POWER OF LANGUAGE IN BOLLYWOOD
CONNIE HAHAM

RUPA

Published by
Rupa Publications India Pvt. Ltd 2016
7/16, Ansari Road, Daryaganj
New Delhi 110002

Sales centres:
Allahabad Bengaluru Chennai
Hyderabad Jaipur Kathmandu
Kolkata Mumbai

Copyright © Connie Haham 2016
Copyright for the photographs and illustrations vest
with the respective copyright holders.

The views and opinions expressed in this book are the author's own and the facts are as reported by her which have been verified to the extent possible, and the publishers are not in any way liable for the same.

All rights reserved.
No part of this publication may be reproduced, transmitted,
or stored in a retrieval system, in any form or by any means,
electronic, mechanical, photocopying, recording or otherwise,
without the prior permission of the publisher.

ISBN: 978-81-291-3477-6

First impression 2016

10 9 8 7 6 5 4 3 2 1

Printed by Replika Press Pvt. Ltd., India

This book is sold subject to the condition that it shall not,
by way of trade or otherwise, be lent, resold, hired out, or otherwise circulated,
without the publisher's prior consent, in any form of binding or cover
other than that in which it is published.

*In grateful memory of my late parents,
Joe Comingore and Betty Ann Terry Comingore.*

CONTENTS

Preface ix
A Note on the Transliteration xvii

Names	1
I've Got a Story to Tell	13
It's in the Writing	28
The Weight of Words	46
Kader Khan: An Urduwaala from Kamathipura, Master of the Clap-Clap Line	86
The Magic of the Human Voice	99
Multilingualism Abounds	109
Poetry	156
The Presence of Urdu	167
Generations: A Father-Son Thing	189
The Place of English in Hindi Cinema	204
Squiggles	240
Bridges	254
In the Learning Zone	277
A Language Looking for its Way	289
Interview Dates	303
Bibliography	305
Acknowledgements	311

PREFACE

'Lafzon ko ahtiyaat se barta kijiye. In mein jaan hoti hai.
(Use words carefully. Because they're living beings.)

—Firaq Gorakhpuri, giving advice to screenwriter and
playwright Javed Siddiqi many years ago
at a mushaaira in Lucknow[1]

I'VE ALWAYS loved the movies. Some of my best childhood memories are of leisurely afternoons spent watching double features with friends in a small-town Texas movie theatre, a palace for me at age seven, but probably rather tawdry, even in its heyday. The films ran the gamut of Hollywood offerings of the 1950s—crime and war stories, musicals, westerns, slapstick comedies. The entertaining worlds that crossed the portal of the cinema screen totally captivated me. With the end of childhood came a dawning awareness that cinema might deserve analysis, not just reaction. However, it was only when I moved to France as a young adult that film-going became an intellectual exercise. Cinema in France, after all, is referred to not as 'entertainment'—such a crass American notion in the eyes of the French intelligentsia—but as 'le septième art', or the seventh art. I caught the wave of the New Wave and revelled in the wide selection of films which Paris offered. The elegant theory behind the art of film criticism was as much a part of Parisian life in the '70s as baguettes and red wine. Deep inside, though, the movie-going child, the one who had danced for a week after watching *Seven Brides for Seven Brothers* (1954),

---

[1]From an interview with Javed Siddiqi, Bombay, April 2006.

remained alive and well, if dormant. That fun-loving child was awakened most unexpectedly in 1979. A chance encounter with Hindi cinema in Paris, more precisely with *Amar Akbar Anthony*,[2] soon had me dancing again.

I really had no intention of studying Hindi. Little by little, though, I found the voices I was hearing too beautiful to ignore. I wanted to understand the meaning behind those sounds. I wanted to be able to pronounce Sahir Ludhianvi's words as sung by Lata Mangeshkar or Kishore Kumar, and what exactly, I wondered, were Gabbar Singh in *Sholay* (1975) and Vijay Kumar in *Trishul* (1978) saying? Subtitles proved most inadequate. They allowed a superficial understanding of the film stories, all the while hinting teasingly at cultural worlds carried within the words. What was this language? Why was the title written in three scripts? Google did not yet exist; finding answers to such simple questions took time. Urdu, I learned, was written right to left, but what about Hindi, listed as the official language on the censor board's title page? Indo-European root words leapt out—main, tu, nahin, (I you, no). At the same time, a Tunisian student and fellow fan told me he recognized many words from Arabic.

Points on the globe where very different cultures have met, overlapped, collided and coalesced have always piqued my curiosity. Spain attracted me enough that I lived there for over a year, in part because of the three monotheistic religions-cum-cultures, which centuries ago blended and lent each other words, stories, musical forms, architecture and ideas. In Spain that vivid past left an imprint on the landscape and produced nuggets of shared memory, the substance of which was stored away like half-forgotten heirlooms in the nation's collective imagination. Years later I was reminded of the many cultures mostly buried in Spain's past when I heard Lata Mangeshkar sing '*Maano to*

---

[2]Directed by Manmohan Desai, 1977.

main Ganga ma hoon, na maano to behta paani[3] at the beginning of Sultan Amhad's *Ganga Ki Saugand* (1978) as the camera takes us down the Ganga[4], past temples, churches and mosques, all united by the river. In India then, or at least in the movie version of India to which I had access, the linking of multiple cultures seemed to be a present—not past—reality. I felt drawn towards the language that carried this richly diverse culture.

Out of curiosity, I thumbed through R.S. McGregor's *Outline of Hindi Grammar* and soon found myself doing exercises to learn the basics of the language structure, script and vocabulary. Dabbling developed into a passion. I found myself immersed in Platts' *A Dictionary of Urdu, Classical Hindi, and English*. How, I wondered, could one language have so many terms for the concept of longing? The notation on the origins of the words—Sanskrit, Persian, Arabic—was a rich resource and gave me a sense of the logic of this blended language. I learned to decipher the publicity brochures that accompanied the fraying film prints that arrived in Paris via Cairo, various parts of Africa and the Middle East. Those brochures, which used English, Hindi and Urdu, provided both motivation and a means for further learning. Listening, though, remained my preferred entry point into the language. I played film dialogues on audiocassettes hundreds of times. This technique, I later learned, was recommended by language acquisition specialist Steven Krashen, who calls it 'narrow listening'. 'In-depth listening' would probably describe my approach more aptly as I attempted to puzzle out sounds, words and grammar, all the while interacting emotionally with the characters whose voices became such a part of my life. Of all the films I have listened to intensively, *Shakti* (1982), directed by Ramesh Sippy and written by Salim-Javed, has held me most firmly in its aural grip. There is the sonority of the spoken word, as when Dilip Kumar pronounces

---

[3]Lyrics by Anjaan.
[4]River Ganga, often translated as the Ganges.

'yaqinan' (certainly). There is vivid metaphor, as in Amitabh Bachchan's *'Main ek zehrila saanp hoon'* (I'm a poisonous snake) monologue. There is depth of intention most simply expressed, as when Smita Patil tells Amitabh Bachchan *'Kuchh chizen kehne ki nahin, sirf samajhne ki hoti hain'* (Some things need not be said, only understood.) And finally, there is the complex, ambiguous, evolving father-son relationship that had me siding now with one, now with the other. Each time I listened, I understood a bit more of the language, and I entered a bit deeper into the characters' worlds.

Playing with film dialogue was a regular dinner table pastime in our movie-loving family. Obvious references were thrown out— 'Toto, I've a feeling we're not in Kansas anymore'—from the *Wizard of Oz* (1939). But allusions could also be more obscure: 'Yeah, and I'm not very tall either'—Humphrey Bogart to Lauren Bacall in *The Big Sleep* (1946). I would venture that Hollywood's famous quotes, though beloved in a certain milieu, carry only a fraction of the cultural weight of Hindi film lines, which provide shared references and social glue to a broad and diverse swathe of the population. *Kitne aadmi the?*[5] (How many men were there?) *Bhaai, tum sign karoge ki nahin?*[6] (Brother, will you sign or not?) My name is Anthony Gonzalves.[7] *Aap mere naajaayez baap hain!*[8] (You are my illegitimate father!) *Phir bhi dil hai hindustaani.*[9] (Even then, my heart is Indian.) The '70 and early '80s were a particularly fertile time for dialogue-baazi or 'throwing dialogues,' i.e. taking powerfully written lines and speaking them in a dramatic and/or memorable way. One line

---

[5] *Sholay.*
[6] *Deewaar* (1975).
[7] *Amar Akbar Anthony.*
[8] *Trishul.*
[9] *Shree 420* (1955).

could be the crux of a movie: *Mere paas ma hai.*[10] (But I have mother.) Another could be a joy to roll around one's mouth: *Roz sochti hoon re, lekin sochte sochte ye sochne lagti hoon ki sochne se kya faayda. Isliye main ne sochna hi chhod diya.*[11] (Every day I keep thinking, yeah, but with this thinking and thinking, I start thinking, What's the point of thinking? So I stopped thinking.)

As I continued both to enjoy and to ponder over Hindi cinema, an opportunity to study at The University of Texas at Austin had me delving deeper. Hindi, Urdu, language learning, sociolinguistics, theories of language acquisition and language change, multilingualism…all spoke in some way to the complex linguistic situation in which Indian cinema bathed.

I have always entered the Perry Castañeda Library at The University of Texas with a sense of awe. It is a palace of learning, filled with books on any and every subject in a vast number of languages and accessible to any who enter. So many answers to so many questions…but not to all. I was curious, for example, about language perceptions and attitudes among writers, directors and actors. I also wondered how a film in Hindi emerged from the multilingual cauldron in which it began.

It is a difficult-to-accept fact of life: we don't always get our questions answered. Then again, sometimes we do. Following the publication of my first book, *Enchantment of the Mind: Manmohan Desai's Films* in early 2006, I travelled to Bombay after a long interval and while there, was able to speak with a few people from the film industry. The stories I heard in those initial interviews were so stimulating that I returned the next year and the next, each time understanding more as people graciously shared information, personal stories, impressions and points of view.

The result is this book, whose title refers to a song from the film *Aaja Nachle* (2007). Though the film did poorly at the

---

[10] *Deewaar.*
[11] *Parvarish* (1977).

box office, it is one of my all-time favourites. Jaideep Sahni, the dialogue writer of the film, also wrote lyrics for several of the film's songs, including 'Show Me Your Jalwa'. A teacher's son, Jaideep Sahni sometimes shifted during our conversations into teacher mode himself, bringing me inside his layered perceptions of certain words he had chosen. 'Show Me Your Jalwa' he translated as 'Come show me your stuff'. The 'stuff' to be examined in this book is words; the process by which they make it to the screen; how thoughts, language and stories intersect; how generations tend to relate differently to language and scripts; how individual differences in temperament, background or education can affect relationships to language; and how language choice in film reflects societal changes. *Show Me Your Words*. Words are, of course, not normally 'seen' except on the written page, unless, that is, you consider words to possess the sort of life that Firaq Gorakhpuri assigns to them, life which allows them to bounce from the writer's pen over many hurdles into the actor's mouth and out again, past the editor's scissors and into our ears—not only into our ears, also into our eyes as we see words mouthed and their meanings perhaps subtly enhanced by an actor's non-verbal cues. Sound and sight do meet in interesting ways.

The second part of the title comes from a young academic researcher I met at the University of Wisconsin-Madison's Annual Conference on South Asia in 2007. Jahnavi Phalkey did her university studies in Bombay, followed by a PhD in the U.S. Research grants have since taken her to various parts of Europe. Her field, the history of science, is quite unconnected to Hindi films. Nevertheless, she agreed to speak on record about her relationship to language and to the cinema she saw as a child in Nagpur, all from the perspective she has today as someone at home on several continents. Asked if she felt different connections to different languages, she answered, 'I don't quite know. I have often wanted to think seriously about this.' She went on to delineate spaces that she associates with various languages: Hindi with friends, Marathi in the home. 'English,' she said, 'is definitely the language of my professional life and the language I feel least vulnerable in.' I had never before heard this sort of formulation. 'Vulnerable? What does that mean?' I asked. What she said next has stayed with me. Like most thought-provoking statements, it is self-evident after the fact, but it had not occurred to me in those terms. She answered, 'I don't know. It would be sort of useless to pretend that I don't know that language is power.' The power of language. The notion came up again and again among interviewees, though no one else named it as Jahnavi Phalkey did.

A NOTE ON THE TRANSLITERATION

The National Spelling Bee—won several times in recent years by Indian Americans—would not exist were English a neatly phonetic language. The highly illogical spelling of so many English words is a fascinating challenge to some, a frustration to most and, from time to time, a source of amusement. Lord Cromer drolly exposed some of the non-phonetic aspects of English in a short poem in *The Spectator* in 1902. It begins:

> When English is the tongue we speak,
> Why is 'break' not rhymed with 'freak'?
> Will you tell me why it's true
> We say 'sew' but likewise 'few';
> And the maker of a verse
> Cannot rhyme his 'horse' with 'worse'?
> 'Beard' is not the same as 'heard';
> 'Cord' is different from 'word';
> 'Cow' is 'cow', but 'low' is 'low';
> 'Shoe' is never rhymed with 'foe'.

His poem ends:

> Wherefore 'done' but 'gone' and 'lone'?
> Is there any reason known?
> And, in short, it seems to me
> Sounds and letters disagree.

With English as the Indic languages' principal portal into the Latin script, transliteration of Hindi–Urdu was a confusing affair from the outset. And still today, in spite of an ever-greater use of Roman Hindi, standardization remains, at best, a goal. When friends text, do they write, for example, 'dungi' or 'doongi'? No one has decided definitively.

Side by side with the generally beautifully consistent Devanagari script, Roman Hindi offers a rather baffling array of spellings. Establishing and adhering to an equivalence of Hindi phonemes and Latin letters would require a concerted effort on the part of publishers, businesses, local governments and all who share the virtual world of the Internet. It may happen one day, but for now it seems not to be a priority.

The unphonetic nature of English is, of course, not the only challenge in transliteration. Some phonemes in Hindi–Urdu simply do not exist in English. To this linguistic problem, linguists provided a solution in the form of the International Phonetic Alphabet, which, though an excellent tool for specialists, tends to make the layperson's eyes glaze over. A simpler alternative is to be found in dictionaries such as John T. Platts', now online at *Digital Dictionaries of South Asia* (uchicago.edu). This system uses diacritics—principally, dots, lines and colons—to clarify letters that could be interpreted in more than one way. It makes for fairly easy reading and assures precision. For publishers, however, diacritics multiply the potential for error.

We are left then with various informal methods of transliteration, which often result in nuances being lost, as when a 'k' is substituted for a 'q' in the word 'haq'. More problematic are distinctions that are masked over when one letter is used to transcribe both dental consonants (pronounced with the tongue touching the teeth) and retroflex consonants (in which the tongue curls to the back roof of the mouth). 'Lat' with a retroflex (लट) is a lock of hair. 'Lat' (लत) with a dental is a bad habit. Native speakers of Hindi-Urdu accustomed to reading in Roman script will quickly supply the correct pronunciation based on context, in the same way that readers of English determine whether 'bear' refers to an animal or to the verb meaning 'to carry'. Though inelegant and inexact, having one letter for two different sounds is not really an impediment to understanding. Having one letter represent three sounds, however, is another matter. How is one to interpret a word written with a 'd' when it could represent either द or ड or ड़, or again, 'dh' when in Hindi it could be read either ध or ढ or ढ़? These too can be inferred from context, but deciphering them requires mental gymnastics.

Why then, one might ask, when Devanagari provides such precision, would one resort to Roman Hindi at all? The answer, obviously, is that Roman Hindi, in any form, offers many people a needed link between the spoken and the written word. If Roman Hindi is by nature lax, it is also by nature inclusive and, in its capacity for inclusion, it deserves our respect.

Connie Haham

Austin, Texas
November 2015.

NAMES

'The naming of cats is a difficult matter,
It isn't just one of your holiday games.
You may think at first I'm mad as a hatter
When I tell you a cat must have three different names.'

—From 'The Naming of Cats' by T.S. Eliot

'...*To to to Akbar mera naam nahin hai*'
(Then...my name isn't Akbar)

—A key line in the 'Parda Hai' song from
Amar Akbar Anthony

How can one ever forget Akbar's (Rishi Kapoor) name after this powerful affirmation by lyricist Anand Bakshi, in the voice of playback singer Mohammed Rafi? Names make us sit up and take notice. Names of people, names of things, names of places. They define. They provide borders. This is the love-struck qawwali singer Akbar, who will prove that he is worthy of his name by winning Salma's (Neetu Singh) heart in the course of one event and emotion-filled song.

Likewise, there can be no doubt as to the name of the taangewaali (cart driver) (Hema Malini) in the classic film *Sholay*. She refers to herself in the third person eight times before Jai (Amitabh Bachchan) mockingly asks, '*Tumhaara naam kya hai, Basanti?*' (Pray tell,—a loose translation of the irony in Jai's voice—what is your name, Basanti?) The academic and administrative term 'to self-identify' comes to mind. However, within the real world of the film industry we only wish that naming were so clear-cut and straightforward. Instead, we are confronted with knots, gnarls and confusion. What to call the film industry? What to call the principle language in which the films are made? What to call the city in which the industry is based? Opinions compete. These can be lightly held; the equivalent of the common debate: is the tomato a fruit or a vegetable? 'Hmmm…I don't know. Let's just eat the salad.' Opinions can also be cast-iron convictions. Disagreeing becomes perilous.

In an attempt to explain some of my research to a friend in Paris, I said, 'Imagine that the French couldn't decide how to refer to French films, that the name for the language itself was subject to debate and that Paris, centre of the film industry, had changed names in the last few years and was sometimes referred to as Paris and sometimes by its new name. Now further imagine that film scripts for this industry might be written in English, with French dialogue added later.' Her jaw dropped.

As someone who has worked in advertising, screenwriter Jaideep Sahni is particularly sensitive to the power of names and 'namers', that is, the people who decide what we will call objects, institutions, groups of people, abstract ideas, everything. Names allow us to mentally divide the world into manageable bits in order to function. As we discussed this complex issue, he observed, 'Nomenclature may really be at the centre of many things… Changing or branding just one right word or name may be equal to a million words because, in one clean stroke, you change the frame of reference of a person or an entire society.'

Thus mentally buttressed, let's face the first question: should the country's major movie industry most appropriately be referred to as Hindi cinema, Bollywood, Indian popular cinema, Hindi commercial cinema, mainstream Hindi cinema, Bhaarati cinema, Bombay/Mumbai-based popular cinema or what? 'Bollywood' has caught imaginations and even made it to the *Oxford English Dictionary*, but it continues to incite the ire or at least the annoyance of many industry folks. In *Luck by Chance* (2009), directed by Zoya Akhtar and written by Zoya and Javed Akhtar, Dimple Kapadia plays an ageing star and mother of an upcoming starlet. When someone utters the word 'Bollywood' in her presence, she explodes in an indignant tirade. In real life, Amitabh Bachchan has repeatedly expressed his view that the proper nomenclature is 'Hindi cinema' because, as he told a BBC World Service *On Screen* interviewer[1], 'We make our films in Hindi, and Hindi is our national language.'

Director-producer Aziz Mirza was incensed:

> I personally take the word Bollywood as an insult. People are not affected by it. To each his own. I imagine a Mehboob Khan or a Bimal Roy or a Guru Dutt hearing 'You make films for Bollywood.' Thank God that generation died; because they were proud. Today, we are not even ashamed of being called Bollywood! Our journalists are not even ashamed of saying it because it sells.

Screenwriter Shridhar Raghavan, though not offended by the name Bollywood, called it a 'corny name'. With all this in mind, I once mentioned my interest in 'Hindi cinema' to a taxi driver in India. He promptly corrected me, 'Oh, you mean Bollywood.' What to do?

Writer and documentary filmmaker Nasreen Munni Kabir also objects to the term Bollywood but, putting aside reservations, made it the title of her 2001 book published by Channel 4 in the UK. She conceded that the term represents a kind of branding. 'You need keys and passwords,' she said. 'Bollywood opens the door.'

The term Bollywood is relatively recent. At some point, '-ollywood' became a suffix meaning 'a nation's cinema'. Hollywood began as a place and then a place with a famous white sign on

---

[1] February 2007.

the side of a hill. However, it has long since come to mean 'home of cinema in the US' and is loosely applied to most US motion picture productions. 'Metonymy' is the technical term by which a part comes to represent the whole, as in 'Wall Street', which means not just a street in lower Manhattan but everything and everyone connected to high finance in the US and, sometimes by extension, throughout the world. For the sake of convenience—or laziness—words sometimes morph from the specific to the general in this way. Watergate was simply a hotel in Washington, DC, until 1972 when Nixon's men tried to burglarize their rivals' headquarters there. The resulting scandal was soon shorthanded into the name of the hotel. Within a few years '-gate' was generalized into a suffix meaning 'scandal'—Irangate under President Reagan, the British royals' Camillagate, the Indian Barkhagate and so many more. Hence, Bombay + -ollywood = Bollywood.

Our love for analogy and linguistic shortcuts aside, there's another way of seeing 'Bollywood' in relationship to Hollywood. Without condoning the name 'Bollywood', screenwriter Jaideep Sahni noted Hindi cinema's Hollywood-like hegemonic tendencies within the broader world of Indian cinema. It is quite true that while some actors and directors have moved back and forth between regional and Hindi cinema, as is the case of South Indian director Mani Ratnam, talent has mostly migrated to the wider platform of Hindi cinema at the expense of regional film. Actress Sharmila Tagore, to take but one example, began in Bengali cinema and finished her career in Hindi films. How did Hindi cinema gain such reach and such status, I wondered? Jaideep ventured:

> Hindi cinema has its plus points in that it has kept the country together emotionally through very trying times. But the flip side is that at times it can be this monster or maybe like a giant banyan tree that hasn't let any other plants grow under it—short films or regional films or documentaries or any other kinds of music or self-expression… But it's like

Hollywood. They were just better at marketing and finance than anyone else. In the same way, the Bombay guys weren't necessarily better filmmakers, storytellers or writers. They were just better businessmen. That's why I say that Hindi films are just the Hollywood to everyone else.

From this perspective, 'Bollywood' looks less like little brother to Hollywood and more like big brother to all of the regional cinemas of India. Bollywood is the one that can throw its weight around. It's the cinema with the bigger bucks and more national and international prestige. L'Oréal would probably not have asked Aishwarya Rai Bachchan, Indian film actress and Miss World 1994, to be the face of their brand, had her Bollywood stardom not brought her to the attention of the cosmetic company executives in Paris. Oprah Winfrey had Aishwarya and husband Abhishek Bachchan on her American TV show in a segment entitled 'Bollywood Love Story'. On Oprah's site the tag line reads, 'America has Hollywood. Nigeria has Nollywood. But in India, it's all about Bollywood.'[2] And so it is, usually. An exception came in 2011, when Tamil star Dhanush did not resort to Hindi in order to make the whole country sit up and listen. He had the nation tapping to his beat with his Tamil-English song 'Kolaveri Di' from the film *3*. Still, it took only a short time for Bollywood to reassert itself. Dhanush was invited north—his first Hindi film *Raanjhanaa* released in 2013. Bollywood could sigh with relief that its power, status and allure were as great as ever, and the story, as reported, was all about 'Bollywood', not 'the Hindi film industry', whether told by bollywoodlife.com, bollywoodhungama.com or *India Today*.

'Bollywood' it would seem to be, then. Still, because the name 'Bollywood' provokes such ire among its detractors, let's pause and imagine 'Hindi cinema' as the definitive name of the

---

[2]http://www.oprah.com/entertainment/Bollywood-Love-Story-Aishwarya-Rai-and-Abhishek-Bachchan, 28 September 2009.

industry. While it is true that film industries in India are referred to by language—Punjabi films, Tamil films, Marathi films—on the world stage this would simply never work. Imagine the confusion were one to argue that movies produced in Brazil should be called 'Portuguese films' following the logic that Brazilians speak Portuguese or, for that matter, that movies made in Bangladesh should be called 'Bengali films' or American movies 'English films'. In the purely Indian context, language may define a film industry, but step onto the world stage and the rules must change. And 'Bollywood', however annoyingly derivative, makes little mental maps of the subcontinent pop into the minds of viewers around the globe.

But what about the name of the language? *Hindi?* Really? Javed Akhtar takes issue:

> It is a question I have not been able to find an answer to—why, since the very beginning, are these films called Hindi films? We have two languages in North India. One is Hindi. Another is Urdu. As a matter of fact, Urdu is an older language than contemporary modern Hindi. Traditionally, most of the writers from the so-called Hindi cinema have been from Urdu.

Actor Tom Alter opted for another term, 'The description "Hindi cinema" was very ironic—the language that was used in Hindi cinema in the 1950s and '60s wasn't Hindi. It was not necessarily pure Urdu, but it was what Gandhiji called Hindustani.'

Farhan Akhtar is typical of a younger generation in the film industry who call the language of cinema 'Hindi' as a matter of course, even if 'Hinglish', the mongrel mixture of Hindi and English, might more accurately define the language being used in film today.

Administratively, 'Hindi' certainly carries weight. Each film produced in India is preceded by a shot of the official Film Certification, a white bilingual governmental form with blanks for the film's name, release date and language. Though 'Hindustani' and 'Urdu' have historically been listed, today 'Hindi' is the almost automatic choice. Even a symbol for Urdu culture like Mohammed Sadiq's *Chaudhvin ka Chand* (1960) lists its language as 'Hindi'. A bit of research into the language history of northern India can leave one either fascinated by its twists and turns or reeling from the tangled complexity of it all.[3] What seems obvious even at a glance is that a language that can be spelled in two ways in its principle script (हिंदी/हिन्दी) is likely to be a bit hard to pin down. Hindi, Urdu, Hindustani, Hindi-Urdu, Urdu-Hindi or Dakkhani. One can hear them all, even if at this point in history 'Hindi' has a definite edge.

If disagreements persist concerning the name of the cinema and the language, it is the name of the city where the cinema is made that is truly politically charged. The decision to change the official name of the metropolis of Bombay to Mumbai took place in the mid-1990s when a Shiv Sena coalition party came to power.[4] Many in the film world, including fictional characters within films, have continued to call the city Bombay. A few films have addressed the issue directly. The spirit is mocking and comedic in *Welcome to Sajjanpur*, Shyam Benegal's 2008 film. The village letter writer Mahadev (Shreyas Talpade) is brushing his teeth as he explains to us that his town was formerly called Durjanpur, that is, until Pandit Jawaharlal Nehru came through and decreed to Mr Collector, 'I don't like this name Durjanpur. Change it to

---

[3] For a brief overview from the point of view of a linguist and a neutral outside observer, see the appendix of Christine Everaert's *Tracing the Boundaries between Hindi and Urdu: Lost and Added in Translation between 20th Century Short Stories*, 2010.

[4] For a cool, scholarly, yet engaging look at the history of city name changes across the subcontinent, visit Kenny Easwaran's website for the piece he wrote in 2001 when he was a PhD student researching conditional probability in the department of philosophy at Berkeley (http://www.ocf.berkeley.edu/~easwaran/papers/india.html).

Sajjanpur with immediate effect.' Mahadev continues:

> ...*aur tab se Durjanpur ho gaya Sajjanpur. Vaise hi jaise Bombay Mumbai, Calcutta Kolkata, aur Madras Chennai. Par koi farq pada? Haan, pada. Jab iska naam Durjanpur tha, yahaan sajjan log zyaada the. Jab se Sajjanpur pada hai, chaaron taraf durjan hi durjan hain.*
>
> (And since then Durjanpur became Sajjanpur. Like Bombay Mumbai, Calcutta Kolkata and Madras Chennai. But did anything change? Yes, things changed. When the name was Durjanpur [rascal town] most people here were good folk. Since it became Sajjanpur [honest town] there are rascals everywhere.)

Vishal Bhardwaj's *Kaminey* (2009) tackles the issue of one city's name head-on, along with the violence the Mumbai-Bombay divide can provoke. The young couple, Sweety (Priyanka Chopra) and Guddu (Shahid Kapoor), are alone in the night, whispering sweet nothings into each other's ears. Guddu is normally the stutterer, but tonight, love makes them mirror each other, and it is Sweety who stutters as she argues against Guddu continuing to look for a condom. '*Jaante ho issey kitne door hote hain ham?*' (You know how far it keeps us from each other?) '*Kitne?*' he asks. And she answers, '*Jaise main New York mein aur tum N...N...N...*' (It's like I'm in New York and you are in N...N...N...). 'New Jersey?' he ventures. 'N...N...N,' she continues to stammer. And he continues to guess, 'New Zealand?' 'New Delhi?'

She finally bursts out 'New Bombay', adopting his name for the city. And he lovingly corrects her, exchanging his words for hers, 'Bombay nahin, Mumbai.' (Not Bombay, Mumbai.) In a voice choked with feeling, she asks, 'You love Mumbai, na? But I love you more than Mumbai, more than Chennai, more than Kolkata, more than Bengaluru, Thiruvananthapuram.' Contentious issues melt away before the power of hormone-enhanced feeling. If the couple can overcome the political differences these new city names represent, which of life's hardships can they not face, side by side? Yes, but when Sweety finds she is pregnant a few weeks later, they will face a much harsher reality. Sweety's brother is an underworld don playing the Marathi nationalist card. Guddu's full name gives away his origins. 'When did you come here?' the thuggish brother asks Guddu. *'Bombay mein?'* (In Bombay?) Guddu responds. 'I was born here. My father arrived (from Uttar Pradesh) in 1984 in Bombay.' 'Mumbai!' the brother berates him. Guddu looks him in the eye and calmly answers, *'Tabhi Bombay hi tha'* (That time it was still Bombay) and one of the brother's henchmen kicks Guddu in the back. 'It was Mumbai then, and it's Mumbai now!' What follows is a predictable diatribe against bloody migrants, i.e. workers from Uttar Pradesh who come to take Maharashtrian jobs.

Bhardwaj's courageous inclusion of the perplexing issue stands in contrast to the careful avoidance one more often finds, both within films and throughout the industry. Even those in charge of subtitling tend to toe the line. Disconcertingly, DVDs regularly have us read 'Mumbai' in the subtitles even as we hear 'Bombay' in the dialogue. More noticeably, in 2009, producer Karan Johar personally apologized to the powerful Maharashtra Navnirman Sena (MNS) party leader Raj Thackeray at the release of *Wake Up Sid* (2009) for the film's characters' having referred to the city as Bombay.

With the passing years some have adjusted, both in and out of the city, in India and abroad, to 'Mumbai'. An appeasing voice comes from Marathi-speaking Mumbaikar director Madhur Bhandarkar, 'I call the city I live in Bombay. Mumbai. Both we say.'

If 'Mumbai' has won a certain acceptance, administratively, it is 'Bombay' that carries the dream. In Chandra Barot's *Don* (1978), written by Salim-Javed, the lyrics of the song '*Ee hai Bambai nagariya, tu dekh babua*', penned by Anjaan, himself from Banaras (or Varanasi), spoke of the magnificence of Bombay, a city that lures people to leave their homes for its streets of gold.

Amitabh Bachchan plays a street performer who dances and pantomimes to Kishore Kumar's playback singing.

> *Ee hai Bambai nagariya, tu dekh babua*
> *Ye sheheron mein sheher hai Bambai wah, arey wah wah Bambai wah*
> *Ye baat sabhi hai ulti hai phir bhi wah re Bambai wah re wah re Bambai wah*
> (This is the city of Bombay. Look at it, my boy.
> This is the city of all cities. Even if things are upside down, wah! Bombay is great).

Amitabh Bachchan in Don, *as the Banaras street performer dancing in Bombay. (Sketch by Simon P. Holzman)*

Almost thirty years later the dream has become hipper, more consumerist. In *Bunty aur Babli* (2005), directed by Shaad Ali and written by Jaideep Sahni, Rakesh (Abhishek Bachchan) and Vimmi (Rani Mukerji) have each fled their homes to search for success in bigger cities. Realizing they have a gift as con artists and work well as partners, they change their names to Bunty and Babli and are ready for the big time—Bombay. As the train nears the city, Babli exults:

> मुझे तो विश्वास नहीं हो रहा कि कल सुबह मैं बम्बई में होंगी।
> कितने साल से, कितने ड्रीम्स देखे थे, सब सच हो जाएंगे।

> (I can't believe I'll be in Bombay tomorrow morning. How many dreams have I dreamed for how many years? All of them will come true.)

Bombay–Mumbai complexities can be found at every turn. The English version of *Dhobi Ghat* (2011), written and directed by Kiran Rao, is called *Mumbai Diaries*. Yet the artist Arun, played by Aamir Khan, raises a toast (in English) at the opening show for his paintings 'to Bombay, my muse, my whore, my beloved'.

What to make of all these contradictions and debates? Ignore the opposing voices and pick terminology according to one's preference? Give weight to history and voices of authority? Bow to the informal democracy of 'whatever people say the most wins'? In *The Argumentative Indian* (2006), Nobel-Prize-winning economist and social commentator Amartya Sen makes the case that from the time of the Mahabharata and the Ramayana to the present, Indian culture has been filled with argument and counterargument, debate and disputation. Indian culture is 'loquacious', says Sen, and he sums up his chapter on argument with a little poem by the nineteenth-century Bengali intellectual Ram Mohan Roy:

> Just consider how terrible the day of your death will be. Others will go on speaking, and you will not be able to argue back.[5]

In a time of rapid change, linguistic solid ground is hard to find. Words are changing. People are moving about. Names are in

---

[5] Sen, Amartya, 2005, p. 32.

flux. The new competes with the old. Choosing one name over another is rather like setting out on a path despite the threat of quicksand. Still, one takes the path. One needs to name, to give some name, any name; maybe one name today, another name tomorrow, but a name just the same.

I'VE GOT A STORY TO TELL

'The writer is the most important person in Hollywood, but we must never tell the sons of bitches.'

—Irving Thalberg, Hollywood producer
from 1919 to 1936

Story Whys...

Stories are everywhere and, child or adult, we crave them. A story can be intentional and carefully constructed by the narrator, or it can be a simple account of a day's event. But add a flourish here, an embellishment there, a few pregnant pauses, a voice rising or falling at just the right moment, and you've got something people readily lend an ear to. It can also be created by a listener or watcher who simply *wants* a story there, as when we look at clouds and see shapes into which we read characters, landscapes and events. Or we observe, say, two squirrels jumping about on a tree; given a moment to let our minds amble, we might assign roles to the pair, create a backstory and project their relationship into the future as we imagine them negotiating good times and bad. Because stories come to us so instinctively, we are vexed when we can't tease them out, when questions asked go unanswered. 'Whatever became of that childhood friend?' Or again, the ever-hopeful-but-rarely-successful 'What happened at school today?' which parents throw out and which children so regularly manage to duck. Still, we go on asking.

We want stories. We need them and thus, we conveniently slice up time into episodes, arbitrarily inserting 'The End' at whatever we deem an appropriate moment. The story keeps rolling on, of course. The only true ending comes with death. But still we narrate. We do little mental replays of scenes, bringing certain elements to the fore, ignoring others, as we recount bits of our lives, consciously or unconsciously editing and embroidering as we go along. We pull together threads which may or may not be objectively connected, play with colours and lighting to alter the mood and effect, and produce patterns in the form of flashbacks, our 'memories' by which we explain ourselves to ourselves. We do all this in answer to those fundamental questions which we are likely to ignore beyond adolescence but which remain suspended somewhere above our heads like faded cartoon bubbles: 'Who am I? Why am I who I am? What paths did I take to get here? And what did I experience along the way?' So it is that we interpret and reinterpret our lives and give meaning to events, both big and small.

If we take a great deal of liberty selecting, deleting or reworking what we consider memory-worthy episodes to our own 'realities', fiction storytellers have the luxury of an even freer hand in moulding characters, relationships and happenings to fit the template of their choosing. Then, eliminating randomness, they can, whenever they wish, draw their stories to a conclusion in ways most likely to satisfy listeners, readers or viewers. Of course, the best stories leave us wishing to go on living with the characters we have come to know. Hence, the retelling of old favourites. Hence, the series. Hence, the sequels.

...And Hows

If we can soar in considering the ways in which we respond to stories, questions of 'how' quickly bring us back down to earth. The medium matters. Spoken or written words, songs, dances, paintings, puppets, hand shadows manoeuvring against a wall. With the addition, however, of moviemaking in the last one hundred-plus years, the stakes have changed. In the days when people had no option but to listen to a story being told or sung by a human voice in real time, stories lasted and travelled only by being retold, resung. With the written word and, still more, the printed word, stories greatly expanded their potential reach in both time and space; and also became more expensive to produce. More expensive still was the technology of microphones, recording instruments and the radio, which gave oral storytelling ever wider audiences. Filmmaking involved several leaps in technology that simultaneously increased audience potential and investor risk. Vast audiences could be reached and fortunes amassed or, just as easily, huge sums could be sunk without a trace. Storytellers, meanwhile, continued to tell stories in much the same way they always had. Yet, stories could now be transformed through the medium of film into something more lifelike—or perhaps dreamlike—than any playwright of the past would ever have imagined possible. Stories gained a thrilling scope, but budget constraints continued to set limits that, while on a different scale, were probably not of a different sort than those Shakespeare grappled with in his time.

One Writer's Ideals—Shridhar Raghavan

Near the end of *Bluffmaster!* (2005) directed by Rohan Sippy and penned by Shridhar Raghavan, a complex plot twist takes us into a film within a film. There, the writer of the film's film, played by Nana Patekar, is holding a brightly coloured umbrella as he crouches on the top branches of a small tree, rather like a scared kitten, just out of reach of anyone who might want to bring him down. The director, played by Riteish Deshmukh, introduces him as '*Ye hamaare Shridhar Sahib hain.*' (This is our Shridhar Sahib.) This image stuck with me as I went to meet the real Shridhar Sahib in February 2008 in his office in Lokhandwala. Far from scared or kitten-like, Shridhar Raghavan showed himself to be well-spoken, bursting with enthusiasm and immersed in his craft.[6] He began by sharing some of his thoughts on storytelling:

> Look at the root of [the] story. You are talking about a group of cavemen. Somebody is going out hunting and somebody is doing the cooking and there's some idiot over there who is not very good at hunting; he has already imagined getting attacked, so he's paralysed, but he's got to eat that particular evening. So sitting around the fire, he tells them wonderful stories and exaggerates their hunt and makes everybody's lives sound more interesting. They throw him a bone and think, 'He's talking about me; it relates to my life.' The first writer was born.
>
> When you're telling a story to a kid, it can be the most absurd story ever. It can start with a sofa. The sofa you are sitting on right now is orange, but it wasn't orange yesterday. Yesterday it was pink. Why did it turn pink? Yesterday... actually...the sun...and so on and so forth. See, the steps that lead to a story can be completely nonsensical. The child's only interest is: what happened next? What happened next? In its entirety the story is utter nonsense, but when you are going through it, it seems to have a life of its own.

Raghavan ventured into the world of storytelling early, publishing short stories as a twelve-year-old growing up in Poona. Like so many writers, he has always been an avid reader. Eclectic in his tastes, he loves Dostoevsky, Manto, James Elroy, Kurt Vonnegut and Ray Bradbury, to name but a few. As a film buff, his passions are equally diverse: Vijay Anand, Jean-Pierre Melville, Stephen Chow, Manmohan Desai, Quentin Tarantino, Krzysztof Kieslowski and many more. He came to Bombay to write fiction in the late eighties, but, as he said, 'There's no such

---

[6] I later learned that the layered inside joke on *'ye hamaare Shridhar Sahib hain'* was actor Nana Patekar's on-the-sets improvisation.

thing as a career in fiction per se,' so he worked in advertising and then journalism, back when feature journalism involved research for 3,000-word pieces. When that began dying out, he moved to television and did eight hundred episodes for *CID*, regarded as the longest-running show on Indian television. A harsh judge of his own work, he considers only two hundred of those episodes to be 'pretty good', but as he said, 'I managed to make those pretty good ones only because I kept writing the bad ones.' And there was cinema too. But as Raghavan said, 'I essentially consider myself a story-writer.' He laid out his approach:

> First, you start researching something. You say, 'Maybe I should write a short story or an article about this. Or maybe I should do this as a short film. Or maybe a documentary.' The form shows itself much later, but first you're obsessed with something. Not for a film like *Bluffmaster!*[7] though. *Bluffmaster!* was simple. We wanted to do a con film. But in a film like *Khakee*[8] or *Apaharan*,[9] I was researching, and at some point I said, 'Hey, this can be a movie.'

If the writer exerts near-total control when writing short stories or novels, writing for film means working in collaboration, with all the accompanying limitations. Raghavan went on:

> Honesty on the writer's part has to be there first. And it has to last the processes by which the story gets to screen. There's the director, the cinematographer, the actor, everybody. There are so many obstacles that the original story has to pass. It's like sperm. Literally one in a million will actually make it. Any good film goes through years and years of writing, and a certain honesty, there in the

---

[7]Directed by Rohan Sippy.
[8]Directed by Rajkumar Santoshi, 2004.
[9]Directed by Prakash Jha, 2005.

beginning, say, 100 per cent, might have become 90-80-60-40, but even if it was 20 per cent in the end, at its heart it still remains an honest movie. But if you begin with dishonesty, then it is the opposite. Even 10 per cent dishonesty in the beginning will turn into 100 per cent by the time the film gets made. Your dishonesty will be compounded by the next guy's dishonesty and then, when it comes on screen, it is a slap on the face of the audience. They see through it. I have to be intrinsically, completely responsible for every moment which is there. It can be discarded at some point, but I should have had a point of view in the first place… In scriptwriting people talk about how you should know the end of the film first. I would prefer you don't know. You just wonder and wonder, and after two months of thinking it over, you come up with the next moment. Then you do that sixty times. You wind up with a script which has sixty to seventy scenes, and the guy watching in the audience can't come up with the solution to the next scene because it took you three months to think of it. You wrote fifty things and abandoned forty-eight. Then the fiftieth has a certain honesty to it.

The Format

The writing, the abandoning and the rewriting which Shridhar Raghavan describes bring to mind a man sitting with paper and pen—or a computer—for long hours in solitary concentration, producing a text which will later be transformed into moving images, full of sound and colour, with characters whose looks have become defined by the actors who play them. Not all film production begins with written text, however. In the film *Luck By Chance*, story and direction by Zoya Akhtar, dialogue by Javed Akhtar, a big-time old-style producer played by Rishi Kapoor has agreed to help his brother-in-law (Alyy Khan) to find much-needed corporate funding for his upcoming project. We soon see the two producers, one wearing a bright silk shirt, the other a white cotton kameez, sitting in a sleek, modern office opposite two men in sober Western business attire. These financiers are not at all impressed by the producers' promises that actors John Abraham and Bipasha Basu have agreed to play the lead characters. The financiers' basic criteria is 'property'. The two producers looked puzzled. One of the executives explains, '*Hollywood mein script ko property kehte hain.*' (In Hollywood the script is called property.) 'You see,' says the second in English, 'there, content is king.' When he goes on to suggest, quite coolly, the need for a change in the mindset of the film industry, the Rishi Kapoor character does not miss a beat, '*Change aa raha hai, brother. Hamne John aur Bipasha ko isliye nahin liya hai kyonki vo stars hain. Stars to vo hain, lekin hamne unko isliye liya hai kyonki script ki demand hai.*' (Change is coming, brother. We didn't choose John and Bipasha because they are stars. They *are* stars, but we chose them because of the demands of the script.) Across the table, the man in the suit looks exceedingly sceptical, and he's right. The 'script' at this point is probably no more than a series of jotted-down ideas.

In her early acting career Shabana Azmi was noted for her performances in parallel or New Wave cinema, but she quickly branched out to work in mainstream popular films as well. In 1977, for instance, she acted in *Parvarish* and *Amar Akbar Anthony*, two films by director Manmohan Desai. When I met with her at her home in 2007 to discuss language and cinema from her perspective as an actor, she looked back to her experience in the popular film industry in the '70s. She is on record as having thoroughly enjoyed working with Desai[10]. At the same time, she remembered how hard it was to act without a 'bound script', a 'property', as the financiers in *Luck By Chance* would refer to it

---

[10]Haham, Connie, *Enchantment of the Mind: Manmohan Desai's Films*, Roli Books, New Delhi, 2006, p. 88.

decades later. She gave the example of her experience on Desai's sets:

> Earlier, you couldn't pay enough attention to giving proper emotion to dialogue because the scenes were being written as you were doing them. You never got them in advance. See, there was no concept of a written script. We used to be given a storyline—and not in too much detail, because it was evolving in Manmohan Desai's head as he was making it… And it was just a question of trying to learn the lines so you didn't forget the dialogue. In a lot of Hindi cinema I feel no meaning is conveyed beyond the absolute obvious because nobody has had time to internalize the lines, to put in pauses and meanings so that they are not just driven by knee-jerk reactions. I think that now, because the trend has changed and we have bound scripts with dialogue in advance, there is a greater chance of doing that… I got the lines for *Parvarish* about thirty minutes before going to shoot. You can (now) get the script sometimes as much as three months in advance. The film industry is becoming far more systematic and organized, and people have finally realized that there is more value in doing pre-production for two years and shooting for three months, rather than do pre-production for three months and shoot for four years. Also, in certain instances we have been able to do a run-through or rehearsal with all the actors in advance.

If much is made of the 'bound script' today, it is by no means the universal standard to which all writers aspire. Nor do all filmmakers demand it. Producer–director Rohan Sippy explained the strengths of the traditional method of producing a screenplay orally through storytelling and discussion:

> People like Shridhar (Raghavan) and Rajat (Arora) don't really work that way, but there are writers who typically sit down with the director, run through stuff and brainstorm

and come up with concepts to scenes. Anuvab Pal (writer of *Mumbai Calling*) and *The President is Coming* is very oral in terms of his tradition. What he told me is that ultimately he will record on audio CD of what his script is. What he likes to keep in writing are a couple of words for a scene. So he'll have something as cryptic as 'nappie' or something like that. His theory is basically that if I can't narrate it, that scene needs improving. It has to come organically, which I really respect. I think that's a great way to tell stories. When you hear people like him tell stories, you realize he has a real panache with which he tells it. There's a real organic flow that doesn't come from reading it off a page. And he probably improvises a few things each time, which keeps the script polished at each stage.

Traditional oral script narration or 'pitching the story' remains a powerful way of bringing actors on board to do a movie. Actor-producer Aamir Khan explained that he prefers listening to scripts being narrated so that he can visualize the film from the director's point of view, rather than getting stuck with the images that come to mind as he reads. He said:

> I remember when I heard this narration from John Matthew [Mathan] who made a film called *Sarfarosh* (1999) with me. John is probably one of the most appalling narrators. He kind of opened the script and started reading it. He fumbled through it. He kind of hesitated on a lot of words. And he kind of missed pages. He did all of that. But the power of the script came through to me. And then there are other directors, for example, Raj[kumar] Santoshi (*Andaz Apna Apna*, 1994). He is someone who doesn't look at the script in front of him... So each director has his own style of narrating the script, but essentially it is taking me through the script right from scene one to the last scene... One of the most important things I look for in the director is:

> Does he have a story to tell? Is the story wanting to come out of him?[11]

Narration can come from the director. It can also be required of the writer. Jaideep Sahni understands the tradition of narrating stories. He nevertheless described the process as rather painful:

> I have a hang-up about projection, that if you're projecting you're trying to make [the story] more important than it is. I can project. Like when I was in advertising, I could do a striptease on a table. It's not about me. It's about some product. But when it's a song or a script which I've written, there's a lot of *me* in it. I just have this tendency to say, 'Here, you want bound scripts all the time, here, here's a bound script. Read it.'

Javed Siddiqi: A Playwright in the Film World

Javed Siddiqi believes in the written word and in the creative process, and he has penned dialogues for many acclaimed films such as Satyajit Ray's *Shatranj ke Khilari* (1977), Muzaffar Ali's *Umrao Jaan* (1981), Khalid Mohamed's *Fiza* (2000) and Shyam Benegal's *Zubeidaa* (2001). But writing for cinema is not his first passion. That would be theatre. His plays *Tumhari Amrita*, *Begum Jaan*, *Saalgirah* and *Shyam Rang*, for example, have given him scope for creativity and artistic control of a sort the film industry could not possibly accord. He explained with an example from *Begum Jaan*:

> There are certain things which I personally observe, and I want to use them and I want to make my comment and I have to use somebody else's shoulder to fire my gun. So

---

[11]BAFTA Goes Bollywood: Aamir Khan in Conversation with Nasreen Munni Kabir, 21 August 2006.

I use my characters. Any character can do. For example, in *Begum Jaan*, so much is said against history because of the type of history we have today. What the bloody history is, in the history book, is all the stupid stories of the kings and the leaders. Do we really know what people used to eat, people used to do, people used to think? We don't. That is my personal feeling. But I've used Begum Jaan when she says, '*History ki tragedy yehi hai ki jeete huye likhte hain aur haare huye padhte hain.*' (The tragedy of history is this, that the victors write and the losers read.) So this was my own personal anger which I wanted to take out, but I can't do it anywhere else, so I use that Begum Jaan character as a platform… In cinema it's very difficult because there are so many other elements involved, so many other people are involved. And most of the time they are more influential than the writer.

Siddiqi came of age at a pivotal time in Indian history. His family background and his early personal experiences helped define the direction of his artistic career. He shares his story:

I belong to a family of journalists and poets and writers. My father's uncles, the two Ali brothers, were great patriots against the British regime in the 1920s. My father's uncle was the president of the Congress for some time. They were very active people who also brought out newspapers. One of them was here in Bombay; it was called *Khilafat*. My father's uncle was Maulana Mohammad Ali. Mohammad Ali Road was named after him. And Shaukat Ali Road is for his brother. My great-grandfather was an author of many books. I belonged to the small independent state of Rampur near Nainital, the hill station four hours from Delhi. My early schooling was the normal Urdu and Persian and a bit of Arabic and [the] Quran. I finished high school there and then went to Aligarh University. That was when my father expired, and the whole family was in very bad shape. It was during Partition. Unfortunately, because more than half the family had migrated to Pakistan, the Government of India confiscated almost all the property because all these characters used to be the favourites of the nawabs and the maharajahs. They had amassed a lot of money, property, villages, havelis, palaces and houses. It was all confiscated. The rule was that whoever left, his property would be confiscated, but unfortunately, in our family the property was undivided. There was one person who used to collect all the rent and distribute it among the family. My father was an activist and was jailed. He came out totally disillusioned and died shortly afterwards. There were no earnings. So my uncle who was running a newspaper here in Bombay asked me to come because he had read some of my short stories I had already had published. You could say I started writing—in Urdu—at the age of twelve.

Siddiqi did not come to Bombay in order to join the film industry, but being in Bombay gave him that opportunity. And if he takes pride in what he has contributed to many good films, he also bemoans the dilution of the writer's work as he has seen it play out in many generic productions. As we sat in his cozy office in Four Bungalows, Andheri, in April 2006, he employed the flourishes of a practised raconteur to bring to life the unfortunate process by which mediocrity can seep in along the way as an idea becomes story, then screenplay and finally film:

Screenwriter and playwright Javed Siddiqi.
(Photo courtesy: Javed Siddiqi)

In India, unfortunately, the star is everything. We have to make stories at the whims and fancies of stars... I am quite choosy now; I only do two or three films a year. I'm happy with my low profile. But if anyone comes to me, first I ask, 'Who are you going to sign for the lead role?' The very name of that star is going to decide what sort of story the director is in search of. So I dig out my old files, my thoughts, every torn pad, and I start tossing ideas, and he may like them or not. If the director has come to me with a particular star in mind, and he wants me to write something for that particular star, I have a very limited scope. Unfortunately, there are very few directors who have their own say. The producer is the man who makes money, or rather, he wants to make money, so why would he not want to please the star? The star might say, 'I have done fifty films where I've played the hero. Now I want to play the hero with negative traits. Can you find a story like that?' The producer will come running to the director, and he will say, 'Let's go to Javed Siddiqi. He must have something in his little cubbyhole.' The producer will say, 'Star X wants this, so buster, can you give us something?' I will say to myself, 'All right, this man is genuine. He has made films. He has money also, so most probably he will complete the film, and it will be seen in the cinema halls.' So after considering all these aspects, I will say, 'All right. Sir, I have this in mind.' Then I will go to the star. The star will listen to me. He will make some observations, suggestions and changes. And the director will have to say something. Otherwise, the writer will feel the director doesn't know anything. So he makes some suggestions. Then I'm signed, and I'll get my first pay cheque. Good. And then the producer will get involved. And some sort of structure will appear. And people will fill up this office. The director comes. The producer comes. Sometimes the star appears, and the editor will come and the cameraman will come, and the two assistants. They will all be here, and I will be facing the firing squad. I will say, 'Sir, this is the structure I've thought of.' They all will be thinking, 'Now the writer is good, but he has to be corrected in a few places; otherwise, he's going to make mistakes.' That's the second stage. Then the third stage: my first draft is ready. That first draft is read out because it's on paper. Is the hero in the right light? The other hero is not usurping? Does the heroine have enough footage or not? How many songs are there? The song situations should be good. Then a series of narrations start for the star, the heroine, the second hero, the villain, the music director, the lyrics writer. Sometimes they give me my due respect, and there are not too many suggestions. Sometimes it is 'You should change this. You should change that.' Then there is the second draft *with* the dialogue. (My assistants type it out in Hindi.) So it is sent to them.

Now the shooting starts. I make a point not to attend the shootings. The assistant director reads it out. And if the actor is good and knows his job and knows the language, and he respects the writing, then he's not going to make any change. But if he's not... There's an episode with the great writer Rajinder Singh Bedi. He had written a scene. Then he got a phone call in the morning, 'You have to come to the sets. There is one line that the hero cannot deliver. He's finding it difficult. Can you come over?' He went to the studio. It was quite far. He was given the scene and told, 'This is the line you have to change, sir.' He read the whole scene. He said, 'Sorry, I'm not going to change this line.' Everyone was shocked. They said, 'A writer of your calibre with such status and such a name; you're a great writer and you say you cannot change this line?' He said, 'I didn't say I cannot. I said I *will* not. I'm not going to change the line.' So naturally, everybody asked, 'Why? Why can't you do this?' He said, 'Because in the whole bloody scene, this is the *only* line written by me!'

Now there are reasons for these attitudes in the industry, which should nevertheless be condemned as much as possible. Here is another small episode I can narrate. There was this famous director. He asked me to write this great scene, and I wrote something really fantastic. What a good scene it was! I read it out to the director. He said, 'Oh Javed, it's fantastic, yaar. Why don't you come to the sets tomorrow?' The actor was supposed to come at 9 a.m. We take it for granted that at 11 a.m. the star will be there. The news came that he would be coming around lunchtime. So the director asked me, 'Can you edit down the scene a bit because I don't have that much time? The buster will be leaving at 6 p.m.' I cut a few lines here and there. Now it's 2 p.m. and no star. It's the last day of the set. There's no chance of reshooting because the star doesn't have dates for another two months. At 3 p.m. the director asks me, 'Can you do something, Javed Sahib? Just keep the essence of the scene.' So I kept the essence, hardly five or ten lines with five or ten set-ups and five or ten different shots. The star finally came at 5 p.m. The director forgot all the shots. He fixed one round trolley and asked the star to stand in the middle and narrate whatever he could. The trolley was going round and round and round. In one single shot the whole scene was over. So this is the situation. In these circumstances people like us are still surviving, and creativity is still alive, which is amazing.[12]

---

[12] For further information on Javed Siddiqi's work, see his website: http://www.javedsiddiqi.com/

IT'S IN THE WRITING

Tom Alter, Mona Ambegaonkar and Ananya Dutta performed in a play called *Got to be Aishwarya* in 2006 in Mumbai. At the centre of the plot is a small-town girl who dreams of making it big in Bollywood with the help of her long-estranged father. At one point, Bombay is being compared—most unfavourably—to a quiet town in the provinces. The big choking city needs no better defence, however, than this clinching one-liner—*'Hamaare paas Bollywood hai.'* (But we have Bollywood). The audience loved it. The reference, of course, is to the classic *'Mere paas Ma hai'* from *Deewaar*, in which the criminal brother (Amitabh Bachchan) vaunts his wealth to his poor but honest policeman brother (Shashi Kapoor), whose trump card is 'But I've got Ma.' This particular line gets a lot of play, and, whenever it is used, it seems to click with listeners. Music composer A.R. Rahman used it when accepting an Oscar for Best Original Score and Best Song in Los Angeles in February 2009. He began his speech by thanking his mother for being there and for her blessings. He could have used other words, but instead he chose to say it with words audiences would love: *'Mere paas Ma hai.'*

Some years back, Cogito Consulting did a marketing study to see which movie quotes have become part of Indian vocabulary. *'Mere paas Ma hai'* not surprisingly, continues to be a favourite, but *'Main aur meri tanhaai'* (my loneliness and I) from *Silsila* (1981) ranks higher in memorability than lines from more recent films. Speaking for Cogito, V.M. Wabgaonkar argues that 'the impact that Bollywood dialogues have had on the society can be gauged from the most used dialogues... They show how we have reinforced our beliefs, derived inspiration or even given vent to bugging issues through their words, style and impact.'[13]

Hollywood actors sell products with their faces, and rock songs have been used to market detergent, but lines of dialogue? Unlikely. Marketing with words penned by film writers may be an Indian phenomenon. Nevertheless, as in Hollywood, many in the Hindi film industry realized early on that good writing was essential to good filmmaking. William Faulkner, Raymond Chandler and even Aldous Huxley were among those invited— or lured—by Hollywood, with its promise of fame and fortune. In the 1940s and '50s, the Progressive Writers' Movement and the Bombay film world had a similar symbiotic relationship. Premchand, Manto, Gulshan Nanda and many well-known poets established short or long-term working relationships with the movie industry. Today people able to turn a phrase tend to begin in advertising. Some move on to writing or directing feature films, e.g. Jaideep Sahni, Anurag Kashyap, Dibakar Banerjee, Prasoon Joshi, Navdeep Singh, Shashanka Ghosh and, much earlier, Shyam Benegal. Amitabh Bachchan remarked favourably that advertising is supplying more and more writers to the film world:

> *Bahut se log jo ki advertising field mein hain...vo log ab filmein banaana chaah rahe hain. Ye ek achchha roop hai kyonki main samajhta hoon ki yadi advertising mein tees second ya saat second ke andar ek padaarth ko itna aakarshak bana dena taaki janta usse pasand kare, ye agar un mein gunn hai, to us hi gunn ko vo...yadi unko do ghante ya teen ghante mil jaayen, to kaisa hoga. To ye ek bahut achchha development hai. Main aisa maanta hoon.*

(A lot of people in the advertising field now want to make

---

[13]'Bollywood dialogues of yesteryears still tops: Study,' *The Hindu Business Line*, 9 December 2005.

films. This is a good thing, because I consider that if in advertising something can be made so alluring that people want it in less than thirty seconds or less than seven seconds, if these people can get two or three hours, then what will we have? So I admit that this is a very good development.)[14]

At another time, however, Bachchan complained:

Ab us tarah ki likhaavat hoti nahin hai. Mujhe is baat ka khed hai aur dukh bhi hai ki aaj pehle jaisi patkatha ya dialogue nahin likhe jaate. Pata nahin kya vajah hai. Ho sakta hai ki logon ke paas samay nahin hai dialogue sunne ka. Haan bhaai, kya bolna hai, jaldi bolo. Zyaada laffaazi ki zaroorat nahin hai. Is tarah ka ravaiya hai ab logon ka.[15]

(That sort of writing doesn't happen now. I regret it. I'm sad too that screenplays like before aren't being written today. I don't know why. It could be that people don't have the time to listen to dialogue. 'Like, yeah man, whatever you have to say, say it fast. No need for so much eloquence.' This is the attitude of people these days.)

In Zoya Akhtar's *Zindagi Na Milegi Dobara* (2011) the poet and the adman are brought together in Farhan Akhtar's character who makes a living as a copywriter but spends his spare moments filling a notebook with poetry. In reality, Farhan himself has written the dialogue for the film, while his character's poetry is by his father, Javed Akhtar. Two generations, each marked by an era, each with a different style and focus, converge in the on-screen character.

Shabana Azmi contrasted Javed Akhtar's dialogue writing during the '70s with Farhan's:

---

[14]Speaking on the BBC Hindi Service, October 2010.
[15]Quoted by the BBC Hindi Service, '*Aaj logon ke paas vaqt nahin*,' 30 June 2011.

You know, dialogue was not like the spoken word, but it had a resonance all its own. And it was, within mainstream Hindi cinema, about being able to win applause at the end of the dialogue. You associate it with the hero who had to speak lines that were not everyday spoken lines. Today it's changing. Particularly with *Dil Chahta Hai* (2001). There's Javed, who has been the king of dialogue, so to speak, and then Farhan, his son, who in *Dil Chahta Hai* completely changed the dialogue so that it's like spoken language.

Shridhar Raghavan sees another strength in the writing of the past:

It is simple to say that at that time it was theatrical dialogue. No, Amitabh Bachchan was in fact very brooding and quiet, like in *Shakti*. There's a wonderful, romantic moment where the woman says, 'Why don't you come home for a cup of coffee? *Main sachmuch bahut achchhi coffee banaati hoon.*' (I make really good coffee.) And he looks at her, pauses and says, 'Some other time.' This is real. This is writing. You can make out the tension between them.

The 'Coffee Scene' from *Shakti* (1982)[16]

रोमा: हाँ, मुझे याद है आपने कहा था आप आएंगे। मगर मैंने सोचा आपने यूंही कह दिया होगा। बाद में भूल गए होंगे।
विजय: मैं भूलता नहीं हूँ। एक ख़ुश ख़बरी थी। सोचा सबसे पहले आपको सुना दूँ। इसलिए चल आया। मैं...
रोमा: आपको नौकरी मिल गई।
विजय: आपको कैसे मालूम?
रोमा: जो काम ढूंढ रहा हो और क्या ख़ुश ख़बरी दे सकता

---

[16] *Shakti*, directed by Ramesh Sippy, written by Salim-Javed, starring Dilip Kumar, Amitabh Bachchan, Smita Patil, Rakhee, Amrish Puri and Kulbhushan Kharbanda.

है? देखा? भूलती मैं भी नहीं हूँ। मैं सचमुच बहुत अच्छी कॉफ़ी बनाती हूँ।
विजय: आज नहीं। आप बहुत थकी हुई हैं और फिर रात भी बहुत हो गई है। फिर सही।
रोमा: ओके। बाई।
विजय: अरे हाँ, एक बात जो कहनी थी वो तो कही नहीं। आप बहुत अच्छा गाती हैं।
रोमा: मैं जानती हूँ।

(Roma: Yes, I remember you said you would come. Still, I thought you were just saying that and afterwards you'd forget.
Vijay: I don't forget. I have good news that I wanted you to be the first to know. That's why I came.
Roma: You found a job.
Vijay: How did you know?
Roma: For someone who is looking for a job, what other good news could there be? You see, I don't forget either. I really make very good coffee.
Vijay: Err, not tonight. You're very tired, and it's really late. Another time.
Roma: Okay, bye.
Vijay: Oh yes, I have to tell you, you sing very well.
Roma: I know.)

This scene is powerful in its very restraint. Vijay has grown up holding in his anger at his father. He has turned his silence into his essence, punctuated by bursts of violence. We understand his motivation. But what of Roma? So much is left unsaid. We have her eyes, her voice, her poise and her pauses. As an actor, Smita Patil never goes into default mode. Her diction and careful enunciation as Roma provide a striking contrast to the voice she gives to Bindu, the village woman, in Shyam Benegal's *Manthan* (1976). We know then that there is meaning to the voice Smita Patil adopts for Roma. And the words she speaks, though few, are intriguing. The sparse writing combined with the rich portrayal give us hints, but finally we are left with the mystery: who is this educated, sensitive, delicate yet independent city woman Vijay has chanced to meet? We don't quite know, but the genius of the writing, the acting and the direction is that we are made to care.

Writing is not given sufficient attention in cinema: so goes the frequent complaint heard worldwide. It is but the rare film that makes us want to know the name of the writer. In June 2011, French critics on *Le Masque et La Plume*, a weekly hour-long radio programme, were ecstatic as they described the Iranian film *Une Séparation* (*Jodaeiye Náder az Simin*, 2011), written and directed by Asghar Farhadi. 'A perfect scenario!' declared Xavier Leherpeur. The next week the film was playing at twenty-one theatres in Paris and more all over France. The public really does care. David Kipen devotes an entire book, *The Schreiber Theory* (2006), to a plea both for good writing and also for the recognition of the screenwriter's work. Kipen complains, 'Rep houses regularly film tributes to directors, actors, studios, genres, countries and God knows what all—everything, it seems, but screenwriters.'[17] At the same time, he criticizes screenwriters who 'climb all over themselves—and sometimes each other—to become directors. How is anybody supposed to respect a profession that everybody's forever stampeding to get out of, or at least trying to parlay into a dual career?'[18]

Jaideep Sahni voiced a similar complaint about the place of the writer in Hindi cinema:

> Most of the writers in our business have traditionally wanted to be heroes. Or they have basically wanted to be poets, great literary figures, which is another way of saying they have wanted to become heroes. There are very few writers who are interested in telling stories. Everyone says

---

[17] Kipen, 2006, p. 68.
[18] Ibid., p. 69.

we don't have great writing in our films. Sure, we don't. Who's paying attention to writing? The writers certainly aren't. The directors aren't. Nor the actors. The critics who come up with this criticism that we don't have great writers certainly aren't because if they were, they would not have named me the greatest writer of the year when I wrote *Company* and the worst writer of the year when I wrote *Bunty aur Babli*. They confused the language which was meant for the characters with a literary statement.

It is true that entertainment reporters arrive at movie theatres after the first showing of a new film, microphones in hand, often asking the exiting audiences point-blank how well the stars did. Even if the questions are posed more neutrally, still, the viewers themselves tend to praise or blame a film depending on their appreciation of the actors' performances. And yet as writer-director Vishal Bhardwaj says, 'If a good script is badly shot, even then it works. If a good script is badly edited, even then it works. But the script has to be good.'[19]

Naseeruddin Shah would seem to concur. As he looked back on his acting career in 2011, he stressed the strength of the writing in the films he remembers with greatest satisfaction, for example, the 1983 *Masoom*, written by Gulzar and directed by Shekhar Kapur, or Mira Nair's *Monsoon Wedding* (2001), of which he said, '*Jab likhaai itni achchhi ho to actor ko kuchh zyaada nahin karna padta.*' (If the writing is that good, an actor doesn't have to do much.)[20]

Robert Altman was a filmmaker whose respect for the written word in cinema was such that among the jewels in his substantial body of work was a filmed play, *Come Back to the Five and Dime, Jimmy Dean, Jimmy Dean* (1982). In Altman's *The Player* (1992), a

---

[19]Bhardwaj, Vishal, from *Views and Thoughts on Scriptwriting*, 2005, p. 56.
[20]Speaking with Saima Iqbal on the BBC Hindi Service *Ek Mulaaqaat*, 30 October 2011.

cruel look at the inner workings of Hollywood, well-paid studio executives cynically consider eliminating writers altogether.

> Larry Levy (Peter Gallagher): All I'm saying is that I think there's a lot of time and money to be saved if we came up with these movies on our own.
> Bonnie (Cynthia Stevenson): Where are these stories coming from, Larry?
> Larry Levy: Anywhere. Anywhere. It doesn't matter. Anywhere. A newspaper. Pick a story, any story.
> Bonnie (reading from a newspaper): 'Immigrants protest budget cuts in literacy programme.'
> Larry Levy: Human spirit overcoming adversity. Sounds like Horatio Alger in the Barrio. Put Jimmy Smits, and you've got a sexy stand-and-deliver. Next...
> Griffin (Tim Robbins): I was just thinking what an interesting concept it is to eliminate the writer from the artistic process. If we could just get rid of these actors and directors, maybe we got something here.

In 2006 Jaideep Sahni continued to write films and lyrics, but his responsibilities had grown after he was named the creative head of film development at Yash Raj Films. Yash Raj Studios was not, like the characters in *The Player*, ready to throw out writers. Quite the contrary. Sahni explained that his new job at the time was to seek out and invest in new writing talent.

> I run it like a pharmaceutical R&D department. So on a business level what I basically do is figure out what we are doing next year, three years, five years, seven years. That's the corporate planning part. Then the other thing is investing in young people who I think have a knack for writing and making it easier for them to learn the craft. Sometimes I give them books to read, movies to watch, even comics to read. I've got people on my team who scan through hundreds and hundreds of scripts that come in. But we actually are

not scanning for stories; we're scanning for writers. What we're looking for is a spark. I've identified about seventeen-eighteen young people, and I've commissioned four of them on scripts. I can't even say I'm teaching, but I'm taking them through it. And it's fun. In fact, two of them are PhD students in sociology from a university in Canada. Another one has come from advertising. Another one wanted to be an actor. There's another one who has just passed out from business school. I'm trying to run it like an R&D department. And I tell them, 'Guys, we invent the molecules.'

There's a reason that dialogue writing is listed last in the writing credits. When someone retells a film, they talk about the story, i.e. about the characters and what happens to them, usually not about the words they have spoken. Trisha Gupta, in an article entitled 'Death by Dialogue', investigates the relationship between screenplay and dialogue writing in Hindi cinema. She writes:

> If, for Jaideep Sahni, the dialogue writer is the invisible soul of the popular Hindi film, there are others like Rekha Nigam for whom it is the screenplay that ought to get more credit than it does. The nuts-and-bolts business of narrative structure, in this view, is seen as something quite distinct from the embroidered overlay of cinematic dialogue. Nigam, who has written dialogue (*Parineeta*, 2005) as well as screenplays (*Laaga Chunari Mein Daag*, 2007), describes the difference between the two functions as akin to the difference between interior decoration and architecture: 'The screenplay is the skeleton that nobody actually sees. The dialogue is what gets the claps.'[21]

The claps, or perhaps the jeers. A Google search of 'Hindi film dialogue' brings up an ever-increasing number of sites—over two

---

[21] Gupta, Trisha, 'Death by Dialogue,' *Caravan Magazine*, 1 May 2011.

million in 2011—devoted to collections of beloved and/or derided lines of dialogue. Whereas the majority of sites in 2007 leaned towards loving nostalgia, the prevailing mood more recently is often mocking. Still, that so many would pay such attention to Hindi film lines is significant in itself. Parents have learned that children often prefer being naughty to being ignored. People in the Hindi film industry could come to the same conclusion about dialogue: better bad than unnoticed, which might explain this offering from *bollywoodboxofficenews.com*, along with a comment from the contributor that this once serious dialogue has become funny today:

> '*Kutte, main tera khoon pee jaaunga!*' (You dog, I am gonna drink your blood!)—by Dharmendra in numerous movies[22]

Farhan Akhtar too sees filmi dialogue as funny. He has Aamir Khan's character take shots at filmi dialogue, even as he spouts them, in *Dil Chahta Hai*. Farhan elaborated:

> You see, what happened with *Dil Chahta Hai*, primarily on a language level, was that it was the first in a long time where it didn't feel like the actors were mouthing dialogue. I did bring a certain sort of dialogue element into it, but it was always on some level taking the mickey of the fact that people speak like that in movies. And when Aamir actually does look at Preity and starts telling her 'Your eyes are like the eyes of...', then he bursts out laughing because nobody speaks like that.

'The Fat Opera Singer' Scene from *Dil Chahta Hai*

In *Dil Chahta Hai* Akash (Aamir Khan) plays the jaded sceptic and practical joker within a group of three friends, all striking

---

[22] (http://www.bollywoodboxofficenews.com/bollywood_funny_dialogues_silly_bollywood_dialogues)

out into the world after university. Akash's father packs Akash off to work in the Sydney branch office. Shalini (Preity Zinta), also from Bombay, is on the same flight. The two discover Sydney and each other but remain 'just friends'. Akash, after all, is above falling in love, and Shalini is engaged to a man back home. An evening at the opera, however, leaves the two visibly moved. Afterwards, Shalini asks Akash who he was thinking of during the opera. He answers like a 1960s filmi man in love and then undercuts all emotion with a punchline and peals of laughter at his own joke. Meanwhile, Shalini looks on, feeling the fool for having bought into his words of romance.

आकाश: तो फिर सुनो। मैंने देखा उसे। और ऐसा लगा कि शायद प्यार इसे ही कहते है। इट वाज़ मैजिकल, मैं उसे छूना चाहता था। अपनी बाहों में लेना चाहता था उसे। उसकी आंखों में ऐसा ही भोलापन था जैसे…जैसे इस वक्त तुम्हारी आंखों में है। उसकी आवाज़ में बिल्कुल तुम्हारी आवाज़ की तरह जादू था। उसकी सांसों की खूशबू मैं अब भी उस ही तरह महसूस कर सकता हूँ जैसे इस वक्त तुम्हारी सांसें।
शालिनी: कौन थी वो?
आकाश: वो मोटी ओपेरा सिंगर।

(Akash: So listen. I saw her. And it was like, this is what they call love. Oh, it was magical. I wanted to touch her. I wanted to take her into my arms. There was the very same innocence in her eyes as in yours. Her voice was just as enchanting as yours. I could feel the scent of her breath just as I do yours now.
Shalini: Who was she?
Akash: The fat opera singer!)

'To the second degree.' Thus the French refer to the distancing effect that comes from both audience and director sharing a knowing laugh over an easily recognizable cliché. For director-producer Rohan Sippy it's about irony, a subject to which he has given much thought, as he has compared and contrasted culture in India, Europe and the US. He said:

> Hindi film, what we love about it is that it's very full frontal. It's very clear what we're trying to get at whereas American cinema is 'Oh, you're hiding or being coded in a way'. How Shridhar [Raghavan] wrote *Bluffmaster!* is a departure. There's a lot of that element in the characters who are kind of anti-heroic. I think maybe that's what I mean by irony. It's to do with true and apparent meanings being at odds with each other. Something like that. That's from *Reality Bites*.[23] I think there's traditionally been a lack of irony in our films, and that makes them accessible to a very wide culture, whether it's North African or large parts of Asia, everywhere.

The knowing ironic stance in Sippy's *Bluffmaster!* begins with the exclamation point in the title. Dittu (Ritesh Deshmukh), aspiring conman, hopes to learn the tricks of the trade from his 'guru', master conman Roy (Abhishek Bachchan). Dittu calls out to Roy on the street, '*O, Father India, abe mere munhbole baap, oh boss!*' Now 'Father India' brings to mind both Gandhi, the self-sacrificing Father of the Nation, and *Mother India* (1957), Mehboob Khan's film portraying the grinding hardship of peasant life and a woman ready to sacrifice all to feed her family, all, that is, except her honour. Roy, utterly free of responsibility, lives in urban comfort, using his brain (not brawn) to feed off the efforts of others. Honour? Not part of his vocabulary. Early on in the film his planned wedding to Simmi (Priyanka Chopra) is called off when a family friend recognizes Roy and reveals his true profession. Throughout the film Roy veers between world-weary cynic and man who just possibly has a heart. He makes the switch within the space of

---

[23] A 1994 American film by Ben Stiller, full of Gen-X slacker philosophizing.

a few sentences in this scene that is at first funny and finally heartfelt—or is this too a con?

'Love, the Biggest Bluff': Dialogue from *Bluffmaster!*

रॉय: प्यार। जानती हो दुनिया का सबसे बड़ा झूठ क्या है?
सिम्मी: क्या है?
रॉय: आई लव यू।
सिम्मी: व्हाट?
रॉय: आई लव यू। इन तीन शब्दों से ना जाने कितने लोग दो-दो करते बरबाद हो गये। उन्हें देखो। आज के हीर-रांझा, रोमियो और जूलियट, लैला-मजनूँ और कल के बुश और सद्दाम। रियली। अभी तो सब कुछ ठीक है। तीन महीने बाद सिर्फ़ आई और यू रहेगा। लव हवा हो जाएगा।...
सिम्मी: तो इसका मतलब जब तुमने मुझे आई लव यू कहा था वो झूठ था?
रॉय: वो सच था सिम्मी। अभी तक सच है।
सिम्मी: तुम जैसे ब्लफमास्टर का क्या भरोसा? कब सच बोलते हो, कब झूठ? किसे पता?

(Roy: Love, do you know what the world's biggest lie is?
Simmi: What is it?
Roy: I love you.
Simmi: What?
Roy: I love you. Who knows how many people have come to ruin from those three words. Look at them [a couple at the next table, smiling into each other's eyes]. Today they are Romeo and Juliet, Laila Majnu, and tomorrow Bush and Saddam. Really. Right now everything is fine. After three months only 'I' and 'you' will remain. Love vanishes with the wind...
Simmi: So that means when you said 'I love you,' you were lying.
Roy: That was true, really. It's still true.
Simmi: How can anyone believe a bluffmaster like you?

When are you telling the truth? When are you lying? Who knows?!
Simmi looks into his eyes in a hopeless attempt to decipher his true thoughts.)

The final chapter of the film, of course, creates the greatest distancing effect of all. We have felt real emotions with various characters throughout the film. In the end, we realize that we, the audience, have been 'bluffed' by the scenario.

Bluffmaster! is very much of the twenty-first century. Everyone is cool, educated and thoroughly at home in the city. And yet at its core are themes found in the 1955 Raj Kapoor classic *Shree 420*, written by K.A. Abbas. Raju (Raj Kapoor in his signature Charlie Chaplin look) leaves the countryside for Bombay where he is transformed into Raj—rich, suave and corrupt. He has everything money can buy but, like Roy in *Bluffmaster!*, he has lost the woman he loves.

Shree 420: Raj Talks to Raju in the Mirror

राज: तुम?
राजू: मैं।
राज: क्या देख रहे हो?
राजू: तुम्हें। क्या बताऊँ, एकदम फ़ैंश नज़र आते हो। वाह वाह वाह, कफलिन्क कॉलर, ये वो, ये सूट, वाह वाह वाह क्या कहना। क्यों राजा, बड़े आदमी बनने के लिए, जो चाहिए सब मिल गया ना? अब तो खुश हो? क्यों? क्या हुआ? खुश हो ना?
राज: नहीं राजू, मैं बहुत दुखी हूँ। ना जाने क्या हो गया। तू तो जानता है कि मैं बड़ा आदमी नहीं। पर क्या करूँ? तू कहाँ चला गया, राजू? राजू! राजू! राजू!

(Raj: You?
Raju: Me.
Raj: What are you looking at?
Raju: You. What can I say? You're looking really fashionable. Ah, ah, ah, cufflink, collar, this bowtie, that suit. Ah, ah, ah,

what to say? Why Raju, you've got everything you wanted to become a great man, right? Are you happy now? What? What's wrong? You are happy, aren't you?
Raj: No Raju, I'm very sad. I don't know what happened. You know I'm not a great man. What shall I do? Where did you go, Raju? Raju, Raju, Raju, Raju!)

Raj Kapoor as Raj in Shree 420.

Raj Kapoor as Raju in Shree 420. *(Sketches by Simon P. Holzman)*

This scene from *Shree 420* is beautifully constructed. Raju's appearance in the mirror comes as a surprise both to Raj and to us. Using simple words Raju makes Raj look deep inside and admit what, in his search for material gains, he has lost. And then he disappears, leaving Raj calling forlornly after him. It is a fifty-eight-second drama in which vague disquiet gives way to shame and finally to full awareness of his great sadness, *'Main bahut dukhi hoon.'* Raju's disappearance is a shock to us, as it is to Raj, standing alone before the mirror. *'Tu kahaan chala gaya, Raju?'* (Where did you go, Raju?) is a punchline, but without laughter.

Writers generally look for some sort of 'punch', whether in a word, a line or simply a calculated look. Take this scene from Rajkumar Hirani's *3 Idiots* (2009) and listen to it build steadily towards the final wallop.

The 'Definition of a Machine' Scene from *3 Idiots*

Rancho (Aamir Khan) is grinning eagerly as he sits down to one of his first classes at the engineering school he has long dreamed of attending. The professor (Achyut Potdar) goes straight to the attack, *'Zyaada maza lene ki zaroorat nahin hai. Bolo, machine kya hai?'* (There's no need to have too much fun. Tell me, what is a machine?)

Rancho answers, 'Sir, a machine is anything that reduces human effort, sir. *Har vo cheez jo insaan ka kaam aasaan kare ya vaqt bachaaye, vo machine hai,* sir.' Rancho gives examples: the fan, the telephone, the calculator. The professor, peeved at not hearing the 'correct' definition, calls on the Mr Goody-Two-Shoes of the class, Chatur (Omi Vaidya), who regurgitates an incomprehensible but perfectly memorized, exam-ready answer. Rancho protests, *'Lekin sir, main ne bhi to vohi bataaya, sir, aasaan bhaasha mein.'* (But sir, that's what I said too, sir, in simple language.) Rancho is told that if he likes simple language, he should join an arts and commerce college.

Rancho objects, *'Lekin sir, matlab bhi to samajh mein aana chaahiye. Aise kitaabi definition ratke kya faayda?'* (But sir, we need to understand too. What's the use of cramming this bookish definition?)

Rancho is sent out of class. 'Idiot!' the professor shouts after him.

But Rancho soon returns. He has forgotten something.

The professor: *Arre, tum vaapas kyon aaye ho?* (So why are you back?)

Rancho: *Kuchh bhool gaya hoon, sir.* (I forgot something, sir.)

Professor: *Kya?* (What?)

Rancho then uses the same speed and meaning-free voice that Chatur used to define a machine: 'Instruments that record, analyse, summarize, organize, debate and explain information, that are illustrative, non-illustrative, hardbound, paper-backed, jacketed, non-jacketed, with foreword, introduction, table of contents, indexes that are intended for the enlightenment, understanding, enrichment, enhancement and education of the human brain through sensory root of vision...sometimes leisure.'

Professor: *Arre, kehna kya chaahte ho?* (What are you trying to say?)

Rancho: *Kitaabein, sir, books. Books bhool gaya hoon, sir. Le loon?* (Books. I forgot my books, sir. May I take them?)

Professor: *To seedhe seedhe nahin keh sakte the?* (Couldn't you say it simply?)

Rancho: *Thodi der pehle koshish ki thi, sir. Lekin aapko seedha seedha pasand nahin aaya.* (I tried earlier, but you didn't like simple.)

The point in this scene, as throughout the film, is to call attention to the deficit of critical thinking and the surfeit of memorization that marks so much of the Indian education system. Humour tempers what could otherwise sound too preachy. Its educational message aside, the scene follows the 'if only I had said that!' schema which appeals to all who have experienced that classic delayed reaction to slights, injustices and humiliations.

Generally, we can't think fast enough to whip out a comeback line when we need it. Instead we squirm, wince, walk away silently, mutter something incoherent or simply burn with indignation. Scriptwriters, on the other hand, can mull things over in our place, get all the words perfect and hand them to an actor who can then use just the right facial expressions, just the right posture, just the right intonation and just the right tempo to give us that oh-so-satisfying—if vicarious—pleasure of having the last word. Well, I certainly told him off! we think as we project ourselves onto Rancho who, in turn, melts into our psyches, soothing and consoling us, almost making us forget the many times we have been so gauche, so tongue-tied, so un-Rancho like.

THE WEIGHT OF WORDS

'Monsters to the left, and monsters to the right.'
The grandchildren trembled, but Stoner paid more attention to the effect the words had upon him. He weighed and tested each spoken word as if it were a stone. Did it have the proper measure? Proper finish? Proper taste? Proper soul? Did the word of a story have the value of a stone? Around his neck, on a rawhide chain, Stoner had suspended a polished stone cut to the sacred measure, three by two by one. The stone had value. Did the word of a story? Did the weight of an idea?

—Mitchell Chefitz, from the story 'The Mouth of the Mountain' in *The Curse of Blessings*[24]

CINEMA, WE know, is an 'audio-visual' medium. Even if 'audio' comes first, we nevertheless tend to associate film chiefly with the 'visual', partly because our eyes so often trump our ears in the hierarchy of the senses and also because images came first in the history of filmmaking. It was, and still is, 'the motion *picture* industry'. Sound-on-film, i.e. the talkies, took several more decades of engineering efforts to achieve, well after silent films had established their place. Even if you've got no sound, you can still have a movie. You've got no visuals; you have radio. As producer-director Rohan Sippy said, 'The first principle of screenwriting is show, don't tell, so that language is not doing more work than it has to. The visual language, which is much

---

[24]Chefitz, 2006, p. 50.

more universal, can then take over.'

Still, I would submit that if we *can* tell stories with images, the *aud*ience nevertheless wants audio—and not only in the form of music. Words are so important, in fact, that one or two of them can sometimes determine the direction a plot will take, as in Nagesh Kukunoor's *Dor* (2006) (dialogue by Ali Husain Mir). Early in the film, Meera (Ayesha Takia) learns that her husband Shankar (Anirudh Jaykar) has died while working in Saudi Arabia. As a widow, Meera is stripped of jewellery, dressed in concealing blue robes and confined to the home, in careful adherence to Rajasthani custom. She is allowed out only for visits to the temple, and it is there that she meets Zeenat (Gul Panag), who has made her way from the snow-covered mountains of Himachal Pradesh in the hopes of saving her own husband Aamir (Rushad Rana) who has been accused—falsely, Zeenat is sure—of Shankar's murder. Saudi law, a lawyer has explained to Zeenat, will allow Aamir to be pardoned if Shankar's wife will sign a paper of release. In a move that is at once sincere and also self-serving, Zeenat befriends Meera. One day the little girl who has tagged along with Meera speaks with Zeenat and learns from her the greeting 'salaam alaikum'. Later, speaking to Meera's father-in-law (Girish Karnad), the girl proudly repeats the phrase. The patriarch responds in anger, 'What is this nonsense you have been learning at school?' 'Not at school,' the girl answers, 'but from Zeenat Didi, the one Meera meets every day at the temple.' Words of welcome—as-salaam alaikum (peace be upon you)—are distorted into a sign of identity and hence a means of detecting an intruder. An expression of greeting betrays the secret of Zeenat and Meera's budding friendship, and now both women are faced with a bleak future—Zeenat losing her husband and Meera being sold to a factory owner to pay her father-in-law's debts. The plot pivots with just two words!

Actor-screenwriter Kader Khan described a poignant real-life incident in which one word changed the direction of his life:

> I saw other boys who would work to make money for food for their families. I also felt sometimes, when there wasn't anything to eat in our home, that I should also go and work in some tin workshop, some garage or some hotel. One day I was about to go and I felt a hand on my shoulder. My mother was standing there. She said, 'I know where you are going. You are going to make two or three rupees a day. But our poverty can't be wiped out by the three rupees a day you'll earn. For those two or three rupees you'll be stranded all your life. *Saari zindagi teen rupaya chaar rupaya tu kamaata rahega. Agar tujhe is ghar ki poverty uthaani hai*, you have to study. *Tu padh*. Now the way she said padh (study) worked like a bit of mercury. It dropped on my head and went into my veins. I can feel it now. My whole body started shivering. And then I decided I would start studying. We didn't have two rooms, so in mathematics when lots of calculations were required, I used to buy a box of chalks. I had no paper, so I used to write on the whole floor of the room and then wipe it out. My mother would sit in a corner at night while I would study. And she would wake me at midnight. 'Come on, start studying some more.' She was an angel for me.

Words can be powerful, whether spoken in real life or moulded for fiction. A writer who has given a great deal of thought to the property of words is Javed Akhtar. Speaking with Nasreen Munni Kabir, he described his relationship with them in terms of metaphor:

> I believe words are like people. You scrutinise them carefully. You're sitting here, the door opens, a person enters. The first thing you notice is the appearance of the person, then you're introduced. You learn he's an engineer or a chartered accountant. He sits down and you start

talking. Soon you find common links. He's an engineer so he belongs to a certain class and he's from such and such a city. Oh, so he knows your cousin's friend and so on. You develop a kind of association with him and you try to slot him. In the same way, take a word that you're not too familiar with; the first thing that touches you is the sound of the word—its physical appearance. Then comes its occupation, its meaning. The dictionary provides its occupation: this word conveys this meaning. That's its job. But that's not the only thing. The word also has other associations. You start thinking, where did you meet this word before, what kind of company does it keep? Where is it from? What kind of moral values does it represent? A good writer is supposed to be aware of three things before using a word: the physical appearance, the occupation and the associations the word evokes.[25]

In Yash Chopra's *Deewaar*, written by Salim-Javed, i.e. Salim Khan and Javed Akhtar (quoted above), young Vijay's father, Anand (Satyendra Kapoor), is an idealistic union leader who forcefully negotiates for better pay and working conditions for his fellow miners. When the mine owner retaliates by sending his henchmen to kidnap Anand's wife and children, Anand breaks. He is passionate about the union's cause, but he loves his family more. He signs a contract that gives the owner everything and the workers nothing. Enraged, the miners call him a thief, assuming that he is lining his pockets at their expense. Ashamed and disgraced, Vijay's father disappears, and the collective anger is transferred from father to son. Vijay (Alankar Joshi), who will be played as an adult by Amitabh Bachchan, is forced by drunken bullies to have his arm tattooed with the words: *Mera baap chor hai* (My father is a thief). Though the family flees the mining town for the anonymity of the big city, the indelible words will continue to

---

[25]Kabir, Nasreen Munni, *Talking Films*, 1999, pp. 4-5.

haunt Vijay as he moves from shining shoes as a child to loading ships as a man. When chance leads him into the company of gangsters, he prospers. He is now the 'thief' his father was wrongly accused of being. The painful words on his arm have inadvertently given him permission to enter a life of crime. Later, when Vijay's father's corpse is found, Vijay does his duty as a son, but as he stretches out his arm to light the funeral pyre, his shirt sleeve inches up, exposing the tattoed words—the source and symbol of his resentment towards his father and of his alienation from society. He returns home to his girlfriend Anita (Parveen Babi), who tries to comfort him.

The '*Kabhi Nahin Mit Sakta*' Scene from *Deewaar*

अनीता: विजय, एक बात कहूँ, विजय, इसे प्लास्टिक सर्जरी से मिटा दो, विजय, वरना कभी नहीं भूल पाओगे।
विजय: अगर कोई हाथ की सारी लकीरें मिटा दे तो क्या उसकी क़िस्मत बदल जाएगी? ये सिर्फ़ मेरे हाथ पे नहीं, मेरे दिल, दिमाग़ और आत्मा पर लिखी हुई है जहाँ से इसे दुनिया की कोई भी प्लास्टिक सर्जरी नहीं मिटा सकती। ये कभी नहीं मिट सकता, अनीता।

(Anita: Vijay, may I say something? Have this taken off with plastic surgery. Otherwise, you'll never be able to forget.
Vijay: If all the lines of fate are erased from a person's hand, will his fate change? This is written not only on my hand [arm] but on my heart, my mind and my soul where no plastic surgery can erase it. It can never be erased, Anita.)

'Sticks and stones may break my bones, but words can never hurt me.' So goes the adage, but psychoanalysts would disagree. The power of words is such that, try as one might to forget, some sear themselves into our memories where they keep on burning and causing pain long after the event. The four words '*Mera baap chor hai*' weave their way through Vijay's life, embedding into his personality the scars of injustice he has experienced. Vijay responds not by running as his father did but by standing up to fight against any and all who would intimidate him, and time and again, he looks to the words on his arm for confirmation of the rightness of his cause.

Finding Words

The quest for just the right word can be arduous and may require several minds to focus on the task. Director Satyajit Ray had an impressive filmography of Bengali movies long before he ventured into Hindi cinema. His first, *Pather Panchali* (1955), like most of his films, was based on a Bengali novel. Ray's identification with the Bengali language, culture and literature was such that his decision to make the Urdu-Hindi *Shatranj ke Khilari* (The Chess Players) in 1977, based on a short story by Munshi Premchand, surprised critics. Premchand's story, based in Oudh (Awadh) of 1856, tells the tale of two men from the landed gentry who spend their days playing chess, oblivious to work, wives and the signs of political turmoil all around. The film script expands the plot to include the nawab (Amjad Khan) in his palace in Lucknow, the British resident (Richard Attenborough) in his quarters and the diplomatic contacts that take place between the two just before the British gobble up the nawab's territory. Satyajit Ray wrote the screenplay, but he turned to Urdu writers for the dialogue. In this, Javed Siddiqi's first experience writing for cinema, the challenge was to find evocative but not obscure words to give a sense of the time and place:

> There's a scene when Mirza Sahib (Sanjeev Kumar) and Mir Sahib (Saeed Jaffrey) decide they should go across the river where there's an old mosque. They say, 'We'll go over there, and we'll sit and play undisturbed.' They would go in the morning and come back by the evening. In English, 'We'll leave by dawn and we'll be back by dusk.' So the Urdu translation could have been very simple: '*Subah chalenge aur shaam ko laut aayenge.*' Or '*Savere chalenge; raat ko aa*

jaayenge.' But I didn't use those. I used the word '*Tadake chalenge*' (We will leave at daybreak) and '*Jhut-phut mein laut aayenge*,' that is, we will return when the two times meet. Somebody asked me why I used that expression, and I said, 'I don't own and I don't want to write the language which was being spoken at that time in that part of the country. It was Persianized and difficult. I said to Manik-da, that is, Satyajit Ray Dada, 'I am going to coin a kind of language which will give you a feel that this is a period language, but it is not going to be a period language.' And my God, he was a very difficult man to please. He got every word translated. Then he asked me to read and to almost act it out.

Words are out there, waiting to be used. Refined and evocative words such as those Javed Siddiqi chose for *Shatranj ke Khilari*, but also simple everyday words which, when passed through a writer's personal filter, can make us see or feel in new ways, as though we're hearing them for the first time. In *Love Aaj Kal* (2009), written and directed by Imtiaz Ali, Jai (Saif Ali Khan) and Meera (Deepika Padukone), once lovers, have gone their separate ways and are now involved with other people, specifically, Jo (Florence Brudenell-Bruce) and Vikram (Rahul Khanna). In spite of this, when Jai visits Delhi where Meera now lives, they cast caution to the wind and decide to meet. The suffix(es) 'waala-waali-waale' offer multiple meanings and possibilities for nuance. One can add the form to a noun (doodh + waala = milkman), to an adjective (laal + waala = the red one), to an adverb (upar + waala = the one above), to an oblique infinitive (aane + waala = about to come). In a few lines of dialogue of *Love Aaj Kal* this suffix appears and reappears, each time more emphatically and more creatively. On the Delhi Metro Meera, at first, tries to maintain an appropriate distance from Jai. He protests and soon breaks her resolve.

The 'Jai Waali' Scene from *Love Aaj Kal*

> Jai: *Okay, main haath rakhne waala hoon.* (Okay, I'm going to put my hand [on your shoulder].)
> Meera relaxes, slipping back into the comfort of the closeness they once knew.
> Meera: *Ye vaisi vaali feeling hai.* (This is that sort of feeling.)
> Jai: *Kaisi?* (What kind?)
> Meera: *Jai vaali. Aisa hi lagta tha pehle.* (The 'Jai kind' of feeling. This is the way it was before.)
> Jai: *You know, hamne realize nahin kiya lekin ham ek doosre ko bahut like karte the.* (You know, we didn't realize it, but we used to like each other a lot.)
> Meera: *Jo se zyaada?* (More than Jo?)
> Jai: *Vikram se bhi zyaada.* (Even more than Vikram.)

The words are simple. The art and the novelty come from combining them elegantly. Kavita Seth, playback singer for films such as *Wake Up Sid*, stressed the power and appeal of unpretentious words as she spoke[26] about her Sufi song *'Pyaar insaan se karna sikha do'*. (Teach [people] to love humankind.) The message is clear, unadorned, easy to remember.

Javed Siddiqi, who certainly has an immense Urdu vocabulary, also spoke in favour of simple language:

> For example, dil (heart/love) is ji, jiya, mann, prem, pyaar, mohabbat, ishq, ulfat, lagaav, chaahat. They mean the same thing, but how to use them and when to use them, and what is going to be the impact of that particular word? ...It's the most common scene in every film: *'Mujhe tumse pyaar ho gaya hai'*; *'Mujhe tumse prem hai'*; 'I love you.' I always personally like to use a language which is easy to understand. There should not be a word which will divert your attention

---

[26]In an interview on the BBC Hindi service, November 2009.

towards the word itself. The word is an instrument to give information and to proceed further.

For screenwriter and lyricist Jaideep Sahni, the measure of a word or a line is in its impact. During the lively song 'Show Me Your Jalwa' from *Aaja Nachle*, actress and dancer Dia (Madhuri Dixit) encourages townsfolk to come and exhibit their talents. On the last beat in the line *'Aake dikha de mujhe tere talve tere teesein'* she swings her foot up just a bit, exposing the sole, however briefly, its talva. Jaideep Sahni separated for me the layers of meaning he saw in the words:

> Talva. Sole. 'Come and show me the soles of your feet.' And tees is like a welt, but it's used in Hindi like an internal injury, something in your heart. Even a washerman in a seriously Hindi place would know that. Obviously, I'm not asking him to show the soles of his feet and cramps if he had any… I'm asking him to show what he doesn't show to anyone, what he keeps hidden. It's not that it's a phrase which is used, but I'm confident that he'll know what it means. I know it's something stored away in everyone's head, a subconscious connection.

Jaideep gave other examples of impactful lines he has written and then explained the pleasure he takes in finding just the right words for a scene, however short. In *Khosla Ka Ghosla* (2006),[27] K.K. Khosla (Anupam Kher) has been almost totally defeated by a system which allows crooks to prey on honest, hard-working fellows such as himself. His dream of finally building a modest home on his own little plot of land has ended in heartache. His land and money have been stolen. Now it is up to his young adult children to take matters in hand and attempt to outsmart the crooked land-grabber, played by Boman Irani. As they plan their moves, the young people order in pizza. Khosla looks at this

---

[27]Written by Jaideep Sahni and directed by Dibakar Banerjee.

strange food and then helplessly up at his wife. '*Kuchh chutney, vagairaah?*' he asks her. If at least he can put chutney on the thing, perhaps it will be edible. Jaideep said, 'I'm very happy with that pizza line. There's nothing to the line. He just says, "Is there any chutney around?" But it sums up an entire life. The world has changed, and this guy's trying to come to grips with it. That's doing more with less. It's a matter between my heart and the audience's hearts.'

Jaideep Sahni recalled another line he loved from his script *Bunty aur Babli*. Again, it was a simple one-liner. Rakesh (Abhishek Bachchan) and Vimmi (Rani Mukerji), aka Bunty and Babli, have given up their life as adventurous con artists and settled down with Rakesh's hard-working upright parents in Fursatganj (idle town) where they are raising their own son as any respectable middle-class people should. The police inspector, played by Amitabh Bachchan, shows up at their house one day to ask for their expertise, as ex-conmen, to catch other conmen. They sit up straight and act wholly proper. They've surely turned over a new leaf and could not possibly be lured back into their fast-paced city lives, even if they would be on the right side of the law this time. Jaideep Sahni said, 'And then Abhishek's character looks at Rani—and now they're living this very shareef life—and he thinks she's going to say "No." Instead, she says, "मैंने एक मरतबान और आम का अचार बनाया तो मैं मर जाऊँगी।" (If I make one more bottle of mango pickle, I'm going to kill myself.)'

Often it is pictures that make words unnecessary. In this scene, a few words do the work of a host of images: Vimmi slaving in the kitchen, Vimmi desperately trying to ignore her boredom, Vimmi playing the role of 'good daughter-in-law' with the same craft she has lent to her earlier cons. One line sums it all up.

Jaideep Sahni did not mention a special preference for the wedding scene in *Bunty aur Babli*, but it is one of my favourites, with its simple words that paint vivid pictures. The couple has mastered the intricacies of stepping from stifling, traditional, small-town life into the modern world of the city, so full of attractive opportunities. Family connections and societal imperatives, often unacknowledged in the fiction/fantasy of Hindi cinema, are portrayed in this film, valued to some extent, but finally refused with what could be seen as perverse delight. In the following scene the couple's attire, the music, the circling of the sacred fire and even the temples in the background hint at ritual and a society-sanctioned union. Yet family, friends and priest are absent. More importantly, the dialogue, as the couple improvise and individualize their vows, brings them into a novel relationship with modernity. Here are small-town Hindi-speaking characters who are voicing the double jump they have made beyond even the Indian metro lifestyle, directly into Westernized individualism. The humour in the scene both undercuts and highlights the subversive nature of their vows. Middle-class values are refused, and yet a fluidity between the past and the present is maintained. Doors to their parents' worlds are not irremediably shut.

Bunty aur Babli—The 'Shaadi'

बन्टी: हम कभी एक दूसरे से चीटींग नहीं करेंगे।
बबली: हम हमेशा अपने से पहले एक दूसरे के बारे में सोचेंगे।
बन्टी: ठीक है।
बबली: हम कभी एक दूसरे का दिल नहीं दुखाएंगे।
बन्टी: और अगर ग़लती से हो गया तो अचानक बिना बताए रोएंगे नहीं।
बबली: ठीक है। हम एक दूसरे के बिना ना कुछ खाएंगे ना कुछ पीएंगे।
बन्टी: सिवाए सुबह की चाय के। बारह-बारह बजे उठोगी तो हम क्या करेंगे? हम हमेशा एक दूसरे से इतना ही प्यार करेंगे।
बबली: क्यों, ज़्यादा भी तो कर सकते हैं? हम आज से ज़्यादा कल, कल से ज़्यादा परसों और परसों से ज़्यादा नरसों प्यार करेंगे।
बन्टी: हम उन लोगों के साथ कोई रिश्ता नहीं रखेंगे जिनको हमारी बातें पसंद नहीं।

बबली: सिवाए हमारे मम्मी और पापाजी के।
बन्टी: सिर्फ़ तुम्हारे। हम हमेशा बंटी और बबली रहेंगे और हमारे जितने भी ख़्वाब हैं सब पूरे करेंगे।
बबली: सिवाए...
बन्टी: सिवाए?
बबली: वो तुम मेरे पे छोड़ दो।
बन्टी: ठीक है। स्वाहा।
बबली: ओए राकेश, जस्ट मैरीड!
बन्टी: चलें?
बबली: चलो।

(Bunty: We will never cheat on each other, and I'll never buy your lies nor you mine!
Babli: We'll always think of the other one first.
Bunty: Okay.
Babli: We'll never hurt each other.
Bunty: And if we do accidentally, we won't suddenly start crying without an explanation.
Babli: Okay. We won't eat or drink anything without the other.
Bunty: Except for morning tea. You get up at 12.00, so what am I supposed to do? We'll always love each other this much.
Babli: Why? Can't we do better than that? We'll love each other more tomorrow than today, more the next day than tomorrow and still more the day after that.
Bunty: We'll have nothing to do with people who don't like our ideas. (literally, our words!)
Babli: Except for our parents.
Bunty: Except for yours! We'll always be Bunty and Babli, and we'll make all our dreams come true.
Babli: Except...
Bunty: Except?
Babli: Leave that to me.
Bunty: Okay. Swaaha.
Babli: Hey Rakesh. Just married!

Bunty: Shall we?
Babli: Let's go.)

Beyond the lightheartedness of the dialogue is a comment on traditional society meeting purposefully-chosen modernity. That the couple feel the need to mention they will *not* cheat on each other strongly acknowledges that cheating is a possibility, as opposed to the more uplifting (or naïve) positive equivalent: 'We will always remain faithful.' Vimmi/Babli makes it clear that she is not going to sit to the side while her husband eats. Rakesh/Bunty is not going to put up with a wife whose only means of rebellion against patriarchy is tears. And Vimmi is not prepared to rise at dawn to prepare her husband's tea. An ongoing relationship with family is seen as conditional, depending on the couple's desires. 'Except' leaves room for negotiation in the future. Vimmi understands what Rakesh, significantly, does not—that parenthood could make them re-evaluate their present stance.

Aaja Nachle[28]

Aaja Nachle did poorly at its release. And yet I am not alone in finding it to be 'spectacular', 'sensational', 'fantastic', 'terrific', a few of the adjectives used in the online reviews that non-professional critics have taken the time to post. Mariam from Bahrain says, on the IMDb website, that she watched it twice in one day, was fascinated by it, felt herself alive and enthusiastic. The *Laila Majnun* musical, she said, was 'captivating', 'a masterpiece'. My own reaction is actually even more hyperbolic. Each time I view

---

[28] *Come, Let's Dance*, directed by Anil Mehta, made under the Yash Raj banner, with writing credits going to Aditya Chopra (story), Jaideep Sahni (screenplay, dialogues and lyrics for several songs) and Piyush Mishra (for the final *Laila Majnun* opera), music by Salim-Sulaiman, costume design by Dolly Ahluwalia, Manish Malhotra, Mandira Shukla, choreography by Vaibhavi Merchant.

Aaja Nachle, it's as though I'm stepping into the film and living the characters' stories along with them. Is it a perfect film? No. Could I find fault with certain scenes and characters? Yes. But the same could be said of the other movies on my Top 50 list, and much as I may love them all, there are only a few I totally inhabit. The film's strong characters, pertinent themes, memorable dialogue, inventive lyrics and emotionally intense music all draw me in, along with the plastic beauty of the sets and costumes and the perfectly executed choreography.

So why did such a rich film bring in so little money? Chris Garcia, a film writer for an Austin newspaper,[29] appreciated my suggestion that he see *Aaja Nachle* when it played at Tinseltown South, but declined, having decided from the trailer that it looked 'a little chick-flicky'. Is this the key? Do men prefer seeing masculine characters with whom they can identify? Given male-female imbalance, both in sheer numbers and in the power to decide, can any movie which affords predominant screen time to women expect great box-office collections, be it in Hollywood or Bollywood? Sweta Kaushal chose International Women's Day to write up her list of 'women-centric films' for the *Hindustan Times* in 2013.[30] While the list is not assumed to be exhaustive—and doesn't include *Aaja Nachle*—it is, all the same, surprisingly short for a film industry that stretches back a century. She includes *Mother India*, *Arth* (1982), *Nikaah* (1982), *Mrityudand* (1997), *Astitva* (2000), *Dev. D* (2009), *Kahaani* (2012), *Dor*, *Kabhi Alvida Naa Kehna* (2006), *Luck By Chance* and *Lajja* (2001). My own list might be somewhat different but would not, I fear, be all that long either. Now I admit to thoroughly enjoying many 'male-centric' films. Truth be told, I've watched Sergio Leone's *For*

---

[29] *The Austin American Statesman*.
[30] Kaushal, Sweta, 'True Heroines: Women-centric Films Defying Stereotypes in Bollywood', *Hindustan Times*, 7 March 2013.

a Few Dollars More (1965) [31] a good seven times, and almost no film in the world can boast that degree of machismo. Still, I find that constantly taking in the world through the eyes of foregrounded male characters can leave me bored or annoyed or, at times, even enraged. A well-made film that offers a look at the world through women's eyes, on the other hand, comes as a relief. It is an all-too-rare and welcome treat. *Aaja Nachle* gives its women ample screen time, good lines, opportunities to interact with each other and lighting and framing in scene after scene that assure our riveted gaze.

Aaja Nachle begins with Dia (Madhuri Dixit) teaching her New York students jazz steps. A phone call from India takes her, along with her ten-year-old Indian-American daughter Radha (Dalai), to the small town of Shamli, where Dia rediscovers a world she had left behind over a decade before. Her teacher/guru (Darshan Zariwala) has died, he who taught her to dance, to live, to soar (*'udna sikhaaya'*). In a flashback we share Dia's past: here she is with close friend Najma (Divya Dutta), fellow star of the troupe of young girls learning to perform. Here is Steve (Felix D'Alviella), the American journalist who arrives and sweeps her off her feet. Here is her father slapping her for her rebelliousness. Here are her parents making hasty plans for her to marry restaurant owner Mohan (Ranvir Shorey) who has always loved her. Undeterred, Dia follows Steve, leaving behind friends, family and country for America where, though her marriage soon dissolves, she nevertheless puts down new roots. Back in Shamli again, an older, wiser Dia is confronted with the sad ruins of Ajanta, the city-owned theatre where she learned to dance. Promoters have convinced the city that what it needs is a mall, a gleaming symbol of the future, not an outdoor theatre, a deteriorating reminder of the past. A past that includes Dia and

---

[31]Italian spaghetti western starring Clint Eastwood, Lee Van Cleef, and Gian Maria Volontè with entrancing music by Ennio Morricone.

the shame she brought upon her parents. Who would risk being the mother or father of another Dia? Better a town where young people shop than dance. In a message filmed shortly before his death, her teacher appeals to her to save Ajanta.

The story that follows fits, to some extent, into the genre of the backstage musical. Busby Berkeley's 1940s films, often starring Judy Garland and Mickey Rooney, would show small-town folk responding to the challenges at hand by putting on a musical play. Rhythm, enthusiasm and an American 'can-do' spirit were a match for any problem. Busby Berkeley's films, though lively and endearing, lacked depth. They posed no existential threats. They did not pit tradition against modernity, provincialism against a globalized world view. No one was deeply and irremediably sad. Parents did not reject wayward children and flee their hometown in shame. Whatever delight I feel while watching the charming American version of young people overcoming obstacles through song and dance, my involvement in the characters' stories is passing. Not so with *Aaja Nachle*.

The first character Dia confronts is the man with the power to decide Ajanta's fate, Raja Sahib (Akshaye Khanna), the local MP, heir to his father's wealth and authority. He and Dia negotiate a deal: if she can put on a successful performance at Ajanta entirely with dancers and actors from Shamli before the order of demolition goes into effect in two months, he will withdraw his support for the mall. Dia's second negotiation is with the present owners of the house she grew up in, Mr and Mrs Chojar (Vinay Pathak and Sushmita Mukherjee). While the wife warmly welcomes Dia and Radha, Chojar Sahib accepts them as paying guests with strict conditions and cold formality. Dia is plainly someone who knows how to make things happen, and she handles Chojar Sahib as coolly, as elegantly, as she has Raja Sahib. But when it comes to her next encounter, that with her dear friend Najma, Dia is at a loss. After so many years apart there is no hug, no smile, just a hesitant hello. But then Najma is not a free woman;

she is tied to her demanding, intransigent husband (Irrfan Khan) who makes it clear that, given her past, Dia is not welcome in Najma's present world. Dia's pain is palpable. And yet she moves on. With the help of her guru's assistant, Doctor Sahib (Raghuvir Yadav), she begins to audition local talent for the play she has chosen, *Laila Majnun*. A heavy-handed politician (Akhilendra Mishra) sends in his tough guys to spread fear among the small group working with Dia. One toughie stands out, a natural for the character of Majnun, she feels. It is the tall and handsome Imran Pathan (Kunal Kapoor) who grudgingly allows himself to be convinced. Soon it is the tomboy Anokhi (Konkona Sen Sharma) who is falling all over herself vying for the role of Laila. Dia finally relents, sensing the girl's desperation to be near Imran, with whom she is hopelessly infatuated. The troupe expands and progresses, though not without complication, towards the day of the performance. Success promises not only to save Ajanta from a poorly thought-out consumerist form of modernization, it can also repair Dia's broken past and assure her renewed respect in Shamli. The stakes in this wager are high.

Interesting details—some realistic, some moving, some quirky—bring the characters of *Aaja Nachle* alive. There's Raja Sahib offering Dia a bit of the pizza he has just baked. There's Radha's plea that her mother buy an air conditioner so they can sleep mosquito-free. (Dia's answer is no.) There's Imran Pathan's concern of appearing sufficiently tough to the bullies under his command. There's Najma's fear and pain as she plays her accustomed role of a dutiful, unquestioning wife. There's Anokhi, who has learned to play hard to get, the better to attract Imran. She cheats a bit, though. On their walk home after rehearsal she first heads away from him with apparent disinterest but then, while he's not looking, she skips backwards to maintain the illusion she is going away, all the while staying as close as she can, for as long as she can. There's the jilted Mohan tearing a piece of Dia's poster from the wall, wadding it up, but not quite able to throw it away. There's the down-to-earth accountant (Jugal Hansraj), always making sure the troupe's funding is in order. There's the well-dressed politician Chaudhary Sahib, who shifts with the winds of self-interest. There is the inconspicuous waiter, one of Mohan's after-hour drinking buddies, played by Nawazuddin Siddiqui,[32] serving at a private party where he hears and then relays how bribery and rumours threaten the fair fight for the fate of Ajanta. Because the characters have taken on life, the choices they face—large and small—become our choices, their dilemmas our dilemmas.

Characters must change in order to develop. Otherwise, instead of a story, we are left with an immobile portrait, fixed in a moment in time. Learning, one of life's great pleasures, goes in tandem with change. A conduit in a chain, Dia learns from her teacher, teaches in turn, learns more in the process and through her example, inspires others to learn still more. She teaches not only dance but also courage, strength and an intelligent use of power. Some of the lessons are tough: the aerobics for the out-of-shape, nuances of dance for the novices or the art of seduction, which Anokhi slowly achieves through a studied shift in her dress and demeanour. Dia's daughter Radha progresses from a disinterested visitor to the town, unable to speak proper Hindi, to an ardent member of the group. 'I'm not leaving,' she says when the players are threatened with violence. At the beginning, Chojar Sahib is, in the eyes of his wife, the most boring man in the world; by the end he has become a diamond, and a dancing one at that. Some of the transformations result in a story that is just a little bit too tidy. Brilliant acting, though, can overcome the over-neat plot and allow us to suspend disbelief, as Irrfan

---

[32]Before he became a known, bankable actor, he was simply credited as 'Nowaz'. In *Aaja Nachle* and *Peepli Live* (2010), where he plays the local journalist Rakesh, he catches our eye and makes us want each of his scenes to last, so credible is his face, so good his voice, so fluid his movement.

Khan proves in his final scenes in the film.

Strength, even in tiny doses, is essential to the transformative experience that makes for a good story. The word shakti (strength) is feminine. It is not surprising then that Hindi cinema has given us many heroines who personify strength. Often the heroine says and does little but inspires action, e.g. Vidya (Nargis) in *Shree 420* or Radha (Jaya Bhaduri) in *Sholay*. With quiet, centred force, the heroine moves wayward men to do the right thing, often later rather than sooner. Najma, Dia's childhood friend, displays this sort of strength when, in an unspoken act of rebellion against her husband's manipulative business practices, she finally joins the dance troupe. Her act of courage is the stimulus to his change. Dia, on the other hand, is the heroine with a voice, a very sophisticated version of Basanti (Hema Malini) in *Sholay*, one might say. Very young, her strength of personality is such that, ignoring her parents' will, she follows her dream all the way to America. A successful immigrant, when she returns to the country of her birth, she has the power that accompanies wealth and the ease of someone at home in a wider world. In her first meeting with the ultimate decision-maker in the fate of Ajanta MP Raja Uday Singh (Raja Sahib), Dia's haute couture clothing and proud gait give a clear message long before she speaks. Her words merely underline her sense of herself as an equal player in the power struggle that will follow. Dia sometimes oversteps her bounds, though, particularly as an NRI.[33] In her eleven-year-long absence she has forgotten to some extent how to think local. Coming from abroad does not make her automatically right. 'I'm a choreographer, a dancer,' she says. 'From New York,' answers Raja Sahib, with understated but unmistakable sarcasm. She must relearn Shamli's rules, even as she maintains the power and perspective that come with being capable of moving freely and comfortably between worlds, New York one day, Shamli the next.

---

[33]Non-resident Indian.

Dia displays her intellectual strength again and again as she assesses situations and reacts to them swiftly. When she spots her Majnun in Imran Pathan, she goes on the attack, using verbal karate, turning his own words against him. 'You can read and write, can't you?' Angrily, he answers, '*Kya bakvaas kar rahi ho tum?*' (What nonsense are you talking?) Sensing his pride to be his weak point, she continues, 'You've been in plays in school? No? Something? Twinkle twinkle little star? Baa-baa black sheep?' With calculated, intrusive body language, she moves into his personal space until he finally gives in and agrees to join the troupe.

Music is an essential tool in Dia's fight to save Ajanta and, not accessorily, to change a community. In a radio interview[34] neurologist Oliver Sacks discusses his book *Musicophilia* (2007). He describes the power of music to unlock responses—motor, emotional or intellectual—in patients whose brains have been impaired. Once music is learned, it becomes embodied in deeper parts of the brain from which it can well up in amazing ways, even among those with severe memory loss. It is a bit as though the people of Shamli have experienced collective brain damage, perhaps not in most areas of their lives, but certainly with respect to a part of their culture. A play alone would not have the power to reawaken awareness among the townspeople. The music Dia brings to them has the effect of sparking Shamli folks' memories, drawing them into a deeper, richer life, and back to a part of their culture which, for all appearances, had been lost. Her guru said and she repeats, '*Kalaakaar ko sheher ki zaroorat nahin. Sheher ko kalaakaar ki zaroorat hai.*' (The artist doesn't need a town; the town needs the artist.)

It was difficult while seeing *Aaja Nachle* not to think of another film released in the fall of 2007, *Pete Seeger: The Power of Song*, a documentary by Jim Brown, about the eighty-eight-

---

[34] Speaking with Carrie Gracie on the BBC World Service's *The Interview*, 25 January 2008.

year-old folk singer whose songs have had a powerful effect on American society over the decades. Pete Seeger explains that discussing politics tends to separate people, while singing—even about highly politicized topics—brings them together and energizes them into action. And Shamli needs action. Dia's decision to stage *Laila Majnun* at Ajanta is hardly fortuitous. The story, based on multiple retellings of a seventh-century Arab tale and the twelfth-century version by Persian poet Nizami, is at one level an expression of the injustice that exists within a highly patriarchal social system. Greatly heightened by drama, the limits imposed on Laila's will are nevertheless analogous to the stifling constraints imposed on various women in Shamli. Mrs Chojar expresses her frustration with her role as guardian and symbol of honour within the home: '*Agar main saans bhi loon na, to inki izzat chali jaayegi kyonki hamaare ghar mein do log hain, ye aur inki izzat.*' (If I even take a breath, his honour will be lost because in this house there are two people: this man and his honour.) Somewhat paradoxically, this play, an evocation of the past, will take Shamli back to its roots even as it brings it forward to more progressive thinking. Blind to the everyday injustices that real women face, the townspeople nevertheless respond to Laila, a fictional woman at the mercy of her father, brother and husband. The filmmaker wisely cuts between the play itself and audience reactions to the *Laila Majnun* story. Very ordinary couples look touched. Powerful men have tears in their eyes. Shamli is in need of a repositioning of women. The play offers consciousness-raising even as it entertains.

This version of the Laila Majnun story, created by Piyush Mishra, moves between rhyming chanted lines and actual song. Dia plays the narrator, dressed in the first scene in a long flowing gown, her face framed by a loose, dark green dupatta. The backdrop is sky blue. Just in front of that is the outline of an ancient Arabian city, its sand-coloured minarets contrasting both with the sky and with Dia's striking colours in the foreground. The story she tells begins:

> *Ye har nagri ki baat yaar,*
> *Ye har kooche ki baat yaar*
> *Par kis nagri ka kaun sa koocha*
> *theek thaak maaloom nahin*
> *jo baat hamein maaloom vo ye,*
> *ki rahte hain dono-saath-saath*
> *vo din ho ya ki raat raat,*
> *ab kaun sa din aur kitni raatein*
> *theek thaak maaloom nahin*
> (It happens in every town, my friend.
> It's the word on every street, my friend.
> But which town and which street?
> Of that I'm not quite sure.
> What I do know is this,
> That they're together day and night.
> Now, which day and how many nights?
> Of that I'm not quite sure.)

The 'they' who are together day and night are Laila and Qais, two children, maybe seven years old, who are running and playing around Dia as she recounts the tale. We then see them in school with their maulvi who is furious at Qais for writing not 'Allah' but 'Laila'. When Maulvi Sahib takes a switch to Quais's palms, it is Laila who cries out in pain. When she opens her own palms, they are covered in blood. The families are horrified at this unnatural occurrence; perhaps, they think, the work of the devil. They pull the crying children apart to the chorus chant of *'Inko door door le jaao. Inko door door le jaao.'* (Take them far away from each other.) Years later, it is chance that brings Laila and Qais together again. Their attraction, now heightened by the passion of youth, is instantaneous. Qais climbs into Laila's room on a moonlit night and attaches an anklet as she sleeps. She awakens and holds out the matching anklet. *'Main Laila. Tum Qais,'* she says, confirming what they both know, and they hold out their scarred palms for the other to see, a sign of their enduring, perhaps mystical union. No sooner have they experienced the thrill of each other's embrace than society intervenes to pull them apart once again. Laila's brother Tabrez, sword in hand, forbids Qais to touch his sister. '*Vo meri hai* (she's mine),' Qais answers, and Laila stands firm, warning that should Tabrez dare to kill the man she loves, he will find not one dead body but two. In the fight that ensues, Qais kills Tabrez in self-defense but is found guilty of murder and sentenced to death by stoning. He is now being called 'Majnun', the mad, crazed lover. '*Maaro, maaro*' (Kill him, kill him) comes the chant from the crowd. Laila throws herself upon the unconscious Majnun to protect him from the blows. She sings, '*Koi patthar se na maare mere divaane ko*' (Do not throw stones at my beloved). The song has been reworked,[35] but the tune and this refrain are a nod to 'Husn hazir hai', sung by Lata Mangeshkar, from the 1976 film *Laila Majnu*.[36] Knowing that only her sacrifice can save Qais's life, Laila agrees to marry the man her parents have chosen, the rich and powerful Jawan Bakht, but she sets the condition that her Majnun be banished to the desert and his life spared. The music soars with the Sufi-like incantation '*Ye ishq-ishq*' (this love-love) as dancers, moving frenetically and clad in flowing red, take this tale of thwarted love into a mystical realm. Jawan Bakht soon realizes that this woman he has married is as cold and grey as ash. And yet, she tells him, inside her is a fire burning for another man: '*Main bivi hoon teri aur apne Majnun ki main Laila hoon.*' (I'm your wife, but I'm my Majnun's Laila.) In a fury, Jawan Bakht gathers his soldiers to march to the desert in search of Majnun. Majnun,

---

[35] And sung by Sunidhi Chauhan, Shreya Ghoshal and Sonu Nigam.
[36] Directed by H.S. Rawail, starring Rishi Kapoor and Ranjeeta, with dialogues by Abrar Alvi, music by Jaidev and Madan Mohan and lyrics by Sahir Ludhianvi.

unarmed, dressed in rags and consumed by his love for Laila, makes a frenzied appeal for Jawan Bakht to end his life. *'Tu maar!'* The sword enters Majnun and as he falls to the sand, the sky in the background veers to red. At the same instant, Laila clasps her pierced side, gasps and falls to the palace floor. The camera slowly lifts above her outstretched body, still clothed in wedding red. Following the deaths of Laila and Majnun, blues and whites evoke a heavenly space. The narrated tale concludes that whether you believe in the Brahman Gyan, the Gita, the Bible, the Quran or the Guru Granth Mahaan, *pehle pyaar bhari insaani zubaan ko maano*. (First, believe in human words filled with love.) As Laila and Majnun meet Dia on a staircase that disappears into the sky, below in the foreground are two white tombs where the couple's fathers, along with Jawan Bakht, prostrate themselves, then lift their hands heavenward in prayer. The scene brings to mind the masterpiece of the sixteenth-century Spanish painter El Greco. In his 'Burial of the Count of Orgaz', heavenly spheres swirl above the heads of those below who, unaware, go about their earthly business of praying and laying the Count of Orgaz in his grave. Laila and Majnun disappear up the staircase, joined for all eternity, and the scene fades to black as we hear a final chant of mystical love, *'Ye ishq-ishq'*.

Savouring Words: Piyush Mishra

It was the 'Laila Majnun' musical play in *Aaja Nachle* that made me focus on Piyush Mishra's name. I already knew his face. I had first seen him in Mani Ratnam's *Dil Se* (1998). At the time, I remember wondering if a real CBI inspector had been given a small role in the film, so convincing was Mishra's performance. In Vishal Bhardwaj's *Maqbool* (2003), too, he made me forget that his character Kaka was fictional. Mishra wears many hats—actor, writer, singer and composer. When I sought to meet him in March 2008, though, it was above all for his work as a writer.

My first impression of Piyush Mishra, when we met, was that he exudes the same profound intensity in real life that he brings to the screen. Charged. I asked him about his relationship to words. He explained, first as an actor:

> Earlier, as an actor, I did not respect words. I always thought that the meaning lay in the line. I never knew that the meaning lies in every word. If I say *'main vahaan ja raha hoon'* (I'm going there) all five words are equally important. You misinterpret one word, and the meaning of the line will change. I just learned that lately, especially from Naseeruddin Shah, my teacher. He has a wonderful way of using words. So, very late in life I've started behaving properly with the language... I think that when I speak today, people are more attentive because as an actor I can understand the magic of words...not of the line, of the words!

Piyush Mishra as Kaka in Vishal Bhardwaj's Maqbool.
(Photo courtesy: Vishal Bhardwaj)

Given the impact he has on screen, it came as a surprise to hear his harsh self-assessment. So who is this man who sets such a high bar for himself? Mishra was born and raised in Gwalior in a family that valued language. In high school itself he loved literature and wrote poetry. Afterwards, he studied at the National School of Drama in New Delhi and took up a theatre career that included writing, acting and directing. Intensity may have been written into his role in *Dil Se* but more likely, it is simply a central feature of Mishra's approach to life. During our meeting he looked back on his early years in theatre as an exciting time of intense learning during which the theatre group talked poetry and politics while expanding and refining language. One of his plays was turned into a book, *Gagan Damama Bajiyo* (The Sky Resounds with the Call to Arms), based on the life of freedom fighter Bhagat Singh. In 2003 he shifted to Mumbai to work full-time in cinema because, in spite of his dedication to theatre, particularly Leftist theatre, he decided that taking care of his family came first. And cinema does pay much better.

Mishra shared a bit of his thinking process as a writer, savouring remembered words, still regretting lines that disappeared in the final cut:

> Sound comes phonetically or at times it comes with the meaning also. *Chanda pe thoda zang laga hai, thoda hataate ja....* (There is rust on the moon, just rub some of it off...) The earlier version was *Chanda pe kaise gand laga hai*, gand, meaning dirt. Gand is not an ugly term, but I was thinking that there could be a better expression. *Chanda pe thoda zang laga hai.* As I used that word it became clear. *Sooraj aaj mand pada hai*—mand is dim—*mand pada hai, thoda jalaate ja.* So it was not poetic enough. I was thinking, *Sooraj thand mein band pada hai*, band, meaning closed or dim. *Sooraj thand se mand pada hai*, to lighten it up slightly. If a line sounds wrong to me, even if somebody else likes it, I'll keep on thinking about it. Then a thought suddenly crops up and I scribble it down. Sometimes I get stuck and I keep thinking until the solution comes. It can come anywhere—in the toilet, while driving, while talking to a friend... In its totality it should come out like a very precise and concise piece of art.

Mishra's move from theatre to cinema meant adapting to a different working relationship with words. He said:

> I've got used to cinema writing, screenplay writing… Certain words, certain expressions are much more poetic in theatre. In cinema there is the simplicity of the spoken language. Very precise, pinpoint-sharp expressions are required. There is a film called *Yahaan*[37] about the turmoil in Kashmir. The girl is a local Kashmiri and the boy is an Indian captain stationed in front of her house. They get involved. The girl has never been outside Kashmir, so her questions are simple: *'Tumhaare Pune mein barf padti hai?'* (Does it snow in Pune?) He says no, so she says, *'To chinaar ke ped hain?'* (Are there chinaar/poplar trees?) He says no. Then she asks, *'To vahaan goliyaan chalti hain?'* (Does firing happen there?) He says no. Then she says, *'Kaisa ajeeb lagta hoga na.'* (Then it must feel really strange). This is the kind of expression I love to use in cinema.

Mishra's voice, never disengaged, became more impassioned still as he described his role in the making of the *Laila Majnun* play in *Aaja Nachle*. Remembering the lines he had written, he recited and translated a key scene:

> It was the most precious experience of cinema writing I've ever had, better than anything in the theatre even. It was like writing an opera. I produced something which I never expected, and it all happened so simply. The qissa (story) was from the tenth century. It later became very popular in India, in Urdu. The job was to rewrite and recreate it for 2007 without breaking its classical structure, all the while condensing it into just twenty-five minutes. Adi (Chopra) asked for three songs; I gave him five. I had to recreate the same language, but which would be understood in 2007. It

---

[37]Directed by Shoojit Sircar, 2005.

should be Urdu and should also not be Urdu. Then, being an ex-Leftist, I wanted somehow to incorporate Iraq, the Arabs, Kashmir, without making it a true political statement. For example, *Banaaras ke ikke mein o Ganga teer chalenge, barf ki dhoop soonghne, arre Kashmir chalenge* (In the boats of Banaras we'll wander on the banks of Ganga and go to Kashmir for the smell of crisp snow in the sunshine.) Some lines were cut, actually. There was a whole dialogue of Majnun during the rumble sequence: *Sun lo bevaqoof naadaan, aaj ye Qais kare elaan ki Laila lene aaunga.* (Listen, you ignorant fool, today Qais is making this announcement, 'I will come to take Laila.') *Agar qeemat hai mera khoon* (If I have to pay with my life) *to main Majnun ye deke khoon aab-e-hayaat ko paaunga*—keeping the rhyme scheme and poetry intact—(by giving my blood, I, Majnun, will find the elixir of heaven). *Arre, vo Arab des ho ya ki ho Iraq, ya ho Rangoon, main saare jahaan pe chhaaunga.* (Be it in Arab lands or Iraq or Rangoon, I will be known everywhere.) In that way I tried to incorporate all the places which are burning today. And in the last line also when Majnun says, *Vo hava ki angdaai hai vo pyaar ki parchhai hai.* (She is the whimsy of the wind; she is the reflection of love.) *Har jang ki jismein khoon baha uske aage sharmaai hai.* (Every war in which there was bloodshed, has been shamed before her.) *Jab paap badhe insaan na samjhe kya galati ho aayi thi.* (When the sins grew, the entire human race could not understand what had gone wrong.) *Arre, haqeeqat mein unko ek Laila na mil paayi thi.* (The truth is they couldn't find a Laila of their own.) So for me Laila, a woman, is the epitome of affection, the epitome of togetherness; she accepts everything. That was my way of producing my Laila, a social and spiritual ideal. I am a spiritual person. I believe in that kind of mental peace. There is no need to take revenge, even if reasons might be there. Accept it. So that was an idea and the choice of words…I distorted certain Urdu words. Then there are certain words: neech zaat (low caste), badzaat; *ye tera haath kaat doonga main, o naapaak tujhe maaloom ki tune kise chhua hai, ye meri hai.* (You impure low-born, I will cut off your arms. O impure one, do you realize the person you have touched is mine?) *Keede, tu haraam* (You bastard, you bug). Haraam means illegal child. Harrraam (with a harshly trilled '*r*') doesn't exist, but it's the sound [you make] when you abuse somebody. '*Ye tera naam, zaat, tera kaam, kaat shamshaan ghaat ke naam, agar main nahin karun to naam mera Tabrez nahin kuchh aur.* (I will separate you from work. I'll send you to your death, and if I don't do this, then my name is not Tabrez, but something else.) *Ye meri behen nahin, kuchh aur.* (And she's not my sister but someone else.) *Bas sehen nahin kuchh aur* (I can't bear it anymore)… She talks to her brother when the rumble sequence takes place: *Bhaai tu mera sagaa hai.* (You are my kin, my own).

The confrontation between Laila, Qais and Laila's brother Tabrez (Konkona Sen Sharma, Kunal Kapoor, Jugal Hansraj) in the Laila Majnun *play in* Aaja Nachle. *(Sketch by Simon P. Holzman)*

Abba dil-o-jaan se pyaare, ammijaan mein dil atkaa hai. (Abba is more dear to me than my life, and my heart is held in Ammijaan's embrace.) *Magar maloom nahin kya hua, bhaai, ek aurat andar chillai ki chhua kisi ne.* (I don't know what has happened inside me. A woman for the first time cried out; that somebody touched me. *Mujhko chhua kisi ne.* (Somebody touched me). *Saare savaal ban ke ubaal kaafoor hue bhaai.* (All the questions they got burnt, evaporated.) *Vo aurat baithti thi; ab khadi ho gayi.* (Earlier that woman remained sitting; now she has stood up). *Chhoti thi; ab badi ho gayi.* (She was little; now she has grown up). *Aaj use ehsaas hua ki use zehen chadhi.* (Today she has realized for the first time that a fever is rising in her brain). *Haraarat hai, vo ishq naam ke qalam se likhi ik purzor ibaarat hai.* (She is like a bold statement written by a pen called ishq.) *Vo raat sharam ki putli hai to sooraj chale qayaamat hai.* (She represents the coyness of light at night. She can shake the world like doomsday with the rising sun.) *Vo chhod khuda ke nahin kisi ke taish se darti hai bhaai* (except for God she is not afraid of anybody's anger), *aur jaan sake to jaan ki Laila Qais par marti hai bhaai.* (If you can, then know that Laila is in love with Quais.)

Such powerful writing! The fact that *Aaja Nachle* was initially poorly received does not seal its fate. Cinema history, after all, is filled with treasures that were slow to be recognized as such.

Every Word by Choice: Nagesh Kukunoor and Elahé Hiptoola

Actor-writer-director Nagesh Kukunoor's first career was in engineering. Upon returning to his home town Hyderabad after a decade of studies and corporate work in the US, he stepped into film-making with *Hyderabad Blues* (1998), followed by *Rockford* (1999) and *Bollywood Calling* (2003), all mostly in English. The films had small budgets and were aimed at a niche market. 'The math worked out just fine,' Nagesh said, and the language the characters spoke was true to who they were. From the time of *3 Deewaarein* (2003) and especially *Iqbal* (2005), the market for his films opened up, and the characters, whether prisoners in *3 Dewaarein* or villagers in *Iqbal*, needed to speak Hindi. Nagesh, along with producer and fellow actor Elahé Hiptoola, stressed the effort that went into choosing words.[38]

Elahé Hiptoola and Nagesh Kukunoor in Hyderabad Blues.
(Photo courtesy: Elahé Hiptoola)

Nagesh: I still write my scripts in English. Every dialogue is in the idiom that I know, and then it gets translated by a Hyderabadi friend of ours, Ali Husain Mir, who actually lives in New York, where he is a professor of business administration.

---

[38]In an interview at Film City, Mumbai, 2008.

He's written a book on Urdu poetry.[39] And he has now taken on the onus. He did a little bit of translation for *3 Deewarein* way back. But by the time we came to *Iqbal*, it became very clear that I would do the script in English, and he would do the translation. And then actually we'd sit and work through every word and every line, Elahé, myself or sometimes Husain, if he was in India. Does it make sense to the background of the person? Does it sound right? Is it clichéd? I understand Hindi well; I read and write Hindi. But obviously my grasp of the language is nothing in comparison to what a Husain or an Elahé can do. So I just listen to the sound of each and every word and how it is spoken, and then we okay it or not. That's the process. We sit in these sessions, which can be really exhausting. The two of us or three of us sit around translating, and then there are one or two places where you get stuck because you know that the sound is not right. And I keep going back to the English script and say, 'My exact intent was this.' One of the primary thrusts in all my films is never to use a line that is a Hindi-film-sounding line. This is something that I feel very strongly about. Typically, virtually everyone speaks the same way, be it the servant, be it the owner. It's the same in an American film when a cop says, 'Drop your weapon', and you know that the next line will be, 'Put your hands in the air and walk out slowly.' In Hindi films you literally hear the first two words, and you know what's going to follow. So while my films are all in Hindi now, I can almost say with certainty that the Hindi doesn't sound like the Hindi of any films.

Elahé: It's not filmi. It's what you would hear in your house or your neighbourhood or in your friends' circle. We try to keep it real that way. And we've had problems so many times with

---

[39] Ali Husain Mir and Raza Mir, *Anthems of Resistance: A Celebration of Progressive Urdu Poetry*, 2006.

actors. They take really normal lines like '*Vo kahaan gaya?*' (Where did he go) and make it totally filmi. The question is, how would *you* say it? When the lights come on and the camera comes on, don't become the actor. Just be the person.

Nagesh: It is a commonly spoken language. It is easily identifiable. Indian audiences are indeed conditioned to the Hindi spoken in Hindi cinema. I think that in my films this sense of the 'real' is appreciated, but at the same time too much importance can be given to that. I mean, when you hear Hindi lines spoken in a Hindi film, you know you are watching a film, so there is a certain level of distance. You say, 'Oh, that happens in a film. Everyone acts big; everyone uses lines in a certain way.' In my films you can see some real people in real situations spouting real lines. But sometimes that can get a little confusing for the audience, and they come back saying, 'Oh but in a real situation it would never happen like that.' And I want to tell them, 'No, it's the movies. It's fiction. Anything can happen here.' Sometimes I feel that that works against me as well.

Elahé: If I may interrupt, in Hindi cinema we've always taken lines and made them our own. So *Sholay* we spout verbatim, like '*Jo dar gaya samjho mar gaya.*' (If someone is scared he is already dead.) So the lines are part of our everyday life. That's our vocabulary now. *Our* films have never given people those lines. Or we endeavour not to have bombastic lines in our films. But almost every film has a line like that. Especially *Hyderabad Blues* in which there was a line, *Dil pe mat le yaar* (Don't take it to heart.) In fact, about two or three years after the film got released, there was a movie made with the title *Dil Pe Mat Le Yaar!*[40] And that became such a national anthem that it just captured the imagination of the youth. They would say, '*Dil pe*

---

[40]Directed by Hansal Mehta, 2000.

mat le yaar; haath mein le.' (Don't take it to heart; take it in your hand), and they would all crack up. So even though we endeavour to speak normally, we end up giving lines to the public to make their own.

Nagesh: The point I'm making is that I am very strong about my choices, right down to the words, the actions of the characters… everything. I analyse and I make a very, very clear choice. Nothing happens by accident. Once the film goes out, the thing gains a life of its own. I am always in shock as to what people have interpreted from what I've done. Sometimes that was not what I intended at all. But if you were to ask me about any choice of words put into my characters' mouths, then yeah, we have gone through these sessions where Elahé might have said, 'A woman would never say that.' And I would say, 'That is precisely the reason why I would want to make her say it.' So we have had these arguments that have stretched late into the night. But every word is by choice. Sometimes words on paper have a certain ring, and the moment they come out of the person's mouth, I think, 'Damn, that sounds bad.'

Elahé: Yeah, when we read, we act it out so Nagesh can get the feel of the sound, and then he says, yes, no, or change that.

Nagesh: And the most classic example of that is when you deal with songs. Otherwise there wouldn't be a single love song written in the world because the same 'I love you' is said a million times, and the songs sound great. It is obviously the way the singer is emoting and what he or she is getting across. My Urdu is not good. But I like the sound of the words. I have heard them often enough to roughly know their meaning. And I have shot down so many words, saying they're clichés. The new one, which we are still wrestling with, goes… '*Pal mein mila jahaan, mit gaya pal mein. Pal mein banna saja, lut gaya pal mein.*' Now I love the words based on the context: '*Pal mein mila jahaan.*' (In a moment I got the entire world.) I am still wrestling with: '*Mit gaya*' (I've been destroyed). I don't like it. A lot of Hindi films use '*mit gaya*' with enormous self-pity. I have another golden rule for my films, be it in the words, be it in the way actors act: no self-pity!

Connie: Get rid of Devdas.

Nagesh: That's probably the worst character that ever graced the Indian screen. It's just laced with self-pity. I don't like words that sound like, 'I'm so unfortunate. Poor me.' That is also an instruction that I give actors explicitly, 'Don't feel sorry for yourself.' It is a very American thought, but it was completely given to me by my dad. Growing up, there were a thousand songs and a hundred movies we must have seen together, and he would just get pissed off. All of us imbibed that. My sister and brother feel the same way when they watch movies. But I have made a conscious choice. Sometimes you err on the side of no emotion because you don't want to add too much emotion because it might reek of self-pity. So that is the battle I always fight. Back to these lyrics, I am not happy with the '*Mit gaya pal mein*'. I am still struggling with it. Now the second line '*Pal mein banna saja, lut gaya*'. I could live with '*mit gaya*' but '*lut gaya*' I hate! Everything is lost! The words I suggested were '*kho gaya*'. Rightfully, that is also a huge cliché: mila means found, and khoya is lost. We are still struggling with it, although when the singer sang these first couple of lines, they didn't sound so bad.

Elahé: That's why we need to have these lines sung. I say, 'Don't read them.' The first time Nagesh says, 'What are these Devdas kind of words?' I say, 'Don't even look at them. Please have them sung.'

Nagesh: One of the scenes in this upcoming film has a Mills and Boon[41] line. At the end of a 'date', they are walking on the beach on a moonlit night, and she says, 'This is how a perfect date must end…with a moonlit walk, my tall, dark and handsome stranger.' We couldn't come up with Hindi for that. What we came up with—which eventually I cut out of the film because it just sounded so terrible, even though I shot it that way—was: *Har date aise khatm honi chaahiye. Chaandni raat mein, haathon mein haath mein.* Perfect. Then she says, '*mere Devdas*'. Because we couldn't come up with a fricking word that instantly evoked a romantic lover!

Elahé: But another example where language did make a difference was in *Dor*. The grandmother (Uttara Baokar) and Meera (Ayesha Takia) are having this discussion near the end before Meera runs off. The English line Meera says was 'Don't make me a hero', and the translation was added on '*Ye mere haath mein kyon, main to vahi maamooli Meera hoon, main farishta nahin hoon.* (Why is this in my hands? I'm just Meera, an ordinary girl. I'm no angel.) And the grandmother says, '*Ye jo tum karne ja rahi ho, vo insaan hi kar sakta hai. Farishton ke naseeb mein ye sab kahaan?*' (Only a human being is capable of doing what you are about to do. It is not in an angel's destiny.) That was a use of language that we all understood. The difference was on a dramatic level.

Nagesh: That was Husain's genius because that was not my intent. He took the hero element out and went with angels.

Elahé: Because again 'hero' in Hindi made no sense.

Nagesh: Yeah. I think what she said was, 'Why am I forced to be a hero? I am just a normal, ordinary girl. If I hate someone, I should be allowed to hate someone. If I love someone, I should be allowed to love someone.' So he wrote the Hindi equivalent:

---

[41] A popular UK publisher of romantic fiction.

'*Mujhe farishta banne ko kyon majboor kiya ja raha hai?*'

The grandmother (Uttara Baokar) gives Meera (Ayesha Takia)
her blessings in Dor.
(Photo courtesy: Elahé Hiptoola)

The 'It's Not in an Angel's Destiny' Scene from *Dor*

Upon learning that Meera has strayed from the strict confines of her existence as a widow by meeting Zeenat (Gul Panag) at the temple, her father-in-law (Girish Karnad) sends Meera to a room, locks it from the outside and keeps the key by his side. His mother, also a widow, has been silent about her son's treatment of Meera. But now she steals the key while her son is asleep, enters Meera's quarters and speaks to the girl warmly for the first time, helping her to face the dilemma that confronts her.

मीरा: मैं क्या करूँ दादी माँ?
दादी माँ: तेरा दिल तुझसे क्या कहता है?
मीरा: क्या जानूँ? दिल की आवाज़ को इतना दबाया है कि वह कब का ख़ामोश हो गया।
दादी माँ: दिल कभी बोलना बंद नहीं करता। ध्यान से सुन। रास्ता वही बताएगा।
मीरा: शंकर की मौत ने मेरे हाथों से मेरी ज़िंदगी छीन ली। तो

मैंने अपने दर्द से समझौता कर लिया क्योंकि यही मेरी ज़िंदगी रही है। अच्छा या बुरा, इसे ही निभाना है।
दादी माँ: क्योंकि बाहर की अंजान दुनिया से डर लगता था।
मीरा: हाँ, अपने आप को सांचे में ढाले रखना आसान है। ज़िंदगी चलती है, चलने दो। अपने जीवन की डोर किसी और के हाथ में रहने दो। लेकिन यह डोर जो मेरे हाथ में थमाई गई है इसका मैं क्या करूँ? कौन जीता है? कौन मरता है? इसका फ़ैसला भगवान करे, मीरा क्यों? मुझे यह फ़ैसला नही करना। मैं एक आम इंसान हूँ चाहूँ तो स्वार्थी बनूं। जिसने मुझे दर्द दिया है मैं उसे दर्द दूँ। मुझे फ़रिश्ता बनने पर मजबूर क्यों किया जा रहा है? मुझे यह शक्ति नहीं चाहिए दादी माँ। मुझे यह अधिकार नहीं चाहिए।
दादी माँ: वो हमारे साथ खेल बहुत खेलता है ना?
मीरा: मेरे साथ कुछ ज़्यादा ही।
दादी माँ: तूने जो भी निर्णय किया है, बेटी, उस पर अटल रहना।
मीरा: यह तो मैं ज़ीनत से सीख चुकी हूँ।
दादी माँ: तो फिर इंतज़ार किस बात का? जा, कर जो तुझे करना है। और सुन। जो कुछ भी तू करने जा रही है, वो एक इंसान ही कर सकता है। फ़रिश्तों के नसीब में यह सब कहाँ?
मीरा: दादी माँ...
दादी माँ: शशशश, कुछ कहने की ज़रूरत नहीं है। मैं तो सिर्फ़ अपने पापों को तेरे पुण्यों से ढक लेने की कोशिश कर रही हूँ।

(Meera: What should I do, Grandma?
Grandmother: What does your heart tell you?
Meera: What do I know? The voice in my heart has been suppressed for so long that it has gone silent.
Grandmother: The heart never stops talking. Listen carefully. It will tell you the way.
Meera: Shankar's death snatched my life from my hands. So I compromised with my affliction because this is the life I know. Good or bad, I have to carry on.
Grandmother: Because you were afraid of the unknown outside world.
Meera: Yes, fitting into the mould is easy. Life goes on.

Let it go. Leave the thread of my life in someone else's hands. But this thread which has been thrust in my hand, what am I to do with it? Who lives? Who dies? Let God decide. Why Meera? I don't want to decide. I'm just an ordinary human being. I can be selfish. If someone hurts me, I hurt him. Why do I have to be an angel? I don't want that power, Grandma. I don't want that right.
Grandmother: He plays lots of games with us, doesn't He?
Meera: Too many with me.
Grandmother: Whatever decision you have made, child, stick to it.
Meera: That's what I learned from Zeenat.
Grandmother: So what are you waiting for? Go do what you have to do. And listen, what you are about to do, only a human being can. It is not in an angel's destiny.
Meera: Grandmother....
Grandmother: Shhh. You don't need to say anything. I am only trying to cover my sins with your virtue.)

Nagesh Kukunoor on the Women in *Dor*

Nagesh: Actually, one of the ways I was pitching *Dor* when the film was about to come out was to say, 'It is a movie with two heroes. The only difference is they happen to be women.' I was not trying to be cute or funny or anything like that. If you look at a lot of the things that women do in the film, they do the things that heroes are supposed to in Hindi films. I mean, a guy would have set out to save his wife's life. The thought process probably also came from the fact that I wrote these women as men. I always give these guys as an example: the Coen Brothers. In rural Arizona a guy who probably never went to high school would use a word like 'recidivisim'[42]. I mean the Coen Brothers have consistently done this. There are some guys somewhere

---

[42]Nicolas Cage's character speaking in *Raising Arizona*, 1987.

who might speak like this. And I use that as an example more out of fun. But for *Dor* I know a lot of words that come out of Zeenat's mouth would probably not be uttered by ninety-nine out of hundred women. But there might be that one. That is my justification. But what I've been happy to find is that people seem to enjoy the fact that the characters don't speak like all the characters you hear in Hindi films and that their thoughts and their opinions are so very different.

Connie: And yet they are laden with the burden of tradition.

Nagesh: Absolutely. I mean, you can go up to a point in breaking with reality, and then you make it so unreal that it destroys any kind of empathy you might buy from the audience. I've had to become smart about picking my battles. Instead of changing twenty-five different things, if we change five, the chance of selling it to an audience is probably better… I'm sorry, I am quoting the Coen Bros again, 'People allow me to play in my corner of the sandbox.'

KADER KHAN: AN URDUWAALA FROM KAMATHIPURA, MASTER OF THE CLAP-CLAP LINE

WHEN I met Kader Khan in Pune in February 2007, he shared parts of his early life, gave many anecdotes from the days he had worked in Hindi cinema, explained his personal philosophy, recited and commented on Ghalib and Iqbal and spoke of his present efforts to raise standards in Muslim education. His life could be a screenplay. Kader Khan was born in Kabul and raised in poverty in the Bombay slum of Kamathipura, known for its huge red-light district. At his mother's insistence, he studied diligently and eventually began his working life as a civil engineer and teacher. Along the way, his love of theatre brought him to the attention of the film industry. He then put his teaching on hold for the fame, wealth and glamour the movies offered. By 2007 he had largely left the world of cinema in order to fulfill a promise he had made to his father, that he would use his teaching skills for the betterment of the Muslim community. The following are some highlights of Kader Khan's story, told in his words:

My theatre helped me a lot. Yeah, because from the age of eight or nine years I started working in theatre. See, there was an old actor who was in Mehboob Khan Sahib's *Roti* (1942). His name was Ashraf Khan, a very famous actor. He was making a play, *Wamaq Azra*, like *Romeo and Juliet*. There was a need of a young prince. So how can you find a boy of eight or nine who can jot down about forty pages and then speak the lines in front of a live audience? In those days, I belonged to a very, very, very poor family from the slums. My mother used to send me to the mosque for prayers. I used to bunk and sit in a graveyard alone, in between two graves. I used to yell out. *Kisi ko dekhta tha main ki ye aadmi ne ye kaam achchha kiya, ya ye lafz achchha bola* (If I would see somebody who did something well or used words with skill) and I used to copy him…*aur phir vo ek dedh ghante ke baad jab namaaz khatm hoti thi* (and when prayers finished an hour and a half later), I used to go back to my house. And most of the time I was caught by my mum. Because I never wore chappals, right? I used to go barefoot. She would catch me because we would make vazu (ritual cleansing) at the mosque, and she would look and say, 'Your feet are dirty. That means you didn't go to mosque at all.' *Kya karein?* (What to do?) *Revolution by birth hota hai insaan ke andar.* Man is born revolutionary.

So some people went and told Mr Ashraf Khan that there is a boy; he's sitting in the night alone between the two graves, and he yells and speaks whatever he likes. So he watched me a number of nights, and then one night, he just turned the light of a torch on me. He said, '*Idhar aao. Tum ye kya bolte rahte ho yahaan baithke?*' (Come here. What do you keep saying while sitting there?)

'*Kuchh nahin. Aise hi, jo achchha lagta hai, bolta hoon main.*' (Nothing. Just like that. I say whatever sounds good.)

He stared at me. '*Drame mein kaam karoge?*' (Would you like to work in a drama?)

Main: 'Drama kya hai?' (Me: What is drama?)

'*Ye jo tum kar rahe the, drama kehlaata hai.*' (What you were doing, that's called drama.)

'*Nahin, main ne kabhi kiya nahin ye,*' *keh raha tha main.* (No, I've never done this, I said.)

He told his collector to bring this boy the next day to his small bungalow in the town itself. I went there. He started training me. And with his guidance, affection and fatherly love, I picked up the role in one month. And after one and a half months, the show was staged and I got a standing ovation from the audience. And when an old man came on the stage, he gave me a hundred-rupee note. He said, 'This is a very big sum for you at this age. Always remember this: that you got this certificate at a very young age. Your future is good. I wish you all the best.' He just put his hand on my head and disappeared. I don't know who he was. That hundred-rupee note was with me for a number of years. But in poverty people sell laurels and trophies as well. My circumstances made me spend that money and buy some food for the house.

Then I started writing and directing too. I did my schooling in a technical school. My principal was very good. He would love the fact that I did theatre. I wrote plays. I started [participating] in the inter-college dramatic competition. In two or three years I was so popular among the college students that it was said in Bombay that if somebody had not performed in Kader Khan's play, that means he had not been to college anywhere in Bombay. Students from other colleges used to come and take my autograph. So that popularity I got very early in life.

And then I started teaching. Basically, by education I'm a civil engineer. I used to teach Theory of Structure, Hydraulics, Strength of Material, RCC Steel, but the subject which I used to like was theatre. Stanislavsky, Maxim Gorky, Chekhov, Dostoevsky: these were my other teachers. So my life was split into two.

My parents, because of poverty, they could not continue [staying together]. There was always tension in the house. They got separated... My mother remarried. I got a lot of affection from my mother, an equal amount of hatred from my stepfather. He was a stepfather like in the dramas or the screenplays... He never used to work. He was in the company of bad people. They would take him to bars. *Sharaab peeta tha, aata tha, Ma ko maarta tha* (He would drink, come home, beat my mother) ...*bhookta rehna faaqa karte the.* Starve!

Is zindagi mein sab kuchh dekh liya hai main ne. (I have seen everything in this life.) And these things made me a revolutionary, and I started writing without learning literature from anywhere. And I was a good teacher because everything I used to do, I used to do with love because I never got love, except from my mother and father. So that area of love was empty. I studied in a college where there were no girls. So no affection, no love. Everybody wants love and affection from the parent. That's true. But it has some devils. You get affection from the Almighty too. That is the top level. But insaan (human being) is not at the top level. He lives in the valley, not at the top of the mountain. So a human being wants love. But there was no love. So all that love I put into revolution. I used to write. Pungent lines I used to write and pungent plays.

People from the film industry used to come see the plays regularly. And they heard my name. They saw me on the theatre stage. They saw me performing. They saw my writings. They saw my direction as well. So they were saying, 'Why is this idiot not coming to the film industry? He's a talented man. He should be in the film industry.' So the day I won the award for my *Local Train*, one of the producers and directors and some writers came the next day and said, 'Why don't you join films?' And it was a joke for me. 'You should be a writer; you should be an actor. You could be anything you want because you know everything.' I had never thought of going into films because in those days film was looked down upon. One of the producers, Mr Ramesh Behl, said he was making a film, *Jawani Diwani* (1972).

'I want you to write the dialogues for that film,' he told me.

I said, 'I don't know how to write dialogues.'

He said, 'Whatever you wrote in the play, those are called dialogues.'

So I went there, and they gave me a chance. They said they wanted to shoot the next week. I didn't have a place (of my own). I went to Cross Maidan where people play football. I sat in the corner and would be hit by footballs the entire time. I wrote the script in four hours. *Main gaya vaapas to mujhko dekhkar vo bole, 'Ye ulloo ke patthe ko vo scene samajh mein nahin aaya.'* (When I went back they saw me and said, 'This idiot has not understood the scene.')

I could read their lips; they were talking badly about me. And I said, *'Is ulloo ke patthe ko subject samajh mein aaya hai, yeh ulloo ka pattha likhke laaya hai.'* (This idiot has understood the subject, and has done the writing, and has brought it.)

'What? *Itni jaldi?* (So fast?) Same day?!'

'Meri life aisi hi hai, jo decide karta hoon, us hi din kar deta hoon. Aaj hi faisla ho jaaye. (This is the way my life is; if I decide to do something, I do it the same day. So make up your minds today.) If you want to take me, you take me, or you let me go because I've got my students waiting for me.'

And I narrated the subject and scenes to them. They jumped and said, 'Again.' I narrated again three or four times and they recorded, and within three days the shooting started. That's how my script was taken into a film. That was a film which was to be shot after one week or ten days, but shooting started just after three days because of the completion of the script. Now during that shooting I got extra publicity. There was a rumour in the industry that a new writer has come. He writes very colloquial language. Sometimes it becomes difficult for the artiste to perform the way he narrates the scenes. I got ₹1500 for that initial film, and that was big money because I had never seen more than ₹500 before. I was on the verge of going back to my institution after seven weeks. Then someone came and said, 'I'm a producer and I'm thinking of making a film. *Meri film ka naam* Khel Khel Mein *hai*. (The name of my film is *Khel Khel Mein*). This is the screenplay. I would like you to write the dialogues for this film.' He just gave me an envelope. It was a thick one. I went and counted. It was [contained] over ₹10,000. I completed the script. I got another offer. In six months' time I was called by Manmohan Desai. He was searching for a writer to finish *Roti* (1974). The producer suggested me. Now Manmohan Desai was fed up with Urdu writers. He said, 'I hate this language. These writers, they write all proverbs and muhaavraas and similes. I want my colloquial language. A Muslim? I'm fed up and you're bringing another one?' He met me, and said, *'Dekho, miyaan, main bahut straight bolne vaala aadmi hoon. Tumhaari story pasand aayegi, tumhaara dialogue acchha lagega, to theek hai. Otherwise, dhakka maarke baahar nikaal doonga.'* (Look, Mister, I'm a straight-talking man. If I like your story and your dialogue, great; if not, I'll kick you out.) That was the first time in my six or eight months that somebody had talked to me that way. *'Agar achchha laga to,'* kehta hai, *'main tere ko leke ganpati ki tarah naachunga.'* (If I like it, he said, I'll dance with you like Ganpati.)

He narrated the complete climax. He used to stay at Khetwadi. That was my alma mater. After two or three days, I went back there. He was playing cricket with the street boys. He saw me and asked, *'Kya hai?'* (What is it?)

'Subject-scenes sunaane ke liye aaya hoon.' (I came to narrate the subject and scenes.)

'Sunaane? Matlab, likhke laaya?' He left his cricket. *'Chal, jhatpat.'* (Narrate? That means you've written it? Okay, let's go quickly!)

He took me inside. First time. A giant of a person. Before that all the crews and directors were in tune with me, you know? It was my first time sitting in front of a big director and narrating scenes. Anyway, the actor in me helped me a lot. So actually, that's why the actor and writer and teacher, they were always in tune with one another. The actor would help me. The writer would help the actor. I narrated the scene, and he started jumping. He said, 'Again! *Phir se sunaao.*' (Narrate it again.) He started yelling, 'Jeevan!' His wife's name was Jeevan. *'Idhar aa.'* (Come here.)

'Kaayko bulaaya hai?' (Why did you call me?) she asked.

'Listen to what he has written.'

I narrated. She was in tears. 'This man is dying for the last six months for this sort of scene. You've done more than that.'

He said, 'Again.' I narrated the whole episode about ten times. I didn't know he had put it on tape and recorded everything. And then he went inside to his other room. He brought a small Panasonic TV, and said, 'This is a gift from me.' He was also carrying a golden bracelet and ₹25,000 cash. 'This is a token from me.' Such a big man he was. If he used to love somebody, he would love with his heart. He was not a stingy man. He was brave-hearted. He just dialled all the writers and directors and producers and said, 'You be careful. One man has come who will just rule your industry.' He was a crack. He phoned the writers also. 'Throw away your pens. You don't know how to write!' He said, 'How much have you been getting for writing?'

I said, '₹25,000.'

He said, 'Now your price is one lakh rupees.'[43] And that's how I came into the class of ₹100,000. I was taken from the ground floor to the hundredth floor, and my missile took off from the hundredth floor. From there, there was no point of return. He could not make any film without my being there. I used to sit with him in screenplay discussions, story discussions, choosing of the songs, everything.

But in those days there was a line of division, a line of demarcation. There were two movie heads: Manmohan Desai and Prakash Mehra. I was working with Prakash Mehra as well. I wrote *Khoon Pasina* (1977), *Laawaris* (1981) and *Muqaddar ka Sikandar* (1978) for him. That was a second rocket. *Ab in do logon mein se kya manaahi thi—jo uski film mein kaam karega, idhar nahin kar sakta; jo udhar karta hai, idhar nahin kar sakta.* (Now between these two there was a rift. If someone worked in one camp, they couldn't work in the other.) But they could not order me. Amitabh Bachchan said, 'Come along with me; where I work, you will work.' Manmohan Desai made *Roti*. Then he said, 'I want to produce now.' And he made *Amar Akbar*

---

[43]One lakh = 100,000.

Anthony. He made *Naseeb* (1981). Then he made *Coolie* (1983). Twists and turns he used to have. He believed in that. Prakash Mehra had straight narrations, depending most on the dialogues and the performance. He was a good songwriter as well, Mr Prakash Mehra.

One day I was shooting at RK Studio. Jeetendra came and told me, 'Sorry, this one producer is trying to meet you for the last two years, but he doesn't have the courage to come to you and talk.'

Then the producer came. I asked, 'From where have you got the idea that I'm a big writer or a big man? I'm just an ordinary man.'

'No, sir. Anyway, my brother wants to talk to you.' I talked to his brother G. Hanumantha Rao, the producer of Padmalaya Films, another very big-hearted man, very nice people. He said, 'I'm thinking of making a remake from Kannada to Hindi.' He gave me the script.

I said, 'See, in South India it is the norm that when you remake some film, you go step by step, word by word and follow the original one. I can't do that. I'll rewrite it.'

He said, 'Do whatever you like.'

I wrote; then I recorded the whole script. Jeetendra worked there. Hema Malini worked in it. And that film was *Meri Aawaz Suno* (1981).

With that film I entered into the South [film industry]. It ran into controversy with the Censor Board, but it was passed. When some film is banned, it gets a lot of publicity. It was a big blockbuster. I got the Best Writer Award for this film.

Now I was divided into three: Manmohan Desai, Prakash Mehra and the South. They're very punctual people. They give you complete money. But there was always a tension in my house, that you're not giving us time. I came up from the slums, so I gave them flats and money, but I wasn't giving them time. So now there were three lines: one line between Manmohan Desai and Prakash Mehra; a second line between Manmohan Desai and Prakash Mehra and the South; and a third line between the family and Manmohan Desai, Prakash Mehra and the South. And these lines still exist. Once a piece of bread has been cut into portions, it cannot be rejoined. It's like a mirror broken into pieces. No regrets. Whatever I am, I am.

My father was a friend, philosopher, guide, teacher… everything for me. I'm such a lucky man that wherever I went in life, there would be teachers. Desai was more than a teacher for me. He taught me commercial cinema. He made me work like that. He used to give me a drop; I would convert it into an ocean. Manmohan Desai would give me the outlines, and I would fit in my lines. And I came to know his weaknesses. He wanted the clap-clap dialogues. I used to speak and write from every actor's point of view. I used to keep Manmohan Desai in the frame. I could see his reaction before going to his house, whether he would clap for these lines or not. He was my audience. And he knew the nerves of the audience. '*Talvaar ki vaar jise maar na sake, vo Amar hai. Aag ko jalaakar jo khaak kar daale, vo Akbar hai.*' Then he says, '*Apun public mein bolta hai, anhoni ko jo honi bana daale, vo Anthony hai.*' (He who cannot be killed by a sword is Amar the immortal. He who reduces fire to ashes is Akbar [the undefeatable]. I tell the world openly, he who makes the impossible possible is Anthony.) Really tongue twisters. From this he made the song, 'John Johnny Janardan…'

[When I was young] there was a very tough dramatic competition organized by the Bharatiya Vidya Bhavan at Chowpatty. My God, what sort of audience used to come there— very dangerous. The moment the actor came on stage, they said, '*Aao.*' (Come.) And the actor got frightened. '*Baitho.*' (Sit.) He sat. He took the receiver of the phone. The audience said, 'Hello,' and this man started talking without even dialling the number, and he was booted out. So I learned a lesson from that audience. It was an auditorium of four hundred people. When my play was staged there, I used to get 1,700-1,800 in the audience. And I used to make them clap for every line. I used to imagine them sitting in the gallery. Every line should keep them busy. After ten applauses, you've got the audience. And then you give your ideas, but go on getting the applauses and giving your ideas, and you've won the case. I used to move the audience. That taught me. So from Bharatiya Vidya Bhavan I shifted my focus to Manmohan Desai.

I wrote in films for about twenty-eight years. I got fed up. Basically, my father made me into a teacher. I was really at home in my teaching. I went to the glamour world. I earned a very good name and place and money also. But at heart I was not at ease. I could feel somewhere that my students were waiting for me. My class was waiting for me. One day I saw the new generation arriving in Bollywood and taking over, some new boys who used to work under my director's assistant, not even chief assistant but fourth assistant, fifth assistant. They became heroes, and they became directors. So there was a generation gap, a gap of thoughts and feelings. I worked with one or two but could not continue. So gradually, I started receding, and that's how I got out of the industry by 70 per cent or 80 per cent because directors and producers and actors of my day are mostly gone. And it becomes very difficult to discuss with them [the new generation], to match their thoughts. *Unke thoughts vo saare foreign hain.* They're all imported thoughts. I belong to this soil. I belong to Kamathipura.[44] Unless I find an atmosphere of that, Kamathipura, I can't act or I can't write. And the modern generation, they're conversant with computer science, business management. These subjects were not there in our time at all. The management is very good. The technique is very much advanced. But the literature, they've lost. There are no original writers here. To become a writer you have to pass through some boiling episodes of your life. They call suffering something else. If a boy falls in love with a girl and he's waiting for her for four

---

[44]Southeast of the Mumbai Central train station.

hours, they call that suffering. No, that's not suffering. Suffering is something else, which should go to your subconscious, and it should be written there, recorded there. At any time of life, you can find yourself in a mood to cry. Why do you feel like crying? Because there is one camera in the subconscious which records everything. And one day there is a projection room also, and that camera becomes like a projector and projects that old episode which the eyes have seen. And that is a dramatic scene or an emotional scene, and you feel like crying. That's how a human being is not one but is divided into departments. And the most governing department in the body is the subconscious. We call it heart or brain, but it's the supreme power of the subconscious… Meer Dard has written a very good line:

Dard-e-dil ke vaaste paida kiya insaan ko, dard-e-dil ke vaaste paida kiya insaan ko, varna taa'at ke liye kuchh kam na the karubiyaan. If God had wanted to be worshipped, there are lots of angels for that. Why should he have created a man? If man was created, it was because man was given a heart, and a high heart is to take pain.

Writers should always sketch. Writers should always act. Most writers come from the stage. Oration is part of acting too. When you speak, you take the audience in your clutches. The choice of the words, the fluctuation of your voice…and the gestures… That is what an actor is… We act in our personal lives many times when we speak lies. At that time, the expression acts as make-up. It covers your face… Manto was a writer who inspired me a lot. What I got from Manto was that to have a good idea, you have to have good words. People use a big vocabulary to narrate a big idea, whereas he said that the ideas should be big and the sentences should be simple. And that I followed, and that was the reason for my success. Ghalib gave me the ideas in the form of screenplays. You should have some imagination in your scene. And you should describe everything in a few words. And those words should be bound together so that the audience who's listening to it will be tied to it. If you can tie the audience to your script, you're successful. That tying is very difficult. The trick is that you should know all. You should be a jack of everything. If you're a carpenter, you should know how to select the best wood, cut it into a nice shape. It should accommodate the complete space, and the design should also be good. Designing and accommodation—that is what scriptwriting is. Sometimes you accommodate everything, but it looks like a box. It should look good also.

You know that the line is right only from the reaction. Sometimes in the auditorium you get a response from those lines that you'd have never thought of. And many times you think that this line is going to blow the audience away, and then nothing happens. There are three reactions. There's your reaction, your director's reaction and the audience's reaction, three reactions in three different zones, three different islands. You should travel to all three islands. It's an imaginary world.'

Kader Khan then recited the dialogue that he wrote and delivered in Muqaddar ka Sikandar (1978), *directed by Prakash Mehra.*

Kader Khan as the faqir in Muqaddar ka Sikandar, *opposite Mayur Verma. (Sketch by Simon P. Holzman)*

I played the role of a beggar. I go to a graveyard, and I see the young Amitabh Bachchan sitting beside a grave and crying.

Faqir: Kiski qabr par baithe ho, bachche?
Bachcha: Hamaari ma mar gayi hai.
Faqir: Utho, aao mere saath. Chaaron taraf dekho. Yahaan bhi koi kisi ki behen hai, koi kisi ka bhaai hai, koi kisi ki ma hai. Is sheher-e-khaamoshion mein, is khaamosh sheher mein, is mitti ke dher ke neeche, sab dabe pade hain. Maut se kisko rastaagaari hai? Inhein? Maut se kaun chhoot sakta hai? Aaj unki, to kal hamaari baari hai. Par ek meri baat yaad rakhna. Is faqir ki baat yaad rakhna. Is zindagi mein bahut kaam aayegi. Ki agar sukh mein muskuraate ho to dukh mein qahqah lagaao. Kyonki zinda hain vo log jo maut se takraate hain, aur murdon se badkar hain vo log jo maut se ghabraate hain. Sukh to bevafa hai. Chand dinon ke liye hai, tavaayaf ki tarah aata hai. Duniya ko behlaata hai, dil behlaata hai aur chale jaata hai, magar dukh to apna hamesha ka saathi hai. Ek baar aata hai, to kabhi lauke nahin jaata hai. Isliye sukh ko thokar maar. Dukh ko gale laga. Taqdir tere qadamon mein hogi aur tu muqaddar ka baadshaah hoga.

(Fakir: Whose grave are you sitting beside, child?

Child: My mother died.

Fakir: Get up. Come with me. Look all around. Here too is someone's sister, someone's brother, someone's mother. They are all buried under mounds of dirt in this city of silence. Who can avoid death? Today it is their turn; tomorrow it will be ours. But listen to these words. Remember the words of this fakir. They will take you far in life. If you smile at happiness, then laugh out loud at sorrow. Because it is those who confront death who are truly alive, and those who fear death are worse than the dead themselves. Happiness is unfaithful. It is fleeting. It comes like a dancing girl, beguiling the world, deceiving the heart, and then it goes. But sorrow is always your companion. Once it comes, it never leaves. So spurn happiness. Embrace sorrow. Fortune will be with you every step of the way, and you shall rule Fate.)

THE MAGIC OF THE HUMAN VOICE

Sound, that most primitive of senses, has a physicality to it that vision lacks. Sound is vibration. We *feel* sound. Vision develops slowly after birth, but sound comes to us, filtered through liquid, long before we are born. We hear and feel the gurgling, the gushing and the pounding. We hear and feel voices too, deformed but very near, first and foremost, those of our mothers. After birth, we learn to distinguish sounds and find that we can create them ourselves. And they work their magic. They bring people to us. They create interactions. Within months we are babbling, that is, investigating how to move and coordinate complex sets of muscles within the mouth, throat, chest and belly. How much air do we need for this sound? Where must we place our tongues for that sound? How do we shape our mouths for that vowel? How do we string sounds together to create effect and later, meaning? Not only is the voice magic, it is mysterious. French theorist Michel Chion considers the place of the human voice in cinema:

> The voice is elusive. Once you've eliminated everything that is not the voice itself—the body that houses it, the words it carries, the notes it sings, the traits by which it defines a speaking person, and the timbres that colour it, what's left? What a strange object, what grist for poetic outpourings.[45] [...]

---

[45] Chion, Michel, *The Voice in Cinema*, 1999, p. 1.

> It's rather the privilege accorded to the voice over all other sonic elements, in the same way the human face is not just an image like the others... Call this *vococentrism* if you will. Human listening is naturally vococentrist, and so is talking cinema by and large.[46]

If you're old enough, you will remember a time before cell phones, when names didn't appear on a little screen, when you actually had to pick up the phone to find out who was at the other end of the line and yet a simple 'hello' would usually suffice to announce a friend. No name needed. Each voice in the world is unique, and we are amazingly good at hearing that uniqueness. The non-musician may forget a few notes in a much-loved song but would never forget the voice of a friend. We are more likely, in fact, to recognize the *voice* of an ageing, long-lost friend than we are to distinguish their *face* in a crowd. Shammi Kapoor plays a wise and elderly flute-player in Imtiaz Ali's *Rockstar* (2011). The part is small; his presence is large. The first time he appears, he looks vaguely familiar. Here is an actor we surely know, but who exactly is he? When he speaks, there is no doubt: this is Shammi Kapoor. Time is generally kinder to voices than to faces.

Some voices attract. Others repel. It is as easy to become indifferent to the beautiful face of someone close to us and to ignore the ugly face of a dear friend, but an annoying voice often continues to annoy, no matter how attached we might be to the person who is speaking. In the same way, a soothing or endearing voice continues to soothe and endear. Voices are hard not to notice, at a conscious and/or an unconscious level. Many an actor has been called in for an audition because of an attractive headshot. And while looks may get the person in the door, once inside, it is his or her voice that will capture ears... or not. 'Audition', the word, points to the subtle shift towards

---

[46]Chion, Michel, *Audio-Vision: Sound on Screen*, 1994, p. 6.

the auditory in selecting an actor for a role. Writer-actor Kader Khan has honed his voice into a beautiful instrument:

> What I've learned from theatre: for an actor, when he comes on the stage, his entry should be extraordinary, and there should be some sound so the audience's minds are diverted, because a human being is a human being, so just to divert. Then when he speaks, every word of his should be audible to the last man. And an actor is also a singer. A singer sings the lines of the lyrics. An actor sings the lines of the dialogues. He has to sing in verse, in the dialogue form. It should have its own melody. It should be pleasant to the ears. *Main ne ye analysis kiya hai ki mard ki aavaaz mein thodi si echo aur garaj honi chaahiye, thoda sa base hona chaahiye, thodi si nasal honi chaahiye. Ye combination jo hai, ye sound ko aisa bana deti hai jaise ki kisi gumbad ke andar koi ghungroo gira ho.* (I have done an analysis. In a man's voice there should be some echo, some thunder-like roar, some base, some nasal sound. With this combination the sound that is made is like a set of anklets falling inside a dome.)
>
> Like a dome! You drop a ghungroo. The sound which is produced and the echo, that sort of sound should be there, audible from the actor's mouth. So when you speak in that tone, people get mesmerized. Then they forget about your performance because words are very powerful, and the narration and the audition of the actor...if he has got the right way of dialogue delivery, he can mesmerize the audience. And then if he's got good gestures and good facial expressions and a good style, he can take the audience away.

Actor Morgan Freeman may have been describing a similar phenomenon, even as he spoke in more prosaic terms of the importance of voice. 'In theatre,' he said, 'you really have to have what we call *chops*, that is, training, if nothing else, in voice development, being able to speak and being heard in the back of the theatre. There aren't that many movie actors who can do that without strain. Theatre actors do it as a matter of course.'[47]

AI (artificial intelligence) is premised on the ability of scientists to delve deep and finally understand the workings of the human mind. Within the broader field of mind research, voice is a hot topic. Now that machines can talk to us, it is not only actors who are analysing which voices will capture listeners' ears. Researchers too want to know. Which GPS voice, they wonder, will we *not* be inclined to yell at after we have made several wrong turns and been 'scolded' back to the proper route? Machines talking to us. Machines trying to understand us when we speak. The human voice is both hard to simulate and also hard to decipher. How many have known the frustration of a computerized telephone program asking a question and then not being able to understand the answer? 'I'm sorry,' says the machine. 'Did you say "No"?' Given the push to replace human voices with computerized voices, any and every bit of information about the mind-voice interaction is precious, and research is funded, and knowledge, hopefully, is expanded. The public can't really keep up with what scientists learn, but occasionally we are brought briefly into the loop. Thanks to experiments at the University of Aberdeen King's College,[48] for example, we now know that women are better at remembering words spoken in a low-pitched male voice than in a higher one, but that for men pitch makes no difference for memory. It might not be mixing apples with oranges to consider Kader Khan's description of the impact of a dome-like voice on the audience side by side with the results of the Aberdeen

---

[47]Speaking with presenter Kirsty Lang, *On Screen*, BBC World Service, 12 September 2008.
[48]'Study: Women's Memory More Receptive To Low Voice,' National Public Radio, 20 September 2011.

King's College research. Might we conclude that while men may appreciate Kader Khan's voice, women would be more likely to actually remember what he said?

Piyush Mishra, who is also from a theatre background, described voice philosophically:

> It is not a matter of pronunciation. See, there is a philosophy called 'naam roop darshan', how words and language must have been created. Every word has its own form inside us; if you are not able to create that universal form, the word becomes expressionless and you are considered a bad speaker. When some people speak, you listen to them. A good speaker gives the word its complete form, like Mr Amitabh Bachchan. When he speaks, he gives a shape to each and every word. It is not only his voice. The tongue hits almost all the corners of the mouth cavity; the words then automatically become clearer and the voice goes deeper and deeper and deeper. Then you need to know how to pause, how to take a proper breath between sentences or between words and how to colour and interpret each word.
>
> You can't paint without practice, and you can't speak without practice. You have to reserve some part of your day for rendering speech. Most actors don't. Naseer (Naseeruddin Shah) is one who does. The precision is there, and not even a single dialogue should be wasted. Even 'aah' and 'ooh' cannot be used as fillers; they should have a purpose. Some actors like Robert De Niro use 'aah' and 'ooh' in such a wonderful way; even the sounds are dialogues.

Singer Bobby McFerrin, best known for his 'Don't Worry, Be Happy,' described what might be a version of naam roop darshan:

> You have to take care of your *self*, I think, to sing well or to be a conveyer of song, to catch songs. I like to think of myself as a person who catches pieces, that the songs are out here, and they are simply out here waiting for someone

to reach out for one and grab it and pull it down and have it come out of my mouth.[49]

Vishal Bhardwaj has that most rare ability to write his films, to direct them *and* to compose their soundtracks. His ear is finely tuned to the melody of language. In *Fantasies of a Bollywood Love Thief* (2007), a book centred on the making of Bhardwaj's film *Omkara* (2006), author Stephen Alter quotes him:

> There is a rhythm to every film, just like a song. You give it a certain tempo. I tried to do that with *Maqbool*. Being a musician helped me a lot in directing. I understand the pace of a scene. If an actor takes a second more than he should, or a second less, it can ruin a shot. The other thing is the pitch of an actor's voice. Take Pankaj Kapoor in *Maqbool*. He plays a character who has been chewing paan for fifty years. You can hear it in his voice.[50]

During the days of silent filmmaking an actor with a love and understanding of the voice had to stick to the theatre. The talkies not only opened up possibilities for voice on screen, but also gave us the choice of absence of sound, something that French director Robert Bresson explored, often to a confounding degree, in his films. Michel Chion theorizes: 'In a well-known aphorism Bresson reminded us that the sound film made silence possible. This statement illuminates a paradox: that it was necessary to have sounds and voices so that the *interruption* of them could probe more deeply into this thing called silence.'[51] Several Indian New Wave filmmakers followed in this path. Shabana Azmi has reflected on the place of silence in performance. She said:

---

[49]Speaking with Krista Tippett, *On Being*, American Public Media, 16 June 2011.
[50]Alter, Stephen, *Fantasies of a Bollywood Love Thief*, 2007, p. 17.
[51]Chion, Michel, *Audio-Vision: Sound on Screen*, 1994, pp. 56-57.

Too often it is said that what is difficult is to capture emotions in silences. I think the opposite is true. Because cinema is such a collaborative medium, it is perfectly possible to take a close-up of a silent face, which is not thinking of anything terribly profound, but the cinematographer lights it in a particular way, the editor places it in a particular way, and it can give the impression of deep sorrow, for instance... I think that it's easier to speak through silences because there are other tricks that will allow you to convey a lot of meaning. But to speak previously-rehearsed lines as though you are speaking them for the first time is really the challenge that the actor has to rise up to.

How, it is often asked, does an actor find a character's voice? The 'film within a film' or 'play within a film' genre often shows us directors and actors probing a character's motivation, gestures and voice, bringing to mind method acting created by Lee Strasberg in his New York Actors' Studio during the 1950s. Deep discussions need not take place between a director and an actor, though. Sometimes a word or two will provide the necessary insight. During the filming of *Chalte Chalte* (2003), Aziz Mirza explained why he insisted that Shah Rukh Khan underplay the word pyaar in the line '*Mujhe nahin maaloom business kaise hota hai, magar pyaar to aise hi hota hai.*' (I don't know how business is done, but this is how love is.) The context: an older and more reasonable friend is telling the lovesick hero that he mustn't leave now; there's an important business meeting coming up. But Khan's character is determined to fly off to Greece on an impulse to follow the woman he loves (Rani Mukerji). The word pyaar could not be emphasized because, as Aziz Mirza explained, 'The man is a great lover, but he doesn't know he's a great lover. We know. The moment the man knows he's a great lover, he's not a great lover.'

Screenwriter Jaideep Sahni was also looking for just the right tone to give one of his lines its full force. In *Aaja Nachle* the jilted lover Mohan (Ranvir Shorey) never married after Dia

(Madhuri Dixit) ran away with another man, leaving him stranded eleven years earlier on what was to have been their wedding day. When Dia returns as a successful dancer/director, she quickly goes to work putting up posters for her upcoming performance meant to attract local folk to perform in the play she hopes will save the threatened Ajanta theatre for posterity. Mohan sees her smiling down at him from a poster on a wall and angrily rips it off. In a few days, though, his anger has given way to sadness. Gently, he pulls out and smoothes the crumpled paper, then goes to meet Dia and asks to join her group. His eyes and his voice now betray nothing but shy admiration. That night in his restaurant after hours, he sits with friends, eyes downcast, a glass in hand and a bottle of booze on the table. Next to the booze is a plate of jalebi, oozing oil, syrupy and inviting. The friends are exasperated. Just what do you say when someone is showing himself to be a romantic fool? Jaideep's writing solution? You call him a jalebi. '*Jalebi hai tu!*' Now, to get the full force of the novel insult, Jaideep had actor Yashpal Sharma replace 'jalebi' with a strong invective. With each repetition the energy was ratcheted up. Then the switch was made: '*Jalebi hai tu!!*'

The 'jalebi' scene in Aaja Nachle: *Yashpal Sharma, Nawazuddin Siddiqui and Ranvir Shorey. (Sketch by Simon P. Holzman.)*

Getting the voice right in Hindi cinema can be a strenuous exercise for an actor. It's not just about finding tone, rhythm and accent. Language itself can be a stumbling block. In the bonus DVD of *Aaja Nachle* Konkona Sen Sharma explains that while she loved the character of Anokhi, a foul-mouthed, fighting tomboy, she couldn't imagine that she would ever be able to say her lines. 'I still just barely understand the words,' she said. The bonus DVD then offers us a glimpse of Konkona struggling to get out, *'Satak ke patak doongi to latak ke mar jaayega. Ma ko mausi bolne lagega.'* Konkona Sen Sharma is not alone in barely understanding. While it is clear to any viewer that the expression is impolite, the exact meaning eluded several people I questioned. Fortunately, Jaideep Sahni, who wrote the line, stepped in to offer both context and a nuanced explanation. He said:

> This is a small-town way of talking, from UP and Haryana. 'Satak' means two things: to be squeezed together—like sardines—and also to gulp down in a single swallow. And 'patak' is a wrestler's throw that would land him [the opponent] on his back. So the girl is saying, 'I'll get really close and then swallow you in a second and spit you out.' 'Latak' is hanging. 'You'll hang yourself and die from the shame of having someone like me do this to you.' *Ma ko mausi bolne lagega*: 'Your brain won't work after I'm finished with you. I'll fix you so you won't be able to tell the difference between your mother and your aunt. You think I'm a good-for-nothing girl, but I'll show you. Don't think you're so special.'

Many audiences will not be familiar with this colloquial street language, and yet Sen Sharma manages to convey the essence of the meaning, if not the interesting details, through her voice. The role of Anokhi, overall, offered great scope for voice work, from grating, rasping and high-pitched in her tough-girl phase to low and melodious as a poised young woman in love, and then, in another transformation, to the Urdu-speaking Laila in the *Laila Majnun* play. Piyush Mishra, who worked closely with the actors as he supervised the recording of the lines he had written for *Laila Majnun*, had reserved special praise for the beautiful texture of Sen Sharma's voice. 'I don't think Konkona spends very much labour upon it,' he observed. 'She is gifted.'

American improv actress and TV sketch writer Tina Fey in her book, *Bossypants* (2011), shares some hard-learned lessons, 'You have to remember that actors are human beings. Which is hard sometimes because they look so much better than human beings.'[52] Tina Fey's canny quip only applies to actors' looks, but the thought could be expanded: they usually *sound* better than regular people as well. At the very least, the best of them are capable of rendering their voices marvellously elastic. There is magic in acting. It can play tricks with our minds, punching a part of the brain's pause button and freeing us to dwell inside the character on screen. How an actor looks, moves and sounds combine to produce this hypnotic pull. Kader Khan's term 'mesmerize' is apt. We are often spellbound, and perhaps more than we realize, it is the actor's voice that casts the spell. As infants, even before we could see, we could, one would hope, hear voices consoling us, soothing us, touching us with their vibrations. As adults, we are never beyond the reach of those initial emotions. Good writing gives substance to what an actor says, and another part of our brain awakens. Not only is that me living another life right now, but 'I could be saying that! I could be saying those wonderful words and just that wonderfully.'

---

[52]Fey, Tina, 2011, p. 122.

MULTILINGUALISM ABOUNDS

'No man fully capable of his own language ever masters another.'
—George Bernard Shaw

'Those who know nothing of foreign languages know nothing of their own.'
—Goethe

'To have another language is to possess a second soul.'
—attributed to Charlemagne

THE SUPERHERO played by Rajnikant in the 2010 Tamil film *Enthiran* (*Robot* in its dubbed Hindi version) is capable of speaking '*duniya ki saari bhaashaayein*' (all the languages in the world). One wishes Superman or Batman had such powers, or that the creators of these superheroes had even thought of so endowing their characters!

What do you call someone who speaks several languages? Multilingual. What do you call someone who speaks two languages? Bilingual. What do you call someone who speaks one language? An American.

So goes the joke making the rounds of American university foreign language departments, as professors and students alike despair of bringing the average American student up to the level of second language ability that one so commonly finds in other parts of the world.

Amazing as it seems to most Americans—who have the advantage of speaking the world's current lingua franca or link language—multilingualism, linguists tell us, is actually the norm rather than the exception worldwide. In his book, *Hyperspace*, science writer Michio Kaku describes how, as a child, he imagined life from the perspective of a carp for whom water was invisible because it was its only known universe. Ambient multilingualism, the sort one finds in any big city in India and many smaller towns as well, also creates a certain blindness to its very existence. 'We're all multilingual,' film writer Shama Zaidi said matter-of-factly. 'It's called living,' said University of Texas professor Dr S. Akbar Hyder, describing the ease with which people, at least educated urban dwellers, tend to move smoothly from one language to another in the course of a day or even from one minute to the next in India. Actor-director Nagesh Kukunoor experienced the normalcy of multilingualism, which for him meant Dakkhani (a Hyderabadi mixture of Urdu and Hindi) along with some Marathi and Telugu. 'When I lived in India,' he said, 'I had the ability to sort of jump around, even though English was dominant. But once I went to the US, I lost that ability.' Like many people arriving from the outside, my first impression was of amazement that people could understand each other at all. The young UK actor Dev Patel, who played the lead role in *Slumdog Millionaire* (2008), described his arrival in Bombay this way, 'I think someone called it the smell of sweat and dreams, which I really love. It's just this massive tide of humanity. Everyone's speaking in a different language, and you're just engulfed.'[53] Dev Patel nails it. And, it must be remembered, it is precisely from Bombay's engulfing cauldron with its blurry language borders that this thing called Hindi cinema emerges.

Naturally enough, some people living in multilingual societies are extremely aware of their relationship to language. South African Afrikaans novelist André Brink's memoir, *A Fork in the Road*, shows the author's first contact with English as a child of

---

[53] Speaking to Liane Hansen on National Public Radio, Feb. 1, 2009.

six, going to school, 'English was a foreign language. To us, to me, everything happened only in Afrikaans. To me it was like discovering a new hemisphere to the known world.'⁵⁴

Such an abrupt transition could have been painful. For Brink, though, English was an exciting discovery. Shama Zaidi, on the other hand, described her own plunge into English matter-of-factly, even if the American accent she developed early on left her a bit self-conscious later:

> I grew up in a very small town; it was in a princely state [of Rampur]. I went to an American missionary school when I was seven. I didn't know a word of English. I had studied only Urdu before. [Later] it took me quite some time to undo my American accent. There were four of us, and when we went to college in Delhi, we tried to be like everyone else and lose our accents. One had to have a neutral Indian accent to be accepted.

Possessing two languages can be as simple as having access to two means of communication. Being bilingual can, however, complicate one's sense of self. Serbian-born American poet and translator Charles Semic described himself in terms of duality. With two mother tongues he was 'negotiating two selves, two personas, two sets of knowledge that I have about the world. You become aware of the differences between languages. Some of them are on the surface. Some are in the depths.'⁵⁵

Israeli poet and scholar Haviva Pedaya was interviewed by filmmaker Nurith Aviv for her documentary *Misafa Lesafa* (*From Language to Language,* 2004). Pedaya says, 'I refer to my Hebrew and Arab identities as two distinct entities linked by a blind spot.'⁵⁶

In a related idea, Brink was asked if being able to switch

---

⁵⁴BBC World Service, *The Forum*, hosted by Bridget Kendall, 25 April 2010.
⁵⁵Ibid., 8 January 2011.
⁵⁶http://nurithaviv.free.fr/misafa/synopsis.htm

between languages gives a writer the advantage of having double vision. He answered:

> It might be a sort of astigmatism in which the two images just never coincide. And this awareness can be very disconcerting. But at the same time, I think there's something very sane and healthy about it because it keeps you aware of the fact that whatever you see, whatever you perceive need not be exactly the way you first think it is.

A wider vision, an expansion of self, a multiplication of selves, perhaps even a confusion of selves. Director-producer Rohan Sippy referred to a Woody Allen character to explain his own ease in slipping in and out of languages and cultures. 'I'm definitely more on the *Zelig* side of the spectrum,' he said. In *Zelig*, Allen's 1983 'mockumentary' or fake documentary, Leonard Zelig is 'the human chameleon', a man whose identity is so fragile that he transforms himself involuntarily into a replica of anyone near him. Rohan Sippy's own 'Zeligness' poses no problem. 'What I'm surrounded by...' he said '...I get kind of caught up in. Maybe I'll have an identity crisis at some point.' Like many of his generation from the film world, Rohan Sippy has moved between worlds. After studying in South Bombay and then in Switzerland, he attended university in the US. He feels very quickly at home when he returns to New York, a city he loves, but, he said, 'Now when I go there, my friends tell me how much my accent has changed. So I guess there's a lot more of Bombay in me now, though I'm not conscious of it except when others point it out.'

For some bilinguals there is a language of the home and a language of the outer world. Martin Scorsese, for instance, grew up speaking Italian in his New York home and English beyond its doors. Both languages can live in harmony in their separateness or in a certain turmoil, somewhat the linguistic equivalent of the inner and outer worlds of Satyajit Ray's beautiful 1984 film *Ghare Baire*, based on a Rabindranath Tagore novel, in which the previous barrier between men's and women's spaces is breached, creating strife within a couple. The life within, the life without. The language within, the language without. Barriers and boundaries can be confusing and lend themselves to humour, as this question from a Spanish-speaking child in New York illustrates, '¿*Mamá, cómo se dice vacuum cleaner en inglés?*' (Mama, how do you say vacuum cleaner in English?) The inner language, the language of home and infancy, when different from that of the outer world, usually touches its users more profoundly. One young woman from Barcelona described having her deepest emotions in Catalán. Spanish, the language in which she was educated, always seemed more cerebral.

Most bilingual or multilingual people in any society have their stronger language and their weaker one(s). Documentary filmmaker Paromita Vohra wrote the script—in English—for *Khamosh Pani* (2003), directed by Sabhiha Sumar. It was subsequently translated into Punjabi and Urdu. Paromita observed:

> English is my first language, the one I speak most comfortably. But the fact remains that I know Punjabi somewhat. I've never had to write a film in a language that I didn't know. Could I do that? Perhaps I could try to learn to do it. But it's much easier if you know that this meaning cannot be translated into Punjabi, so I'm not going to write a dialogue which is not translatable.

Being Multilingual: Pipe Dream or Reality

All of these personal observations touch on a central question: Just what does it mean to be bilingual or multilingual? After all, knowing a bit of Russian studied at school is hardly the same as being able to converse comfortably in the language. But is conversing comfortably enough? At what point does one move from apparent comfort in more than one language to being truly bilingual? Some have argued that being 100 per cent bilingual is impossible. One would have to experience everything in life in two languages and have the vocabulary to match. A child might grow up sounding completely bilingual, yet might only have learned to change a fuse in one language. The adult might then need to consult a dictionary for fuse-related vocabulary in the other language before calling the electrician. Top-notch interpreters attempt to make up for the impossibility of living such double-experience lives by spending years memorizing words for every occasion. Is this the criteria for being bilingual? Dr Elaine Horwitz asked this very question to a class of students from various parts of the world who were working towards graduate degrees in Foreign Language Education at The University of Texas at Austin. Some of the students' answers were: to be able to produce and interpret abstract concepts in two languages, to be able to use different levels of discourse from street language to highly literary language, to have adequate vocabulary, to know what is culturally appropriate, to be able to understand and use humour, to be able to argue and show strong emotions, to dream in both languages, to speak without an accent, and my own favourite: not to irritate native speakers! Following this brainstorming, Dr Horwitz gave her own succinct answer: 'Authentic self-presentation via L2' (the second language).[57] In other words, you are fully yourself in both languages. If you sound smart in one language, you don't sound childlike in another. Nothing is lost along the way. Likewise, if in your stronger language you don't know how to be funny, don't have a huge vocabulary or don't argue well, you would not be expected to do so in any other language you might speak.

Multilingualism: A Wealth

There is more than one form of multilingualism. The experience

---

[57] In September 1999, at The University of Texas at Austin.

of a Korean-English bilingual living in the US would be quite different from that of someone speaking two or more languages within India, where many references are shared across the country. Sachin Tendulkar and Amitabh Bachchan could be part of your conversation in Marathi in the morning and in Bengali in the afternoon. However, be it individual bilingualism (the Korean-American example) or societal bilingualism (what most people living in India experience), the science is in: bilingualism is good for you.

Cognitive neuroscientist Ellen Bialystok has spent forty years researching the subject. The benefits of being bilingual, it seems, go well beyond being able to communicate with more people. Bialystok explained:

> In terms of monolinguals and bilinguals, the big thing that we have found is that the (brain) connections are different [...] One of the things we've seen is that on certain kinds of even nonverbal tests, bilingual people are faster. Why? Well, when we look in their brains through neuroimaging, it appears like they're using a different kind of a network that might include language centres to solve a completely nonverbal problem. Their whole brain appears to rewire because of bilingualism.[58]

Jaideep Sahni did not mention having a 'rewired brain', but he was well aware that being at ease in Hindi, English and Punjabi was enriching and that along with language came a knowledge of cultural nuances. He gave an example, 'A lot of my friends' parents I call by their first names. But if somebody's parents come from Kanpur, I wouldn't dream of it! I'd touch their feet. Now that's being bilingual. So I'm comfortable with both. And I'm happier with both. I'm better off.'

---

[58] Claudia Dreifus, 'The Bilingual Advantage', *The New York Times*, 30 May 2011.

Sahni and director Dibakar Banerjee worked together in the advertising field and later on the making of *Khosla Ka Ghosla*. Like Sahni, Banerjee spoke enthusiastically of his multilingual background. In a BBC Hindi Service interview he described growing up in a Punjabi neighbourhood in Delhi, where he was known to his childhood friends as 'Bangaali', the name given to the character played by actor and dialogue writer Manu Rishi in Banerjee's *Oye Lucky! Lucky Oye*! (2008). At the Bal Bharati Public School, Banerjee studied in a dual language programme; some classes were taught in Hindi, others in English. He remembers Hindi being very well taught. For many, being multilingual merely means being able to communicate in various languages; for Banerjee, being multilingual cannot be separated from being multi-literate. He said:

> *Pahle Bengali kitaabein, phir Hindi kitaabein, phir angrezi kitaabein. Isliye mujhe teen bhaashaaon mein baat karne ka abhyaas ho gaya...to kya hua ki bahut saare cultures ko main ne ek saath apne mein le liya? Aur ye mere liye sab se bade garv ki baat hai ki main Dilli ka Bangaali hoon, main Hindi bol sakta hoon, main Punjabi samajh sakta hoon. Aur main angrezi mein bol sakta hoon. Aur agar koi aaj mujhe kehe, bhaiya, tu hai kaun? To main kahoonga main Indian hoon, yaar. Tabhi to main ek saath teen-chaar bhaashaayein bol sakta hoon. Aaj jab hamko kaha ja raha hai, aap agar is praant ke hain, to us praant mein nahin rah sakte, aap agar ye bhaasha bolte hain, to vo bhaasha nahin bol sakte, main to kehta hoon ki jitni aap bhaashaayein zyaada bologe, jitna aap zyaada cultures mein apne aap ko daaloge, aapki personality utni hi badi ho jaayegi.*[59]

(First [I read] Bengali books, then Hindi books, then English books. That's how I got to experience speaking

---

[59]From an interview with Pratiksha Ghildiyal on the BBC Hindi Service's *Sunday ke Sunday*, 2010.

three languages. So I took in a lot of cultures at once. And it's a matter of great pride that I'm a Delhi Bengali, I can speak Hindi, I can understand Punjabi and I can speak in English. And if ever someone asks me today, 'Hey what are you?' Then I'll say, 'Man, I'm an Indian!' That's why I speak three or four languages at once. Today when people tell us that if you come from this region, you can't live in that region, if you speak this language, then you can't speak that language, then I say the more languages you speak, the more cultures you make a part of yourself, the greater your personality will become.)

Feelings of Inadequacy

The self-confidence Banerjee exudes when speaking of his multilingualism is rather rare. The rule tends to be a feeling of some degree of inadequacy. While director Shashanka Ghosh's background is also Bengali-from-Delhi, he admits that he always has someone read over his Hindi writing to check for gender mistakes. Bengali, blessedly, is a language in which common nouns are neither masculine nor feminine. Many languages have them, but gendered nouns are frankly a strange concept, however automatic they seem to those who have grown up with them. One just *knows* that kitaab (book) is feminine, din (day) is masculine, paani (water), despite the typical feminine ending, is masculine and bhoomika (role), despite the typical masculine ending, is feminine. Years ago as a language teacher I assumed that English's neutral 'it' for table, chair, water and other inanimate nouns was a gift for which learners would actually be grateful, perhaps not enough to forgive English its extremely unpredictable pronunciation, but a gift just the same. A five-year-old French girl disabused me of that illusion. The table, she indignantly insisted, was clearly elle, i.e., feminine. That's all there was to it. The genderless 'it' was nonsense, and what's more, it wrought havoc on the order that language gave to her world. Tom and Ray Magliozzi, National Public Radio's wise-cracking Car Talk guys, passed on some jokes about the need for gendered nouns in English:

> 'English words should be male or female...like, a Swiss Army knife, is it male or female?'
> 'Oh, it's male.'
> 'Why?
> Because even though it appears it is useful for a wide variety of things, it spends most of its time just opening bottles.'[60]

English speakers can laugh at the notion of gendered nouns until they confront them in a foreign language and find themselves weeping in frustration. Comedian David Sedaris describes his maddening search for the logic of masculine and feminine nouns during his study of French. On his list of absurdities, he offers this, 'Because it is female and lays eggs, a chicken is masculine.'[61] For Ghosh gendered nouns are not absurd; they are simply a source of insecurity. He described feeling confident while writing screenplays but incapable of writing dialogue:

> I went through about seven writers because no one seemed to be able to capture the language (for *Waisa Bhi Hota Hai Part II*). I was panicking. Now, I'm not a very big movie watcher, but I have this guru (and assistant), Manjeet Singh. He was one of the last assistants to Manmohan Desai. So I was telling him, 'Manjeet, there is something wrong here.' And he kept saying, 'You write it!' And in my head was my inability to write dialogues. But I had this fresh first-time producer, and I told him to just skim through this for gender errors or in case there are any communication errors and then give it to a writer. So he called the next

---

[60] http://www.cartalk.com/ #1145, 11-5-11.
[61] Sedaris, David, 2000, p. 188.

morning saying, 'What the...!' And I was like immediately on the defensive. And then he said, 'No, this is amazing! We are doing this!' I said, 'No, no, I am not a writer. You have to give it to a writer.' He said no. And, you know, I got nominated for best dialogue (Star Screen Awards). Everyone cracked up at home. *'You* have been nominated for Hindi dialogue! Unbelievable!'[62]

Another source of language insecurity relates to place. Most languages have their 'prestigious' registers, which are at least partly defined by geography. The privileged few who come from 'the right place' and 'the right family' and who have enjoyed the 'right sort of education' find their speech to be an asset attained with relatively little effort. In contrast, moving from the periphery to the linguistic centre is possible only with a great deal of effort. The 'Oxbridge' form of British English rests at one end of the scale, the 'classy' end. Backwoods Mississippi speech is assumed to be pitifully situated at the other end. Of course, if you're a blues singer, those classy Oxbridge vowels are utterly useless. And so it is in India. Many Bombay-born film folk spoke to me apologetically of their own Hindi while barely hiding the awe in their voices as they praised the language of certain Delhi screenwriters. And yet, as Anupama Chopra pointed out:

> You know, when Vinod (Vidhu Vinod Chopra) made *Munna Bhai M.B.B.S.*, he showed it to a lot of prospective buyers, and they said, 'Well, you know what? It's not going to work beyond Bombay because the language is too Bambaiya. His "bole to" (meaning) it won't work in the North.' And they didn't pick the film up. It was amazing, though. Not only did the film work everywhere, it even worked in Pakistan. When they had the first India-Pakistan cricket series, people were holding up these banners with 'Bole to',

---

[62]Speaking in March 2008, Mumbai.

this Bambaiya language!⁶³

A non-prestigious form of a language can have a certain cachet, particularly if it is cleverly written, if it creates a sense of place and gives value to what's local.

Working Multilingually

It's midday, lunchtime, in a many-starred hotel in Juhu. I chance to overhear one man pitching a story, complete with cinematic details. The listener across the table enthusiastically interjects an idea from time to time. A phone call interrupts and English gives way to a South Indian language. Curiosity wins over discretion, and I ask the man who is not on the phone where he is from. Graciously, he explains that he is a Punjabi from Bombay. English is their shared language, cinema their shared medium. The actual words that will be spoken on screen? These, he tells me, will either be improvised by the actors or hurriedly written before each scene is shot. 'In that case,' I ask, 'how will the actors have time to memorize the lines?'

'Someone in the background can call them out, and everything can be fixed at dubbing time.'

While the English-Hindi matrix may be predominant today, Paromita Vohra emphasized that English has not been the only other language spoken among actors and filmmakers in Bombay cinema, 'In this huge industry films are made by people whose languages are Tamil or Gujarati or whatever—Punjabi because there's a huge migrant population. So I don't know if one should make too much of the fact that people speak English and make Hindi films. In fact, they speak many other languages and make Hindi films.'

Some, like South Indian director Mani Ratnam, have been comfortable entering the world of Hindi cinema. Director Satyajit

---

⁶³Speaking in April 2006, Mumbai.

Ray, on the other hand, was adamant at one point in his career that he would work only in Bengali, a language he knew and could control thoroughly. Asked by Lindsay Anderson if he would work elsewhere in India, Ray answered, 'Since I write my own screenplays, making a screenplay in Hindi would involve using another scriptwriter because I couldn't author a film in a language I wasn't fluent in. I'd feel lost, and I'd lose confidence. I need confidence.'[64] In 1977, however, he changed his mind and made *Shatranj ke Khilari* (*The Chess Players*). In a Q&A at the American Film Institute in 1978, he was asked his reasons for the decision. He gave many: his interest in the story of the 1856 overthrow by the British East India Company of the ruler of Awadh, Nawab Wajid Ali Shah. There was also Ray's love of chess and his desire to reach a wider audience than his Bengali films afforded him. And there were technical considerations related to the poorer quality of black-and-white film stock he had begun to receive. He said:

> My Bengali films reach a very, very small section of the Indian public[...] The moment you use colour, the cost goes up, and then you have to think in terms of a larger audience...and consequently to use a language that is understood more or less all over India, which is Hindi. Well, it's not strictly Hindi; it's Urdu, a classical form of Hindi [...] I was anxious to work with some of Bombay's professional actors.[65] They're intelligent people, and they're unhappy because they're mostly acting in very stupid kinds of films.[66]

---

[64] *Satyajit Ray Interviews*, ed. by Bert Cardullo, 2007, p. 109.
[65] Principally, Sanjeev Kumar, Saeed Jaffrey, Shabana Azmi, Amjad Khan, with voiceover by Amitabh Bachchan for the ironic, animated historical explanations.
[66] *Satyajit Ray Interviews*, p. 71.

Ray later spoke of feeling limited by language during the making of the 1981 short television film *Sadgati*:

> In *Sadgati* my English script had to be translated into Hindi dialogue. And I never knew whether that dialogue was good or right. Even the coaching of actors—where I often act out the pieces myself in advance—becomes impossible during the making of a Hindi-language film. Since I do not have enough knowledge of the language, I can only give a certain amount of verbal direction to the actors. [...] So for Hindi films I can't even go in search of new faces; I must work with experienced actors only.[67]

Multilingual Acting

George Clooney works on a movie in English, goes home and lives the rest of his life in English. Mexican actor Gael García Bernal, while shooting, for example, *Amores Perros*, would have spoken Spanish all day and then returned home to speak Spanish in the evening. A Tunisian actor is unlikely to make films in Arabic and then to switch to living the rest of his or her life in French, even if bilingualism is commonplace in Tunisia. As far as language goes, parallels between Bollywood and film industries in other parts of the world just don't jump to mind. Worldwide, actors do sometimes work on international pictures, whether they are fluent in a second language or not. The experience can involve extra effort or a sense of frustration. Spanish actor Javier Bardem hardly spoke English when he did the Coen Brothers' *No Country for Old Men* (2007). In 2011 he described the difference between acting in English and in Spanish, 'There's this office in my brain full of people working at the same time that I'm talking to you, trying to not be wrong with the intonation, the words, so it's

---

[67] *Satyajit Ray Interviews*, p. 174.

very exhausting. If I speak Spanish, that office is closed. There's nobody in the office. I'm fine by my own [sic].'[68] Foreign-language teachers often call this office 'the monitor'. The 'office', however, is a great metaphor, with its image of staff sitting at desks and labouring over proper tenses, juggling verb endings, testing word order, giving the tongue instructions before each upcoming sound.

Shabana Azmi had no grammatical worries when working in English, and yet she, too, told a story of missing her own language when she found herself on the sets of a British film:

> I've been educated in English and spoken Hindustani and Urdu at home. I speak a dual language constantly; it's a switch between English and Hindustani and Urdu. And I used to always think that I had a greater facility with English than I have with Urdu until I went to work in *Madame Sousaztka* with Shirley MacLaine and John Schlesinger in 1988. And I suddenly realized how difficult it was for me to act in English. And act in English in an atmosphere where everybody else was speaking English. See, when I speak English here in India, it is framed by all the other Indian Englishes, so it doesn't sound so alien, but when I speak English when everybody else is an English person, it sounds like I have a very strong Indian accent. It sounds peculiar. And I wasn't able to own certain phrases. I found it tough, and I longed to act in Hindustani. It came as a complete surprise to me, and then I realized that I have an emotional connection with that language because it's what has gone into my ears ever since I was a child. It has certain images for me. That's my language, and I have a strong emotional connection with it.

---

[68]Interviewed on National Public Radio's *Fresh Air* by Dave Davies, 3 February 2011.

From In-Between Spaces, Looking Out: Shimit Amin

'Je n'ai qu'une langue, ce n'est pas la mienne.'
(I have only one language and it isn't mine.)

—Jacques Derrida[69]

During a conference in Canada, deconstructionist philosopher Jacques Derrida said to the only French person present, 'You are French. I'm not. I come from Algeria and therefore have another relationship to the French language.'[70] Much later, an interviewer from France Culture radio reminded Derrida of this curious yet accessible anecdote as a way of delving into his complex relationship to French, his 'only language', as he says (though he spoke English well enough to teach in American universities during part of his career). Derrida explained that as a boy in Algeria he spoke only French at home and did all his studies in French, and yet he felt that French was not his mother tongue. It was the mother tongue of 'the other', imposed by the colonial power from the other side of the Mediterranean. In *The Monolingualism of the Other*, Derrida moves from the personal to the universal, questioning the very notion of linguistic and cultural identity, of belonging to a group.

Derrida's case came to mind many times as I spoke with Shimit Amin in Mumbai in 2008. However, my first reaction on meeting him was simply—where's the 'heavily American-accented' English I had read about in the Indian press? As we talked, though, his consonants and vowels veered, slowly

---

[69]Derrida, Jacques, *Le Monolinguisme de l'Autre,* Galilée, Paris, 1996, p. 42.
[70]http://www.jacquesderrida.com.ar/frances/narcissisme.htm "Il n'y a pas le narcissisme" (autobiophotographies) Jacques Derrida Diffusé dans une émission de France-Culture (radio) par Didier Cahen, "Le bon plaisir de Jacques Derrida", le 22 Mars 1986 et publié sous le titre "Entretien avec Jacques Derrida" dans Digraphe, 42, Décembre 1987, (translated by the author).

sounding more familiar to my American ears, particularly when he mentioned *Spiderman* and the American Constitution: 'We the people...' He explained that as an immigrant child in America, he had been picked on for his accent; he had had to learn to transform his speech, depending on the context. And yet, perhaps by choice, he continued to sound just a little difficult to place. Languages were many and often problematic when he was a child. With his father he generally spoke English. With his mother it was Gujarati, though he remains embarrassed at how bad his Gujarati is. At his English-medium school in Pune, Hindi was like a second language. There was also Marathi. 'So,' he explained, 'it was quite a jumble of things. But when you have to abandon that and go abroad, you leave it all behind. It's gone.'

Being uprooted is typically hard for children, even if it is to move to a nearby town. Moving to a new country compounds the efforts required to adapt. At twelve, Amin suddenly found himself in small-town Georgia in the American South. He had to learn fast, and television was his medium, as he said, 'to understand what was going on without embarrassing myself and asking questions.'

There were other moves: to Daytona, Florida (which he hated); to Gainesville, Florida for university studies; to Miami and then to Los Angeles to work in films; and then between Los Angeles and Bombay, back and forth—a foot in each world and a hesitancy to call one place home. Moving from continent to continent gave Amin an acute, perhaps painful sensitivity to subtle differences in culture and just how much they matter. As a child in India, he drew indirect lessons from *Amar Akbar Anthony* and many Amitabh Bachchan films, which, he said, 'made you question what it was like to be multiethnic within India in a very subversive way.' If he had already started questioning and challenging everything within his own family's background, the move to the US was crucial. 'I understood the power of being independent. Being an American gave me that freedom.'

Growing up, Amin had occasionally imagined himself coming back to India. At other times he had assumed he would spend the rest of his life in the US. An opportunity came up, however, at the beginning of the millennium, to visit India for some possible film work. He had, after all, acquired some solid experience in his nine or ten years in Los Angeles where he worked in assistant editing, post production, supervising and script development, and though he didn't care for the city, he had had a wonderful time working in cinema and learning as he went along. The timing corresponded with a West-to-East movement that, while not massive, included a significant number of ethnic Indians who had grown up abroad and were now starting to return to India to seek their fortunes, offer their expertise or simply to be part of the new booming India. When Amin arrived in Bombay in 2000, he found a changed country, as exemplified by the omnipresence of cell phones and the Internet. While he thought he could come up with a lot of stories in Bombay, culturally, he felt 'a little lost'. He said, 'I wasn't sure how I could work on a Hindi film. They had their own method and I didn't want to impose my method. I kind of went round and round.' The 'round and round' ended temporarily when he was asked to make *Ab Tak Chhappan*,[71] a film he saw as influenced by 'the Italian crime films of the seventies', a genre which he calls 'a kind of work of art, but with political correctness going out the window'. It was also 'halfway between being and not being a Hindi film,' which meant that the next steps for him were full of uncertainty. 'I was stuck in the middle again and not sure if I could parlay that into another job. I went back [to the US] again, and I said, "I'm not going to come back".'

In spite of his resolve, he did return to India. Yash Raj Films offered him *Chak De! India* (2007) to direct. The film turned out to be a huge success, particularly in India where many people saw

---

[71]Produced by Ram Gopal Varma and written by Sandeep Srivastava, 2004.

it more than once. He then stayed on and directed the delightful *Rocket Singh: Salesman of the Year* in 2009. His more behind-the-scenes work includes the editing of Mira Nair's profoundly moving *The Reluctant Fundamentalist* (2012).

Shimit Amin describes himself as a 'film geek' who has grown up loving 1970s films, art films, American films of the 1930s and '40s, 'which I love and cherish and I watch in my own private space,' he said, while admitting that those films are quite unconnected with his own filmmaking. 'But,' he said, 'I think they influence me heavily in different ways.' He also loves Satyajit Ray films, Shyam Benegal, John Ford. Comparing one's own work to one's idols can be daunting. Amin expressed his angst on many levels and in deeply nuanced ways. He worried about the 'suitcases of money' that it takes to make a film and the responsibility he feels having other people entrust him with their money. 'I mean, I've never seen a million dollars in my life. And then I spend, like, 5 million dollars on a film? I'm like, oh my God, what am I doing?' He also admitted to having a guilty conscience about some of the films he has made. 'I identify heavily with Woody Allen, the Jewish guilt that is such a big part of the American culture.' There's another worry that very few Bergmans or Fellinis break out, that he can't be John Ford. Then again, he can't forget that John Ford and Howard Hawks worked in the studio system and made some terrible films, but which were somehow wonderful just the same. 'They just kept making movies.' He fears, too, that his Hindi films may have a Western quality to them, that they are 'almost a dubbed version of an American film'. By this, Shimit is not saying that he has copied American films. Rather, he is concerned with the thought process involved in making a Hindi film, 'what the language of a Hindi film would be, what the expression of a Hindi film would be'. Perhaps, he thinks, he is not being honest to the characters and their emotions. He then considers the issue from a slightly different angle, that is, what happens to characters and emotions when films set in India have Indians speaking English. 'When you have a film like *City of Joy* (1992) or even *Shakespeare-Wallah* (1965), it's very difficult to see those characters with a certain amount of believability,' he said. 'It's almost like an intellectual exercise, but you just never get the true emotions of those characters out. *So that's where I feel we will always have a barrier. I think we'll always feel like we'll never be able to completely understand.*' (Emphasis mine.)

There was a time when Amin imagined that Indian languages didn't provide the thought process that English does, but then he decided he hadn't been exposed to Hindi enough, that maybe he was just too lazy to get deep enough into Hindi. Then again, Amin said, 'One doesn't hear people expressing themselves 24/7 in Hindi. There's no Oprah on television.'

The 'round and round' that Amin has felt about spaces—where to live, where to work—is carried into his thinking about film and more generally about life. When he is ready to give himself a break for not knowing Hindi well enough, he quickly offers an 'on the other hand' harsher judgement, noting that Billy Wilder and Fritz Lang and many more directors came to Hollywood in the 1930s from different backgrounds and made excellent films in English. 'Billy Wilder's command of English was so amazing,' he said. 'He actually wrote in English shortly after he came to Hollywood.' On the other hand—yet again—Michael Curtiz, who made one of his favourite films of all time, *Casablanca* (1942), really didn't know English that well. '*Casablanca* had some wonderful writers and terrific actors. The director was almost nonexistent in the film, but he is there. It makes me feel closer to understanding what making movies is,' Amin said. He also seemed to find comfort knowing that 'in a weird way Hindi films in India are accepting of people who are from different backgrounds within India, or even from abroad'. But there's the language issue, which he does seem to perceive as overwhelming. He said:

> I don't think in a million years I'll be able to get it right. I've always felt insecure about language, even in English. I never was comfortable with any language because I was misplaced so many times. I don't have a language per se. In my mother tongue I can't read or write, and English isn't my mother tongue.

I didn't ask Amin whether he had read Derrida or perhaps seen the documentary in which a couple of young Americans have us join them as they meet the deconstructionist post-modern philosopher and listen to some of his complex analyses of language and thought.[72] Or if perhaps he had simply reflected on the famous Derrida quote, 'I have only one language, and it isn't mine.' Like millions around the globe, Amin has a mother tongue, from which he feels alienated, and also a principle language, which is not his mother tongue. Unlike millions of others, however, Amin is hyper aware of the resulting sense of 'in-betweenness,' which would, in itself, seem quite post-modern.[73] Woody Allen has often highlighted, to comic effect, our very human and limited ability to communicate just what we mean. In his *Love and Death* (1975), a take off on Dostoevsky and Tolstoy novels, Woody Allen's Boris confides his suicidal feelings to his doctor.

> Boris: Something's missing.
> Doctor: What?
> Boris: I don't know, I feel a void at the centre of my being.
> Doctor: What kind of void?
> Boris: Well...an empty void.
> Doctor: An empty void?

---

[72] *Derrida*, directed by Kirby Dick and Amy Ziering Kofman, 2002.
[73] A simple but classic example of the meeting of post-modern philosophy and linguistics is to be found in this question: at what precise moment do we stop saying someone is 'walking' and start saying 'running'? Words and their meanings, then, are interestingly slippery.

> Boris: Yes. I felt a full void about a month ago but it was just something I ate.

As though to illustrate the inherent challenge in human communication, there was this exchange between us on the topic of Satyajit Ray films. Amin offered, 'Ray films are very special. I think they are in their own stratosphere.' I agreed, definitely. He then added, 'I feel somewhere the language of commercial films is so filthy, so adulterated.' I must have looked blank. Seeing my bafflement, he continued, 'The grammar of commercial films.' I was still stuck in linguistics. 'No, in the camera angles, the editing... everything. We also talk to the audience in a very unspoken way through those things.' I had indeed heard of 'the language of cinema' with the meaning Amin was giving to the words, but the mental shifting of gears from 'language in cinema' to 'language of cinema' took a moment. Of course, never having edited a film, I understand 'language of cinema' in only the most theoretical way. Shimit Amin does not simply observe camera angles and editing the way I would as a film buff. He actually makes them happen.

On the Sets: So Natural and Yet So Much Extra Work

Working in a multilingual environment is both a challenge and a simple fact of life. Rohan Sippy described a particularly split-language experience, what he referred to as 'a PG version of *Babel*,' that is, a cleaner, more acceptable version of the 'family-unfriendly' film by Alejandro González Iñárritu, involving loosely interlocking stories of people living across three continents:

> So yeah, there's the whole spectrum in the interaction, explaining to maybe a Bengali grip or gaffer. And the writer for my first film, Neeraj (Vora), is from Gujarati theatre. My mother's Gujarati, so there would be a bit of that going on, and a very Bombay kind of Hindi and English as well. Now there's this script written by Anuvab Pal from Chennai.

He's a wonderful writer and a director as well. So he's writing in Tamil and then translating with two guys who have a Gujarati kind of background. And there are multiple translations working all the time. What starts in English is then put in Hindi and later translated back into English to give the essence of the scene to some of those working on the sets who are non-Hindi speakers.

Wow! Mind-boggling. And yet, a bit like the water to which Michio Kaku's carp are so oblivious, ambient multilingualism goes largely unnoticed by those bathed in it. When complications arise, you just deal with them.

Language divides can, nevertheless, be such that workers on the sets do not always get even 'the essence of a scene'. Anupama Chopra, in her book *Sholay: The Making of a Classic* (2000), recounts that because the film was shot near Bangalore, the workers on the set were from the village of Ramanagaram. Only one spoke Hindi. The rest spoke Kannada and a smattering of English, but still, somehow the work got done.[74]

Equally matter-of-factly, Jaideep Sahni explained that his interactions with director Ram Gopal Varma, with whom he worked on *Jungle* (2000) and *Company* (2002), were in English, their shared language. The director, a Hyderabadi, speaks Telugu but understands 'enough Hindi to know very well what dialogue works and what doesn't', though as Sahni saw it, 'He does have a tendency at times to just translate a line he has in his head literally into Hindi and get on with it.'

Farhan Akhtar stressed the technical implications of working in two languages:

> I type in Roman Hindi. Then I get it transcribed for actors who prefer to read in Hindi. The other thing is for the timing of the script. In Hindi the size of the text increases

---

[74]Chopra, Anupama, 2000, p. 73.

tremendously, so when your continuity person times it, it times in differently when it's in English and in Hindi. So we try to time it to the Hindi one, and at the script level I edit the Hindi version.

As an outsider listening to these stories of working across languages, my reaction was: how exhaustingly time-consuming and inefficient! But that was indeed an outsider's perspective because those on the inside who were actually doing the extra work to accommodate various languages never complained. I was reminded of a scene at a Juhu hotel where I overheard a group of people, half of them Indian, half young American men—Hollywood mid-level executives, I guessed from the tone of the conversation. I noticed that a great deal of time was spent in light banter among the Americans. The references were very much tied to American culture. The Indians looked rather lost. I remember thinking that the young Americans seemed unaware that communication was not happening, except in their in-group. Very inefficient, I thought at the time. Just maybe, then, it is the fact of living and working multilingually day in, day out, that gives people the automatic reflexes and tools needed to work around language obstacles—many of which perhaps only an outsider would even dub as 'obstacles'.

Translingual Writing

The trouble is our lives are polyglot,
to write them down we have to
cheat a lot.

When life occurs in more than one notation,
all writing is a kind of
translation.

—Mukul Kesavan[75]

---

[75] Kesavan, Mukul, *The Ugliness of the Indian Male*, 2008, p. 68.

Stephen Kellman popularized the term 'translingual writing' in his book *The Translingual Imagination* (2000). By that, he meant:

1) living in one language and writing in another,
2) writing in a language not profoundly one's own or
3) self-translation.

One could define much of the young generation of writers in Hindi as translinguals, inasmuch as most have done English-medium schooling and have their widest vocabularies in English. Screenwriter Shridhar Raghavan, for example, said:

> If we mapped our languages, I could go 100 on 100 with English, say 50-70 on 100 with Tamil and with Hindi, and maybe the same with Marathi. We've come from a background where there are multiple languages behind us, but our language of choice, in spite of all this medley of sounds, is actually English [...] So what happens is, my first drafts I always write in English, including the dialogue. For example, (*showing me a bit of his draft*) I started off in English, and suddenly I will go into Hindi midway. Hindi, Hindi, Hindi, and then I will come back to English. See, every language has a different metre. When you approach a scene in English you find a slightly subtler way to write it. If somebody who doesn't know Hindi at all is writing a screenplay in English and dialogues in English, and then he thinks that, 'Oh, I will just get this translated,' then the guy is an idiot of the highest order, because you cannot translate language. Take, for instance, a story about gangsters…or losers. If I am a Western background guy, and I start thinking, Oh, this should be like *Ocean's Eleven*, then suddenly my reference is all wrong. I'd prefer to have a more rooted Indian story about people who wind up taking to crime and doing a heist because of what their needs are. When my character starts talking in English, it becomes stilted. You cannot hope to write only in English

and expect to make a good Hindi film. If your character is a taxi driver, and if you are trying to write him in English, you are going to get a Samuel Jackson character... I work in English, my first draft is normally around 60 per cent, no, 70 per cent in English and 30 per cent Hindi. My next draft will be 50 per cent English, 50 per cent Hindi. My third draft will be around 30-40 per cent English and 70 per cent Hindi. At this point I would say, 'Okay, this is as good as I am in this language.' There are certain thoughts over here which I can express wonderfully in English, but I am unable to find a suitable colloquialism in Hindi. Take this gangster I'm writing about now. One day he's found that suddenly at the age of fifty-eight or sixty he is broke, and he needs to start all over again. Life doesn't make sense to him. He is looking at himself in the mirror in his bathroom early in the morning. He is wearing his pyjamas, and you can see this deep bypass scar that runs through his chest, and he's feeling the flab and the jowls. And he says, *'Buddha ho gaya, behenchod.'* He says, I have become an old man. Now 'behenchod' actually means sister fucker. I don't like this line in Hindi; it sounds much too crude. The next line I have written in English, 'I am closer to a heart attack than a hard-on.' There's a girl who is twenty-eight or thirty hanging out with him. He thinks, Why the hell is she with me? 'Just go on, do something with your own life, I am half-dead.' And she says, 'To hell with you. Stop overreacting.' Now I have written this in English. If I literally translate this line in Hindi, it's going to sound stupid... When I talk to my dialogue writer,[76] I would tell him I need this mood to come across...and I would tell him, 'Let's try this. Let's try this. Let's try this.' When I work on a Hindi draft, I throw aside my English draft completely,

---

[76]Rajat Arora.

and I just sit with the dialogue writer and start afresh, thinking this scene in Hindi now. In Hindi, whatever he says, I am more interested in that. It might be completely against what I have written in English but genuine to its Hindi roots. That's crucial because finally we are making a Hindi film. In *Bluffmaster!* it didn't matter. *Bluffmaster!* is a very urban sort of story. The whole draft was written in English. Then I did the whole draft in Bambaiya, our Mumbai hotchpotch colloquial version of Hindi, which I can do well. But if I were writing *Kaagaz Ke Phool*[77] today, I would be an idiot if I thought that I could write the film in English and then translate it and expect it to have any poetry to it.

Catering to Multilingual Audiences

Some writers or directors show a particular sensibility in their work to barriers to communication. I spoke with actor-director Anupam Kher for no more than a minute or two during a chance encounter. When I mentioned my interest in multilingualism within Hindi cinema, he gave a tantalizing response, saying that multilingualism 'has made Hindi cinema wordy'. Time didn't allow for elaboration, but Kher's brief and pertinent observation did get me thinking. How, after all, does one write dialogue for a vast public, some of whom have rich Hindi-Urdu vocabularies, while others understand perhaps 20 per cent of what they hear on-screen? It is a challenge that filmmakers from many language backgrounds need never consider. Hollywood writers work under the assumption that they can say 'eighth grade' and have a country full of people produce a recognizable mental image. Jaideep Sahni commented, 'Yeah, it's easier for them. It's like being a copywriter in Singapore. Your neighbour is

---

[77]Guru Dutt's classic film, written by Abrar Alvi, 1959.

your customer. They really have it easy in that sense. We have a lot to deal with.'

In an attempt to cover its bases linguistically, Hindi cinema has often offered the solution of repetition. In Raj Kapoor's *Awaara*[78] Judge Raghunath's (Prithviraj Kapoor) wife Leela (Leela Chitnis) is kidnapped by the manipulative Jagga (K.N. Singh). In his den, Leela falls down unconscious. An old female servant examines her, then tells Jagga, '*Ye garbhavati hai. Ma banne waali hai.*' (She's pregnant. She's going to be a mother.) If all viewers do not understand *garbhavati*, then hopefully the simpler *Ma banne waali* will make the message crystal clear. In *Kaala Patthar*[79] the villainous Prem Chopra character declares, 'Impossible!' and then reiterates with the Persian-based '*Naamumkin hai*' and the Sanskrit root '*Asambhav hai*'.

Repetition can also take place throughout a film. Nasreen Munni Kabir pointed out that Hindi film characters often have their signature lines, what she called 'a theme tune, theme sentence, a mannerism'. She gave the example of the Raj Kapoor character in *Awaara* with his '*Uska qasoor nahin hai. Meri soorat hi aisi hai.*' (It's not his fault. It's just my face.) Raj repeats this each time he is—correctly—taken for a thief. Such lines can be found in other cinemas in the world. In Howard Hawks' 1938 madcap comedy *Bringing Up Baby* the Katherine Hepburn character's refrain—'Everything's going to be all right'—is a sure sign that she is about to make the oh-so-proper David Huxley's (Cary Grant) world ever more impossibly chaotic. Such repeated lines add a theatrical touch. For multilingual audiences with diverse language abilities, they serve the additional purpose of making key phrases satisfyingly easy to grasp. The original *Don*, directed by Chandra Barot and written by Salim-Javed, gave the Amitabh Bachchan character a signature line, '*Don ko pakadna*

---

[78] Written by K.A. Abbas, 1951.

[79] Directed by Yash Chopra and written by Salim-Javed, 1979.

mushkil hi nahin, naamumkin hai.' (Catching Don is not only difficult, it's impossible.) Farhan Akhtar, when remaking *Don* in 2006 with Shah Rukh Khan in the lead, wanted the dialogue to be more realistic than in the original. He decided, however, not to drop that character-defining line. Speaking in 2007, Farhan explained, 'Someone saying "*Mujhe pakadna naamumkin hai*" is very pompous, regardless of how big a gangster he or she is. But for me that dialogue really is magical.' In another recent example, Shaad Ali's *Bunty aur Babli*, we hear Rakesh (Abhishek Bachchan) repeatedly exposing his jaded view of life, '*Ye world hai na, world*,' as in this exchange with a boy serving him tea:

> *Ye world hai na, world. Is mein do tarah ke log hote hain. Pehle, jo chaai pilaate hain, doosre jo chaai peete hain. Jitni jaldi doosri taraf aa jaaoge, utne hi sukhi rahoge, samjhe?*

> (This is the world, i.e. life, the world. There are two kinds of people in it. The first make tea for others and the second drink tea. The faster you come over to the second side, the quicker you'll be happy. Got it?)

Intentional simplification, independent of repetition, is another means of accommodating a range of viewers. Aziz Mirza, director of films such as *Yes Boss* (1997) and *Chalte Chalte*, comes from a film family and considers himself fortunate to have grown up hearing literary Urdu. His own characters, whom he describes as have-nots and strugglers or people trying to live in dignity, do not speak the refined language in vogue at the time when his father Akhtar Mirza was writing scripts for films such as *Waqt* (1965) or *Ab Dilli Dur Nahin* (1957). Mirza explained:

> My father was a writer in his own right. He even went to Harvard and translated Ghalib and gave lectures. I've heard the language spoken. But I for one do not like dialogues. Anything that sounds very literate, I run away from. That

(pointing to a small tree outside) can be called darakht or ped or jhaad. Darakht is more refined. Ped is the normal language. I would use the word ped. My father would use the word darakht. But today with the people I'm around, the language is basically for you to understand. We're all using language only to communicate.

In the following clever and compact scene from *Yes Boss*, the characters played by Juhi Chawla and Shah Rukh Khan chat as they walk along a busy Bombay sidewalk one evening. We hear of their carefully nursed ambitions and their conflicting inner desires. Love could be an impediment on the road to the top. What is potentially simple-boring is made simple-vibrant thanks to good camerawork and complementary acting styles. Juhi Chawla relies on her clear diction and expressive eyes, Shah Rukh Khan on his fast-paced delivery and animated body language.

Dreams of success: Juhi Chawla and Shah Rukh Khan in Yes Boss.
(Photo courtesy: Venus Worldwide Entertainment Pvt. Ltd)

The 'Best of Luck' Scene from *Yes Boss*

Seema: *To tum bahut bade banna chaahte ho.*

Rahul: *Bahut hi bada aur bahut saare khwaab hain mere. Vaise main hi kyon. Is sadak par har chalnewaala kahin na kahin pahunchna chaahta hai, nahin?*

Seema: *Haan. Tum jaante ho main kahaan pahunchna chaahti hoon?*

Rahul: *Kahaan?*

Seema: *Vahaan, Galaxy Towers.*

Rahul: *Baap re. Kehte hain ki vahaan pe har ek flat ek ek crore rupaye ka hota hai.*

Seema: *Main vahaan bahut bada sa ghar chaahti hoon.*

Rahul: *Achchha, farz karo. Tum ko ye sab nahin milta, phir?*

Seema: *To main us se shaadi karoongi jiske paas ye sab kuchh ho.*

Rahul: *Achchha, farz karo. Aisa hoga ki nahin, magar aisa ho jaaye ki is beech mein kisi naukri-pesha seedhe saadhe ladke se tumko pyaar ho jaaye?* Just a thought.

Seema: *Nahin. Naamumkin hai. Do kamzor insaan ek kaamyaab zindagi nahin bana sakte.*

(Rahul stops and looks upset.)

Seema: *Tumhein kya ho gaya?*

Rahul: *Tum, tum bahut hi frank ho. Kitni sachchaai ki baat itni aasani se keh di.*

Seema: *Rahul, apne aapko sukhi dekhne ka sapna dekhna koi gunaah to nahin hai?*

Rahul: *Nahin, bilkul nahin.*

Seema: *To phir kya mera sapna sach hoga?*

Rahul: *Arre, time kya hai? Time, time, tumhaari ghadi mein time kya hua hai?*

Seema: *Saadhe saat baje hain.*

Rahul: *Saadhe saat baje. Achchha, din kaun sa hai?*

Seema: *Somvaar hai.*

Rahul: *Punam ki raat hai?*

Seema: *Haan.*
Rahul: *Punam ki raat ko, saadhe saat baje, somvaar ko, is sadak par khade hokar sachche dil se jo maanga jaayega, vo milega.*
Seema: *Kisne kaha hai?*
Rahul: *Main ne kaha hai.* Best of luck!
Seema: Thank you.

(Seema: So you want to make it big?
Rahul: Very big. And I've got loads of dreams. But not just me. Everyone walking along this sidewalk wants to get somewhere, right?
Seema: Yes, you know where I want to get to?
Rahul: Where?
Seema: There. Galaxy Towers.
Rahul: Wow! They say that every flat there costs a crore.
Seema: I want a big house there.
Rahul: Okay, just suppose you didn't get it. Then what?
Seema: I'd marry someone who had it all.
Rahul: Okay, just suppose—this might happen or not—that you fell in love with a simple boy who works for a living. Just a thought.
Seema: No, that's not possible. Two weak people can't make a success of life.
Seema (seeing Rahul stop): What is it?
Rahul: You, you're really frank. Such a harsh fact of life and you say it so easily.
Seema: Rahul, dreaming of a happy life isn't a sin, is it?
Rahul: Absolutely not.
Seema: So will my dream come true?
Rahul: Uh, what time is it? Time, what time is it by your watch?
Seema: 7.30.
Rahul: 7.30. Okay, what day is it?
Seema: Monday.
Rahul: Is there a full moon?
Seema: Yes.

Rahul: Anyone standing on this sidewalk at 7.30 on a full-moon night on a Monday, will get whatever they ask for with a pure heart.
Seema: Who said so?
Rahul: I said so. Best of luck.
Seema: Thank you.)

Language Aware

The simplicity of the scene above is in stark contrast to the ornate language of a period piece like K. Asif's *Mughal-e-Azam* (1960). '*Ma ba daulat ba nafs-e-nafiis is jang mein shareek honge*,'[80] Akbar says to his scribe as he prepares to lead the army *personally* into battle. From the last part of the sentence audiences would grasp the basic meaning—that Akbar will join in the battle—but the actual words make us feel rather like modern audiences guessing at some of Shakespeare's vocabulary. There was a time when screen language was understood or it was not, but not understanding was not considered a problem, particularly if a film had splendid visuals to carry viewers along. Today, audiences are either, in fact, more impatient with obscure language or, at the very least, directors assume them to be. Hindi cinema has a rich tradition of well-spoken characters, characters whose lines make us wish we could be even half as wise, as clever, as romantic, as poetic. Add in the beautiful diction of the greatest actors, and you have a model that is vexingly hard to attain in real life.

Of late, though, we are seeing characters with markedly less command over language. What to make of this development? Is the goal more realism? Are the writers less skilled in the language they work in? Or are they simply more language-aware, more accustomed to reflecting on the hurdles involved in communicating? An extreme example is to be found in Nagesh

---

[80]From *The Immortal Dialogue of K. Asif's Mughal-e-Azam*, 2007, pp. 158–59.

Kukunoor's *Iqbal* (2005), the story of a cricket-loving boy from a poor family. There is a happy end. Iqbal (Shreyas Talpade) succeeds against all odds and is accepted into the Indian national cricket team. 'Poor and ultimately successful' may not be new, but Iqbal must also overcome being deaf and mute. He is able to communicate satisfactorily only with his sister and de facto interpreter Khadija (Shweta Prasad). We feel his pain at not being understood, and it becomes our own.

There are other language-challenged characters. Anurag Basu gives us the silent Barfi, played by Ranbir Kapoor in the 2012 film of the same name. Opposite him, Priyanka Chopra is the autistic Jhilmil, whose language is that of a slow five-year-old. And in Vishal Bhardwaj's *Kaminey* (2009), twins played by Shahid Kapoor are distinguished not only by their looks and their environments but also by their speech impediments: Guddu is a stutterer, and Charlie has a pronounced lisp.

A greater awareness in Bollywood of the problems that language can pose seems to be producing more attention to register, a catch-all term linguists use to distinguish levels of language. By way of example, the English-speaking character who says 'yeah' as a matter of course might manage a proper 'yes' should the situation require it. Think of the Julia Roberts character in *Pretty Woman* (1990) who finds herself moving from street hooker to well-paid 'escort' and who tries, fails and tries again to adjust her speech patterns to fit her new classy surroundings. In Hindi, a simple example of register is our expectation that buddies would say 'baith' or 'baitho' among themselves but, ideally, 'baithiye' if an older person is being asked to sit down. Because one of the repeated criticisms of Hindi films has been that all the characters tend to speak the same, it is interesting to see meta-awareness, that is, awareness of the awareness of language, making its way into some scenes. Imagine this meta-awareness as a two-step process. In the first, the writer thinks about phrasing and then, pulling back, stops a bit to think about thinking about phrasing. In Puri Jagannath's *Bbuddah Hoga Terra Baap* (2011), Vijju (Amitabh Bachchan) is back in Bombay after being away for some time and looking up his old gangster pals. He finds gangster-turned-guru Mirchi Baba (Rajiv Verma) dressed in saffron and spouting Sanskrit. Vijju rolls his eyes and starts to protest: '*Theek se baat kar na yaar*' (Talk normal, buddy!). When he gets yet more Sanskrit in response, he makes a prune face, gives a dismissive 'Whatever,' and moves on to business. In Prakash Jha's *Aarakshan* (2011) a character who uses the obscure Sanskrit-based sampradaayam for 'chance/opportunity' is corrected by a group of young people who shout in favour of the more popular 'mauq'a!' and then sing and dance to the lively '*De de mauqa de!*' song written by Prasoon Joshi. In Farah Khan's *Om Shanti Om* (2007), with dialogue by Mayur Puri, the problematic vocabulary is not Sanskrit but literary Urdu. Junior artiste Om (Shah Rukh Khan) dreams of becoming a star and winning a Filmfare Award. He and his friend Pappu (Shreyas Talpade) are in the street one night. Both have been drinking. Instead of a Filmfare Award, his friend Pappu presents him with a bottle, the 'batli' award.

Om Shanti Om: the Bottle Award

ओम: लेडीज़ एण्ड जैंटिलमैन, इतनी शिद्दत से मैंने तुम्हें पाने की कोशिश की है, कि हर ज़र्रे ने मुझे तुमसे मिलाने की साज़िश की है।

पप्पु: ए ओमी, कुछ समझ में नहीं आया।

ओम: ओ, मैं सिम्पल करूँ? टेक टू. लेडीज़ एण्ड जैंटिलमैन, कहते है अगर किसी चीज़ को दिल से चाहो तो पूरी कायनात उसे तुमसे मिलाने की कोशिश में लग जाती है। आप सब ने मुझे मेरी चाहत से मिला दिया। थैंक्स। थैंक्स व्हैरी मच। आई फ़ील लाइक दी किंग ऑफ दी वर्लड! और इस बात का यक़ीन हो गया कि हमारी फ़िल्मों की तरह हमारी ज़िंदगी में भी एंड तक सब कुछ ठीक हो जाता है। हैपीज़ एंडिग्ज़। और अगर ठीक ना हो, तो वो दी एंड नहीं। पिक्चर अभी बाक़ी है, मेरे दोस्त। आई लव यू, आई लव यू ऑल!

> (Om: Ladies and gentlemen…it has been with such earnest desire that I have attempted to obtain you (the bottle)

that every particle in the universe has conspired to bring us together.

Pappu: Eh Omi, I don't understand.

Om: Oh, shall I make it simple? Take 2. Ladies and gentlemen, they say that if you want something from the bottom of your heart, then the whole universe conspires to help you find it. And you all helped me fulfil my wish. Thanks. Thanks very much. I feel like the king of the woooooorld!...and one thing I've come to believe, that like in our films, yes, in our lives too everything should come out good in the end. Happys endings. And if they aren't good, then they aren't endings. The rest of the film remains, my friends. I love you, I love you all!)

Om's 'Take 2' is still full of Urdu, but it's the everyday kind that his listeners will understand.

There is no one way of giving the appropriate linguistic touch that will perfectly fit every character or satisfy all the diverse Hindi film audiences. Still, writer-director Vishal Bhardwaj has embraced a slew of languages over the span of his career. From Urdu in *Maqbool* to the Purbi in *Omkara* to Bombay slang and Marathi in *Kaminey*, Bhardwaj consistently gives us an acute sense of place and his characters' status in society through their speech. One result is that not all viewers understand all the dialogue. Some of the more vulgar language of *Omkara*, for example, went thankfully undetected by aunties sitting in comfortable multiplexes in Bombay or London, an observation made by Hindi film buff and researcher Sreya Mitra as we sat drinking coffee and sharing thoughts in Madison, Wisconsin, a few months after the film came out in 2006.

Shimit Amin struggles with conflicting needs: how to remain true to the reality one wishes to portray while allowing audiences to understand. 'There are cheap ways to do it,' he said, 'by throwing in words from a region, or the accent. The audience understands you can't do more than this. Otherwise, we'd have to put subtitles, and the character would have to speak another language, which is the proper way, I guess, if you really want to capture realism.' Shimit credits director Mani Ratnam for using language well, giving a distinct sense of place, for example, in the film *Guru* (2007), set in Gujarat, or with *Yuva* (2004) which conveys the flavour of Bombay. 'He's someone who looks for region in his work. A lot of filmmakers don't care and try to make films as generic as possible,' Amin said. 'As a purist, though, one feels that it hurts the culture of the area itself.'

Multilingualism: Not Always a Boon

It has been established that multilingualism is good for the individual, but just how good is it for an entire society? Victor Gingsburgh and Shiomo Weber address this issue in a book whose title goes to the heart of the dilemma: *How Many Languages Do We Need?* (2011). If knowing more than one language is good for our brains, is having tens, hundreds or even thousands of languages in one country really an advantage? Gingsburgh and Weber remind us that mythologies in various parts of the world have seen multilingualism as a curse from God, whether through the Biblical story of the tower of Babel or the wonder tree that reached to heaven and was cut down by Brahma, creating many languages as it fell to earth. Likewise, in stories from the Iroquois of North America, the Greeks or indigenous Australians,[81] multilingualism is seen not as a wealth but as a burden to be endured by humanity. Ginsburgh and Weber particularly explore the price of multilingualism within the European Union. With its twenty-three official languages and its rules-based approach to bureaucracy, it offers a textbook study of the complexity of dealing with language diversity. The generosity of the laudable European ideal allows that any citizen should be able to address

---

[81]Ginsburgh and Weber, 2011, p. 17.

any EU institution in his or her own language. Bearing the cost for all documents to be translated into all languages, however, is burdensome in the extreme. Language standardization or limitation may then seem a practical solution, but the downside is a sense of disenfranchisement for those on the outskirts of the linguistic centre.

And so it has been and still is in India. Multilingualism ups administrative costs in both the government and the private sector. And it leads to inefficiencies as information is poorly communicated or only partially understood. While literacy rates in India are not on par with those in Europe, India has the distinction of being a multilingual country in which languages have been written for hundreds and in some cases thousands of years, in contrast to Africa and Latin America, where great language diversity exists but largely within oral traditions. David Clingingsmith, professor of economics at Case Western Reserve University, looks at the period between 1931 and 1961 in India to see how industrialization affected both literacy and bilingualism. He comes up with these figures: 'In 1931, 8 per cent of the Indian population were bilingual and 9 per cent were literate. Bilingualism had increased 50 per cent and literacy 300 per cent by 1961.'[82] He goes on to show that industrialization pulled people from disparate language areas to work together in factories, where the need to communicate in a common language acted as an incentive to language learning. Over a period of time, less common languages generally lost out to the dominant language in these workplace settings. In other words, as in the case of the European Union, language standardization makes for more efficiency and can increase industrial productivity but at the expense of human diversity. Those who don't speak the dominant language(s) well enough are often left behind. So is multilingualism actually good for society? Yes, in that speaking several languages can allow for a wider range of perspectives on

---

[82] Clingingsmith, 2011, p. 8.

the world. No, inasmuch as maintaining multilingualism is an expensive proposition. The number of languages we might *want* is often at odds with the number of languages we *need*.

Bi/multilingualism can bring other complications. In September 2003, Dr Keith Walters, then professor of sociolinguistics at The University of Texas, presented a paper based on his experience both as a researcher and as an expert witness. He found himself called in to testify in court cases involving disputes over language. (Only in America, you may be thinking to yourself!) He described the grievance of a group of housekeepers at a private university in San Antonio, Texas, who were not allowed to speak Spanish at work because their employer enforced an 'English-only in the workplace' rule, which could be considered an infringement of their civil rights. The 'right' of speakers of minority languages to express themselves in their language can be pitted against the 'right' of speakers of the majority language, in this case English, to understand what is being said in their presence. Walters relates another case involving Chinese speakers in a US company, in which the English speakers complained of being 'uncomfortable' when Chinese was being spoken in their presence, possibly out of fear that they were being talked about. Walters wrote:

> Although many of us who are bilingual to any degree can recount stories demonstrating that such a fear is often no more than good old American paranoia, we can likewise discuss cases where we and others have used our 'other' language as a secret code or as a device of exclusion. More importantly, we have to admit that in the case cited, those who do not speak Chinese may feel they are being deprived of information that is crucial to their success at the company—and they may well be right.[83]

---

[83] Walters, Keith, 'Is Using Minority Languages In The Workplace A Civil Right? A Human Right? Neither?' Draft paper, 24 September 2003.

As though to illustrate the 'language as a secret code or as a device of exclusion' that Walters points to, the Barbara Mori character in Anurag Basu's *Kites* (2010) asks Hrithik Roshan's character how to say 'I love you' in Hindi. He answers, '*Ullu ki patthi.*' (Idiot.) He then asks her the same question about Spanish, and she answers with a cruder, '*Me estoy haciendo caca.*' (I'm shitting myself.) Both characters play with the words they have learned from the other, savouring them as true expressions of love.

Shabana Azmi was shocked to learn that workers could lose their jobs for speaking their own language or be ordered to speak only English at the workplace. Upon hearing the same story, Jaideep Sahni's first reaction was to say that the employers sounded 'constipated'. 'Why would somebody create an issue with this? These people should talk in whatever they're comfortable in. What do you have to do with how they talk to each other? How dumb is that?' Reflecting further though, Sahni cast a different light on the question:

> It might be this: we were a very feudal society till just a little while back, and we still are in large parts of our country, so maybe in India with employers there's a kind of a gap, and you are okay with it. If workers understand what you're saying, and your world doesn't stop because of this language issue, then it's okay. They can speak to each other in whatever. I don't know. It just occurred to me. But I suspect that there might be a bit of a feudal thing to it because if I were at a party, and there were three of us who knew Hindi and two who spoke to each other in Bengali, and they kept going on and on in it for five minutes, we'd have a problem. I wouldn't get upset about it, but it'd be strange. And if they're laughing, then I'd say, 'Guys, you know, we're also here.'

Language Attitudes

'I feel more at ease speaking in my mother tongue. It's like being at home with all the usual familiar worn and comfortable clutter around you. Speaking a second language is like being you but in someone else's house.'

—a Welsh speaker named Ellen, cited by researcher Aneta Pavlenko[84]

A sense of home, i.e. the place where the heart is. An Israeli-American, who spent the first fourteen years of his life in Israel, may have a bigger vocabulary in English, but even after twenty years in the US, when speaking English, he still feels like a tourist. For director Shashanka Ghosh, who speaks English much of the day, Hindi is the language of intimacy. 'With my friends, by the second drink, everything lapses back into Hindi.' Shimit Amin has continued to work on his Hindi since returning from the US to India because he feels, 'Hindi allows you a certain place to go and a comfort that maybe English doesn't. When you speak in Hindi to somebody who knows Hindi, I think you get that kind of closeness that you don't get in English.' Both directors seek the 'at home' feeling that language can give. But attitudes towards language are multifarious and can cover the spectrum of reactions, from impassioned to nonchalant. What language is 'mine'? Just how 'mine' is that language? How correct does that language have to be and can I stand to hear it misused? And how do I/we feel about other languages in general and *certain* other languages in particular? Such questions are rarely formulated. Yet, were each individual in the world to be asked, the answers would probably be as intense or as detached as if one were to ask the meaning of life and our place in the grand scheme of things. From absolute certainty to a shrug of the shoulders. It

---

[84]Pavlenko, Aneta, Ed., *Bilingual Minds*, p. 19.

is the shrug that allows so many in India to move easily from language to language, often within one sentence, paying more attention to the desire and the need to communicate than to grammatical properness or strict language boundaries. Dialogue writer Shama Zaidi expressed both the shrug, so to speak, and also absolute certainty. Having studied in detail the history of language in northern India, she could take a particularly long and cool view of language change in the region. Speaking in 2006, she said:

> Earlier, it was Persian and whatever language you spoke. And now it's become English. All that's happened is that Persian has got replaced by English. Earlier, it was Sanskrit. So we always had a high language and a low language. I think all languages evolve, and now we have something called Hinglish and Pinglish...

Moving from linguistic history to the more personal family domain, Zaidi's attitudes became more entrenched. She said:

> Well, there's this pecking order. Earlier, English was at the top, followed by Hindi or Urdu. Then you had the dialects. So, say, in a place like Rajasthan, everyone at home would speak in dialect, and on the street they would speak in Hindi or to tourists in English. Now the whole middle class in Rajasthan has starting speaking in Hindi. They refuse to speak dialect. It's only the aristocracy and the villagers who speak dialect, the aristocracy as a kind of identity thing and the villagers because they don't know anything else. And everybody else speaks Hindi. And it's like (the pecking order) here in Bombay. But since our family belong to the theatre, we look down on people who don't speak Hindi. We think the cachet thing is to speak proper Hindi. The hoi polloi speaks only English, but I've forbidden my granddaughter to talk to me in English.

Actor Tom Alter complained of English being a fad, often spoken poorly and at the expense of other languages. Speaking in 2007, he pleaded for true multilingualism:

> See, I was a bit fortunate to have been born in India in 1950, so I've seen in my childhood people who were my father's friends, people who spoke very good English, but at the same time, without any conflict of ego, would then speak beautiful Hindi or Bengali or Urdu or whatever their language was. In their English there was no affectation, no fake accent, no attempt to talk like a Westerner. They talked as they spoke, and they spoke beautifully. Look at Nehru, for instance. The man wrote this incredible book, *The Discovery of India*. He could then give fluent speeches in Hindi. And Kashmiri. And he knew Urdu... Manmohan Singh. He is an intellectual. He's at home in Punjabi; he's

Tom Alter in Mangal Pandey: The Rising.
(Photo courtesy: Kaleidoscope Entertainment Private Limited)

at home in Urdu; he's at home in Hindi; he's at home in English. He just goes back and forth between these four languages the way one drinks tea or coffee. These are the people who really are the backbone... Our greatest actor, Amitabh Bachchan, is the greatest example. His English is flawless. His Hindi is perfect. And he can very easily move from one to the other. So I don't get too discouraged. Every now and then I lose my temper with young people who insist on talking in English. And I just tell them, 'Why?!' Their English, with all due respect, is not so good that they can think and create in that language. But they want to do that and in doing that, they neglect their mother tongue... When they want to express a thought or a feeling, they're unable to because they don't have one language which is coming from their heart. And it's very very sad. But it is an inferiority complex which they have to get through, and they will get through it.

We live in a more connected world today than at any time in the past. As a result, on one level we feel the exciting tug of the global. Billions of us have access to images and information from every continent. If English speakers are ever more numerous, it is precisely because the language connects so many worldwide. Administratively though, and very often emotionally, we continue to be tied to the countries of our citizenship. So there's the world and there's the nation, but on another level, we feel bound to the local, listening to local live music, harvesting vegetables from our own little gardens, and perhaps stubbornly refusing to modify our accents, no matter how far we may move from the region or even neighbourhood of our childhoods. Neapolitan singer Nino D'Angelo, whose language seemed foreign to his pan-Italian audience at the San Remo Song Festival in 2010, said, 'I think dialect is at the root of each and every one of us. It's in my DNA. Turning your back on your dialect is like turning your back on your values, your traditions, or losing a parent. Of course, we have to learn Italian too, but I find it hard as I grew up speaking only my dialect.'[85] At the Annual Conference on South Asia in Madison, Wisconsin, in 2007, Anshuman Pandey from the University of Michigan gave a presentation entitled 'Fashioning a Transnational Bihari Identity Through Bhojpuri Film Songs' in which he documented the rising phenomenon of Bhojpuri cinema, particularly as represented by actor-singer-director Manoj Tiwari whose song 'Purab ke Beta' (Son of the East) offers a sense of cultural belonging to migrant Biharis across India and far beyond Indian borders. The tug of the local is powerful.

Generational belonging, educational background, individual psychology, the politics of the moment and chance circumstance all influence our feelings about language. Linguistic pride, for instance, ebbs and flows throughout history and across the world. The status of Hindi–Urdu has tended to fall as that of English has risen in India. The paradoxical experience of graduate student and Hindi teaching assistant Shilpa Parnami at The University of Texas is worth noting, however. Hindi, she has observed, is so valued within the South Asian Studies department that she has found herself wanting to speak the language more in Austin than she had in India. Likewise, actress Sushmita Sen's pride in Hindi grew from an experience abroad. She explained that, contrary to the impression she gives of being fully at ease in English, she actually studied the language rather late and was even afraid to speak English on stage while competing for the title of Miss Universe (1994).[86] It was while taking part, though, that she realized the Spanish-speaking contestants were just fine with not knowing English, which led her to reappraise the role of

---

[85] Reported by Emma Wallis, *The Strand*, BBC World Service, February 2010.
[86] The Philippines hosted the Miss Universe pageant in 1994. Sushmita Sen won the title. The first and second runners-up that year were from Columbia and Venezuela.

English in India. '*Mere desh mein ye kyon hota hai ki ham log itna zyaada zor dete hain ki English mein baat karo.*[87] (Why is it that in my country we put so much emphasis on speaking English?)

Whatever misgivings one might have, English, of course, continues in its role as the language of power in India. Jaideep Sahni, in 2006, stressed that something is lost and something is gained with its ever-greater use:

> English will take care of itself because it really is your passport to a better future. And that is fine by me. I'd rather everyone talk to everyone else than not talk and just think that their own world and their own culture is great. But there's a loss of authentic, original cultures everywhere. My kids won't know the Ramayana and the Mahabharata the way I do. They won't know Hindi as well as I do. I don't know Hindi as well as my grandmother would. But then I know more about a hell of a lot of things than she does. It's a trade-off. But all in all I'm fine with it.

Versatile multilingual Tamil actor Kamal Haasan also noted his sense of limitation in the many languages in which he has worked, '*Fluency pata nahin.* (I don't know about fluency.) I have the dubious distinction of being illiterate in five languages. I can speak them, but I can't read and write them. *Hindi thoda padh-likh sakta hoon* (I can read and write a bit of Hindi), but not Telugu and Malayalam).'[88]

Haasan was, of course, exaggerating. He is very literate in English and probably in Tamil as well. With a bit of written Hindi, he would then be able to handle three scripts in three unrelated languages. Not bad. While celebrating his fifty years in cinema in 2009, he was interviewed repeatedly. At one point, he pleaded for a balanced multilingualism in these terms,

---

[87]Speaking on the BBC Hindi Service 70 MM in 2011.
[88]Speaking on the BBC Hindi Service in April 2011.

We were under the yoke of the British for 300 years. And what we should do is take the strength from it and not the weakness. We have a strength which is that this is an English-speaking nation. Our national language is English, and don't be ashamed about it. Use it as a tool. But don't forget your mother language.[89]

---

[89] Confessions in conversation with Shaili Saini on E-24 Bollywood Channel.

POETRY

'Bachpan se hai sir par Allah ka haath, aur Allahrakha hai mere saath. Baazu par hai saat sau chhiyaasi ka billa, bees number ka bidi peeta hoon, kaam karta hoon coolie ka, aur naam hai Iqbal.'

–Amitabh Bachchan's character Iqbal introducing himself to Julie (Rati Agnihotri) in *Coolie*, dialogue by Kader Khan[90]

Just what is poetry? Possibly something a bit difficult to define, but something one 'knows when one sees', as an American judge famously said of pornography. An online search of *poetry* brings up site after site with list upon list of its elements. Wikianswers, for example, offers rhythm, metre, rhyme, alliteration, simile, metaphor, theme, symbolism. Paul Reuben of California State University, Stanislaus, adds personification, metonymy, paradox, overstatement, understatement and irony. He quotes poet William Wordsworth, who called poetry 'the spontaneous overflow of powerful feelings, recollected in tranquility'. He continues more personally, 'Poetry might be defined, initially, as a kind of language that says more and says it more intensely than does ordinary language.'[91] Poet and professor Adam Sol goes a step further: 'Poetry, at its best, imagines a perfect language, which can impart all nuances, meanings and music that it never quite achieves in our everyday speech.'

---

[90]Directed by Manmohan Desai and Prayag Raj, 1983.
[91](http://www.csustan.edu/English/reuben/pal/append/axf.html)

The quote from *Coolie* in the beginning of the chapter relies on alliteration, creative word order, repetition and rhythm. Since childhood the hand of Allah has been on Iqbal's head, and Allahrakha (his falcon) has been by his side. On his arm is a badge with the (sacred) number 786. He smokes twenty cheap cigarettes a day, works as a railroad porter and is named Iqbal. Dynamic, succinct, beautiful to the ear and fun!

The most developed poetic form within Hindi cinema is probably metaphor. It is humbling to observe the amazing capacity for memorization people thoroughly immersed in Urdu-Hindi literary traditions have. Metaphoric language, which can speak to even the most untrained mind, no doubt works as a memory aid, leaving behind vivid mental images. At the same time, metre and rhyme, when integrated at a very young age, would seem to work not only at a neurological level but also at a physiological level, with breathing and muscles becoming finely tuned for poetic rhythms, probably facilitating feats of memory.[92]

These mental images have become the focus of a great deal of academic research. What was once viewed as a poetic device is now seen as essential to the way in which humans beings make sense of the world. In 1980 cognitive linguists George Lakoff and Mark Johnson wrote the influential *Metaphors We Live By*. Our experiences of the physical world can turn into abstractions through metaphors. Life, then, is a journey. More is up and less is down. We fight disease or we fight for a principle. Expressions of imagery are so much a part of our lives that we are generally blind to them; it is only when we consider metaphors to be deserving of study in their own right that they suddenly leap off the page, from the airways or out of daily speech and grab our attention. In 'Metaphors: We Are What We Speak'

---

[92]This is a hypothesis. It makes sense, and I like it, but then again, perhaps I am merely looking to excuse my own inability to summon up more than two or three lines of verse at a time.

sociolinguist Deborah Tannen says, 'the terms in which we talk about something shape the way we think about it—and even what we see.'[93] Language 'moulds our way of thinking about people, actions and the world around us'.[94]

Songs tend to be the repository of poetry within Hindi cinema. Poets such as Sahir Ludhianvi, Kaifi Azmi, Shakeel Badayuni and Gulzar have enriched us with a trove of lyrics. At times, dialogue too has been filled with a poetic sensibility. The 1970s saw a pair of writers, Salim-Javed, i.e. Salim Khan and Javed Akhtar, make their mark not only with characters and stories that spoke to a generation but also with a metaphor-filled style of dialogue writing that was unique and lasting.

In *Shakti*, written by Salim-Javed and directed by Ramesh Sippy, two powerful stars, Dilip Kumar and Amitabh Bachchan, play stern father and rebellious son. When gangsters kidnap the eight-year-old Vijay, his policeman father endangers his son's life by placing duty to the law ahead of love for his son. This moment of broken trust is the first step along a path of increasing father-son conflict that sees the alienated adult Vijay sucked into a life of crime. Vijay loves his mother (Raakhee) and his companion (Smita Patil), but neither woman is capable of preventing him from spiralling ever further away from family and law. The script, the direction and the acting combine to give us a powerful story in which each flawed man first garners our favour and then provokes our anger as our sympathies shift from father to son and back again. How can we not feel Vijay's sense of injustice over being wrongly jailed? When his smuggler boss pays for his release, Vijay's father tries to warn the son not to go down the road from which there is no return. Defiantly, the son answers that he has no intention of returning—and we are on his side. Nevertheless, we ache with the father as he sadly tells his wife

---

[93]From Walters, Keith and Brody, Michael, ed., 2005, p. 14.
[94]Ibid.

that night what has happened:

Tumhaara beta kho gaya hai, Sheetal... Haan, kho gaya tumhaara beta. Ye sab kaise hua, kaunsi kami reh gayi hamaare pyaar mein? Kya bhool hui hamse...meri samajh mein nahin aata. Lekin aaj jab vo log meri aankhon ke saamne use le gaye, to mujhe laga kisine mere bete ka daam lagaaya aur daam lagaakar use khareed liya. Unhone mere bete ko khareed liya aur main dekhta raha. Main dekhta raha, Sheetal, kuchh nahin kar saka...

(Your son is lost, Sheetal... Yes, lost. How did all this happen? What was lacking in our love? What mistake did we make? I don't understand, but today those people took him away right in front of my eyes. It was like someone paid for my son, and having paid, bought him. They bought my son, and I watched. I watched, Sheetal; there was nothing I could do.)

Vijay (Amitabh Bachchan) and his policeman father (Dilip Kumar) in Shakti. *(Sketch by Simon P. Holzman)*

These simple words, spoken in Dilip Kumar's understated way, create images and produce emotions which will last much longer than the words themselves.

Vijay's mother's reaction to 'losing' her only son is to fall gravely ill. When the gangster Vijay, now immensely wealthier than his father, visits his sick mother and begs her to allow him to take her to the best doctors, she refuses, preferring to sink slowly towards death rather than leave her husband and follow Vijay. Not one paisa of dishonest money has ever come into her home, and she will not accept his money, stained with crime and dishonesty, now. *'Mera ghar ek mandir ki tarah pavitr hai, Vijay.'* (My home is holy, like a temple, Vijay.) He reminds her of how weak she has become, and she replies, *'Main abhi itni kamzor nahin hoon, Vijay, ki main apne pati ki imaandaari ka bojh na utha sakun.'* (I am not so weak, Vijay, that I cannot lift the burden of my husband's honesty.) *'Beimaani ka paisa mere liye zeher hai, beta,'* (Dishonest money is poison for me, son), she tells him accusingly.

In despair Vijay returns to his luxurious apartment. Roma finds him drinking, hardly able to speak or to stand. Zeher (poison) is a powerful word and a part of the poetic tradition. In a monologue which heaps metaphor upon metaphor, Vijay, by all appearances a strong man, bemoans his helplessness, cries out his pain as he compares himself to a poisonous snake and finally collapses to the floor at Roma's feet.

Sharab khareednewaale rupaye mere paas bahut hai. Haan, dava khareednewaale rupaye mere paas nahin hain... Jaanti ho, Roma, mere baap ne do shaadiyaan ki. Do—ek meri ma ke saath aur ek apni naukri ke saath. Apni ma ka beta main hoon aur meri sauteli ma, yaani, mere baap ki doosri bivi ka beta hai qaanoon, qaanoon. Qaanoon mera sautela bhaai hai, sautela bhaai. Aur main to us ghar se bhaag gaya hoon, lekin meri sauteli ma aur mere sautele bhaai ne meri ma ko mere baap ke ghar ke andar qaid kar diya hai. Aur meri ma bahut bimaar hai, to main kuchh... kuchh nahin kar sakta tha... isliye ki main vo badnaseeb beta hoon ki jis dava ko chhoo doon, vo meri ma ke liye zeher ban jaayegi. Zeher. Mere ma-baap, mere apne ma-baap, mujhe apna beta nahin, ek zehreela saanp samajhte hain. Tum bhi mujhse daro kyonki main ek zehreela saanp hoon. Main tumhein bhi das sakta hoon. Zehreela saanp.

(I have plenty of money to buy alcohol but no money to buy medicine. Do you know, Roma, that my father got married twice, once to my mother and once to his job. I am my mother's son; and my stepmother's, that is, my father's second wife's, son is the law. The law. The law is my stepbrother, my stepbrother. I have fled from that house, but my stepmother and stepbrother have imprisoned my mother inside my father's house. And even though my mother is very ill, I could do nothing for her because I am that ill-fated son whose very touch turns medicine to poison. Poison. My mother and father, my own mother and father, see me not as a son but as a poisonous snake. You, too, should fear me because I'm a poisonous snake. I could sink my fangs into you as well. A poisonous snake!)

Javed Akhtar comes from a long line of poets. His grandfather, uncle, father and mother were all well-known Urdu writers. Still, a brief comparison of this literary tradition and Salim-Javed's writing reveals that Salim-Javed use few formulaic expressions from the past. Rather, key words return. Within the Persian-Urdu tradition, words evoking pain, the heart, longing, the journey and the power of eyes to communicate are common. Zulm, dil, vaqt, intizaar, armaan, duniya, zindagi, hamsafar, qadam, raahon, nazar, nigaahein are more evocative than their English translations, simply because of the multitude of poetic references they bring to mind.

Poetry comes not only from words but also from the voice in which the words are spoken. Nasreen Munni Kabir speculated on the source of the power of Amitabh Bachchan's delivery of his speech near the end of *Deewaar*. In the very temple the Vijay character has always rebelliously refused to enter, he now angrily exhorts Shiva to let his ailing mother live:

> *Vo aurat aaj zindagi aur maut ke sarhad par khadi hai aur ye tumhaari haar hai. Haan, ye tumhaari haar hai. Kya qusoor hai uska? Kaunsa paap, kaunsa jurm kiya hai usne? Kya vo jurm ye hai ki vo meri ma hai? Kya vo jurm ye hai ki usne mujhe janm diya hai? Kya vo jurm ye hai ki main usse pyaar karta hoon? …Main ne kabhi tum se kuchh nahin maanga, lekin aaj, aaj maangta hoon. Mere gunaahon ki saza meri ma ko mat do.*

> (That woman today stands between life and death, and this is your defeat. Yes, this is your defeat. What is her fault? What sin, what crime did she commit? Is it her crime that she is my mother? Is it her crime that she gave birth to me? Is it her crime that I love her? …I have never asked anything of you, but today I'm asking: do not punish my mother for my sins.)

Nasreen Munni Kabir said, referring to this famous scene:

> I feel that it sounds very much like a mushaa'ira (poetic gathering). The intonation, the diction is like that of a poet. If Amitabh, as a child, was running around with his dad (famous poet Harivansh Rai Bachchan) to mushaa'iras, he must have been hearing poetry—Hindi-Urdu poetry—and how the poets delivered impact. In speeches, Amitabh has got much more the poet's style than the theatre man's style of delivery. Every word has weight; every word is distinct, clear, audible.

Poetic moments in recent films are tame in comparison with those in Salim-Javed films. In *3 Idiots*[95] engineering student Rancho

---

[95] Directed by Rajkumar Hirani.

(Aamir Khan) is described this way by one of his friends:

> *Kuchh baat thi us mein. Saala duniya ke taur-tareeqe qadam-qadam pe challenge karta tha. Ham sab to professors ke remote control pe chalnewaale logon mein se the. Vo bas ek hi tha jo shaayad machine nahin tha.*

(There was something about him. Damn, he would challenge the ways of the world every step of the way. The rest of us were like people who moved when the professors punched the remote control button. He was the only one who was maybe not a machine.)

This is not lyrical writing, but it is poetry. Succinctly, the words create mental images—students as machines in a lifeless system and one man who loves machines but refuses to be one.

In the 2009 *Love Aaj Kal*, writer-director Imtiaz Ali plays with words from the past and renews them. His modern character Jai (Saif Ali Khan) says the word dil (heart) while speaking to the older Veer Singh (Rishi Kapoor). By his side and listening on without understanding is Jai's French-speaking girlfriend-of-the-moment (Florence Brudenell-Bruce). She picks the word up from a conversation and repeats dil, amplifying its meaning for the audience because we hear it through her fresh ears. She has grasped that dil is key to the conversation from which she is being excluded, just as she will ultimately be excluded from Jai's heart. Dil expands to 'dilli' as Veer Singh speaks of losing his own heart years ago in the city whose name evokes heart. 'Delhi?' asks the young cosmopolitan Jai, using the English pronunciation of the name. Veer Singh taps his chest—his heart—in exasperation. 'Dilli!' he says, preferring the Hindi pronunciation of the name of the city. Veer is shown to believe in love and lasting commitment. Jai, the love sceptic, believes in having a pretty girl by his side. Blind to his feelings, he responds to Veer (who worked in a factory when he first fell in love) and takes the metaphor yet a step further, *'Dil ki factory band ho chuki hai.'* (The heart factory has shut down.) The image is spare and striking.

Another form of poetry is to be found in the opening lines of *Bunty aur Babli*, written by Jaideep Sahni, voiced over by Amitabh Bachchan and set against images of Bombay's Marine Drive sparkling in the sun like the pearl necklace to which it has been compared:

> *Ye hai India, chamchamaata, jagmagaata, phusphusaata ki agar tera koi sapna hai, to aa, aaja aur karle poora. Agar tere mein koi bhookh hai, to aa, aaja aur karle poori. Izzat, shohrat, rupaya, taaqat, sab tere dost ban jaayenge aur teri zindagi kabhi na khatm hone waala sunehra sapna.*

> (This is India, shining, glistening, whispering that if you have some dream, then come, come and make it real. If you are hungering for something, then come, come and get your fill. Respect, fame, money and power, all of these will become yours and your life be a never-ending golden dream.)

There's a beat to these lines which are chock-full of evocative words and brimming with onomatopoeia, the effect of which is heightened by Amitabh Bachchan's mature poetic voice. And there's power that comes from the use of repetition, from the dream conjured up, from the irony suggested. Powerful, too, is the contrast between first images of shining India and the next scenes of small-town youth frustrated in their desires for their part of the dream. Jaideep Sahni, who wrote these words, gave his definition of poetry, particularly in relation to lyric-writing:

> Poetry is just another name for creativity and impact. It's a state of mind. It's not about flowery words. I come up against a lot of my lyric-writer friends who keep confusing lyrics with poetry. I think poetry is seeing a certain thing in a way or from an angle that makes another person sit up and say, 'I've never looked at it like that.' I don't have anything against poetry. I have a thing against people who,

at least in my book, don't know what poetry is. Can they not see poetry in the way Sachin Tendulkar takes a certain shot in cricket? The apple fell down. Why did only Newton say, 'Why did the apple fall down?' That is poetry. Or a guy called Kekulé figures out the structure of benzene. That is poetry.

What Jaideep here refers to as poetry is a sort rarely mentioned in English literature classes. The word *poetry* in dictionary.reference.com includes 'poetic qualities however manifested: the poetry of simple acts and things' and 'poetic spirit or feeling: The pianist played the prelude with poetry'. Shridhar Raghavan remembers the advice he received early in his film-writing career:

> [Director] Kundan Shah[96] used to say, 'But where's the poetry in the scene?' I'd write a scene, and it seemed perfect. He would say, 'This has got no poetry, man.' And I understood gradually what he meant. Poetry is something else. It's beyond language. It's creating a certain feeling which resonates inside you. And then the movie becomes not something you are watching; it becomes something which connects with you. Poetry is a very random word I am using. When I see something where I feel, yeah, the guy made it with utter genuine honest intention. He's communicated a bit of that to me, and I walk away with a bit of that movie in me.

Shridhar Raghavan's 'I walk away with a bit of the movie in me' touches on one of the powers and mysteries of the movies, that is, the memories they are able to generate. Like our dreams, entire films quickly evaporate as though we had never seen them. And even films that make a deep impression rarely leave us with more than a few images, a bit of storyline, perhaps a sense of atmosphere, a few emotions and one or two scenes that for some

---

[96] Kundan Shah, especially appreciated for his 1983 *Jaane Bhi Do Yaaro*.

reason 'stick'. Why? Why do we remember what we remember? Why do we forget what we forget? And why do I remember this scene when you remember that scene, and yet we both remember yet another scene? Because Indian cinema relies heavily on music, and because music can access our emotions in intimate ways, song sequences may offer particularly strong hooks for our memory. Who can resist, who cannot connect with Geeta Dutt's delicate rendering of Kaifi Azmi's lyrics and S.D. Burman's music for the song 'Vaqt ne kiya' in Guru Dutt's *Kaagaz Ke Phool* (1959)? The black-and-white film allows for a striking use of light and shadow with long close-ups of the faces of Waheeda Rehman and Guru Dutt. As film viewers we all have, no doubt, experienced such poetic moments of connection, and when we feel let down by a film, it is perhaps poetry of one sort or another that is missing.

An image of poetry: Waheeda Rehman in Kaagaz Ke Phool.
(Sketch by Simon P. Holzman)

THE PRESENCE OF URDU

'For a long time, let's remember that it was the Hindi film which was the custodian of the Urdu language.'

—Shabana Azmi, Bombay, February 2007

'Main keh doonga ki Urdu ko thodi bahut jagah mil gayi Bollywood mein, kuchh der tak panaah mil gayi.'
(I would say that Urdu found a bit of space in Bollywood. It found some shelter there for a while.)

—Ali Husain Mir speaking with Dr Akbar Hyder, Austin, March 2008

Teri edi ki vo khankhan
Teri chhoti si vo anban
Teri palkein teri bindi
Teri Urdu teri Hindi
(Your tapping heels, your little rifts, your eyelids, your bindi, your Urdu, your Hindi)

—Jaideep Sahni, 'Show Me Your Jalwa' from *Aaja Nachle*

Vo yaar hai jo khushbu ki tarah
Jiski zubaan Urdu ki tarah
(That friend (lover) who is like a fragrance/Whose language is like Urdu)

—Gulzar, 'Chaiyya Chaiyya' from *Dil Se*

It is hard to imagine this cinema without the presence of Urdu. The language is rarely named today within the films themselves, but it remains a well from which writers draw. For dialogue writer Shama Zaidi, one must look to Indian cinema's theatrical roots for an explanation of language as it developed in the newer medium:

> Well, you see, the thing is that Hindi cinema, I really think, is Urdu cinema, because Hindi was a state language, a language of the upper castes, and Urdu was a street language, at least the language of the popular theatre. It was bombastic, but it was used in village squares and Hindi wasn't. It [Hindi cinema] started out as folk theatre. Company theatres were influenced by Victorian melodrama. In Lucknow, they were influenced by the French and French popular theatre. That popular theatre then became cinema. In the beginning there were the same themes and the same sort of language. Like *Sikandar*, it was very theatrical. Even *Mughal-e-Azam* is based on a play. So the language of the theatre set the tone for cinema. And then, when the theatre became more realistic in the '40s, it took about a decade or more for similar themes to come into cinema. Specifically, if you talk about realism and cinema, it was the result of the Leftist movement. And that started in the theatre. The same people then joined films—the poets, the actors—Balraj Sahni, Kaifi Azmi and all these people. They came from the popular theatre and then they moved to film, and the language changed.

Dialogue writer and lyricist Ali Husain Mir looks at the linguistic and cultural changes that Bollywood has undergone more recently:

> To talk about Urdu as a language is difficult. The language survives. Take any Hindi film. The name may be in Urdu. The conversation in films—the language of romance, the language of passion—will all be in Urdu. But I think a language is more than its vocabulary. The sensibility that

was Urdu's, particularly the poetic sensibility, is quickly coming to an end. But even now Bollywood is the kind of place in popular culture where Urdu has got a very significant advantage over other languages, partly because it has so much history and vocabulary and legacy and things it can draw upon, its traditions, which allow it to be expressive in a way that resonates with the melodrama of film.[97]

Scholars and curious language students alike have long asked to what extent culture can be separated from language. When we think, are we merely making use of the grammar and vocabulary at our disposition, or does our language and its accompanying culture determine our perception of the world, to some degree? One formulation of the latter viewpoint is the Sapir-Whorf hypothesis, which, briefly stated, suggests a correlation between

Dancing on a train to A.R. Rahman's beat: Shah Rukh Khan and Malaika Arora in the 'Chaiyya Chaiyya' song from Dil Se.
(Sketch by Simon P. Holzman)

---

[97]From an interview in Urdu with Dr Akbar Hyder at The University of Texas, Spring 2008 (translated by the author).

the language we speak and our thought processes. Ali Mir's comments would seem to suggest an inclination towards this view. Much maligned by linguists, the hypothesis, at least in its less deterministic form, satisfies many bilinguals who find their own understanding of reality strongly filtered by each of their languages. To a certain extent culture is contained in language, expressed through language and transmitted via language. The poetic sensibility to which Ali Mir refers is highly language-specific and culturally bound. As Gulzar suggests in the 'Chaiyya Chaiyya' song, beyond being a means of communication, Urdu possesses a fragrance of its own.

The Pull of Urdu

In Sanjay Leela Bhansali's *Devdas* (2002), Shah Rukh Khan plays Devdas; Madhuri Dixit, the courtesan Chandramukhi. Purists tend to prefer Dilip Kumar and Vyjayanthimala in Bimal Roy's more understated 1955 version of the story, which allows us more readily to believe we are in Bengal in the early twentieth century. The 2002 version of the film, with dialogue credited to Prakash Kapadia, is as sumptuous as the film's decor. In the following scene Devdas drinks red wine from a beautifully shaped glass in Chandramukhi's lush, richly coloured palace. They lie next to a small pool of water, reminiscent of scenes from Kamal Amrohi's *Pakeezah* (1972) or his *Razia Sultan* (1983). The Bengali atmosphere of the *Devdas* novel has given way to the sensibilities one would expect in Urdu poetry. The dialogue is replete with layered, situational metaphors.

Let It Overflow: The 'Wine Glass' Scene from *Devdas*

चंद्रमुखी: बस भी करो। बहुत पी चुके।
देव: यही कह दिया होता, बहुत जी चुके।
चंद्रमुखी: कैसे कह दूँ? तुम्हारे पास तो पारो है, पारो की यादें हैं। मेरे पास तो सिर्फ़ तुम हो, पारसमणि, जिसे छू के लोहा भी

सोना बन जाता है।
देव: अपनी क़ीमत बढ़ा रही हो या मेरी?
चंद्रमुखी: रिश्तों की दुनिया में तवायफ़ की क़ीमत ही क्या होती है? कुछ भी नहीं। और वैसे भी आपने तो हमें छूने का अधिकार ही नहीं दिया।
देव: इश्क़ करती हो मुझसे?
चंद्रमुखी: यही पूछ लिया होता, सांसें लेती हो, चंद्रमुखी?
देव: सांसें लेती हो, चंद्रमुखी? क्या पाओगी? ना मेरे पास घर है, ना दिल।
चंद्रमुखी: सिर्फ़ पाने का नाम ही तो प्यार नहीं है ना, देव बाबू। प्यार का कारोबार तो बहुत बार किया है, मगर प्यार सिर्फ़ एक बार।
देव: चंद्रमुखी, इस भरे पैमाने में और शराब डालोगी, तो क्या होगा?
चंद्रमुखी: छलक कर ज़मीन पर आ गिरेगी।
देव: ममम, इसी तरह पारो के नाम से भरा पड़ा है ये पैमाना, देवदास भी। और भरोगी तो छलक जाएगा। ख़ुद तो गिरेगा, तुम्हें भी गिरा देगा।
चंद्रमुखी: पर ज़मीन पर गिरी शराब को देखकर, लोग तो यही कहेंगे ना कि पैमाने को छू कर निकली है।
देव: तो आओ, छलका दो।

(Chandramukhi: Enough. You've drunk too much.
Devdas: You might as well say I've lived too much.
Chandramukhi: You have Paro and memories of Paro. All I have is you, Parasmani, a stone whose touch can turn even iron to gold.
Devdas: Are you raising your price or mine?
Chandramukhi: In this world of relationships what is a courtesan's value? Nothing. And in any case, you have not even allowed me to touch you.
Devdas: Do you love me?
Chandramukhi: Why not ask, 'Do you breathe, Chandramukhi?'
Devdas: Do you breathe, Chandramukhi? What could you find in me? I have neither home nor heart.

Chandramukhi: Love is not only about acquiring. I have traded in love many times, but only once have I loved.
Devdas: What would happen should I pour yet more wine into this already full glass?
Chandramukhi: It would spill out onto the floor.
Devdas: Hmm. In the same way that this glass is full of wine, Devdas is full of Paro's name. Filling it more means it will spill over. It could even spill over by itself and carry you down as well.
Chandramukhi: But people seeing wine spilt on the floor will say, will they not, that the wine, coming out of the glass, must have caressed it?
Devdas: So come. Let [the glass] overflow!)

One must remember or imagine the voices of Shah Rukh Khan and Madhuri Dixit for the words to carry their full weight. And then there's the translation problem. English needs to be forgiven its relatively harsh sounds and the limited connotations of some words which in Urdu offer intricate allusions. 'Glass', 'breathe', 'floor' and even 'love' are no match for 'paimaana', 'saans', 'zameen' or 'ishq'. And neither 'spill' nor 'overflow' have the phonetic power to bring this scene of verbal foreplay to an end with the pounding urgency of the final '*chhalka do!*' Why the Devanagari script for a quote related to Urdu, you might ask? Why not? For most in the film world today, Urdu poetry is more likely to be read in Devanagari than in Nastaliq. As Javed Akhtar said, 'Let's not confuse language with the script. Even people who write in Devanagari, their vocabulary in films is more Urdu-ish than Hindi-ish.' As though offering confirmation of this observation, playwright, dialogue writer, lyricist and actor Piyush Mishra gave his own example of pursuing Urdu through Devanagari. He read Manto, Ghalib and other poets, complete with notes at the bottom of the page for less common, more Persianized vocabulary, in an edition by Prakash Pandit, *Urdu ke Lokpriya Shaayar*, a popular book of Urdu poetry in Hindi. 'I just loved the phonetic quality of Urdu,' Piyush explained.

What is the pull of this language, its culture and its sensibility, that would so attract generations from the film world, including those whose educational or family backgrounds do not easily open doors into Urdu? Altaf Tyrewala's novel *No God in Sight* (2005) guides us through Bombay and deep into the interlocking lives of the metropolis' fictional residents. We move from one brief but intimate encounter to the next. One of these stories, told in multiple voices, centres around an American-returned son who despises his boorish bourgeois family and wishes for the beauty of Urdu poetry to lift him above his vain existence…as well as to impress his American lover. He finds the young Nawaz, who, in a show of uncharacteristic entrepreneurial spirit, dresses in his father's sherwani, buys a mouthful of paan and, book in hand, sets off as a transformed Nawaz 'saab' to introduce Abhay Joshi, and soon Mr Joshi senior as well, to the poet Faiz. Their meetings end abruptly, however, when Nawaz finds himself at a loss to explain the beautiful words that so captivate the Joshis. *Bukhara-e junoon shabo khayaalon roo maaheer*[98]… The meaning escapes them all, 'teacher' and student alike. Only the desire to know remains.

Director Anurag Kashyap was speaking on the BBC Hindi Service when he chose as one of his favourite songs '*Ye mehlon, ye takhton, ye taajon ki duniya*' from *Pyaasa* (1957). '*To aap Guru Dutt se prerit hain?*' (So you're inspired by Guru Dutt?) the journalist asked. '*Nahin, main Sahir Ludhianvi se prerit hoon,*' (No, I'm inspired by Sahir Ludhianvi)[99] the young filmmaker responded, in reference to the Urdu poet-lyricist. Times change. New generations arrive. But the poetic Urdu of Sahir Ludhianvi keeps calling out to be admired.

Aziz Mirza considers himself fortunate to have grown up hearing Urdu, even if it did not become his language.

---

[98]Tyrewala, Altaf, 2006, p. 107.
[99]*Ek Mulaqaat*, February 2009.

> It's a beautiful language; I do love it. In fact, for a movie I'm making right now, my two characters are from UP where Urdu is still spoken. I would like them to speak [in] a little more refined [manner] than my other characters, to address each other with 'aap', with a little more mohazzab. It's a little bit elevating. Mohazzab is 'gracious', 'gracious and respectful'.

Shridhar Raghavan spoke admiringly of what Urdu could continue to give to cinematic writing:

> When we think Urdu we think the language of kings. It wasn't. It was the language of the common man. People were writing pulp fiction in Urdu. Javed Akhtar got that also. He didn't say, 'I can only use the language if I am doing a period film about Jodhaa–Akbar.' He said, 'When my characters talk with dignity, a few of these words can come in.' Today if I found a guy who knew Urdu, I would go home and thank my gods…If I am working on a film and I write something in English and the guy working with me has read the best of Urdu, he's read Manto, I would hope that all he has read would somehow percolate to the lines I have written in English. And he will give depth and weight to these lines… I'd become a student all over again. I'd say, I wrote this in English. I have done my best in the language which I think in. Now I would like you to take it ten steps higher.

Many people have their Urdu stories. A nice one came from voice artist and stage compère Harish Bhimani who, as a child, begged a neighbour to teach him Urdu. Much later, he found himself in contact with Naushad, the music director. Harish Bhimani said:

> Naushad Sahib would always speak in high-flown Urdu, obviously showing off, particularly to someone who was not so adept. I would speak absolutely Sanskritized Hindi with him. In a matter of minutes he would speak good

Sanskritized Hindi, and I would try to speak as pure an Urdu as possible. It was like a game. The language of Urdu is so lucky in our country. The less you comprehend it, the more fascinated you are. In Hindi it sounds even better: *Hamaare mulk mein Urdu zubaan ne kya qismat paayi. Jitni kam samajh mein aati hai, utni zyaada achchhi lagti hai.* Like French.

Actors, like singers, tend to have a special appreciation for words and sounds. When I asked Tom Alter if he had his favourites, he was quick to respond with a series of Urdu words:

> There's a lovely word combination that we grew up using: ghusalkhaana, the bathroom. The khansaama was the cook. Saleekh bakhsh. Saleekh, of course, means satisfaction. And bakhsh means to give something, like bakhsheesh. Saleekh bakhsh means something that gives you satisfaction.

Producer and actress Elahé Hiptoola, too, knows the effect of sounds. She said:

> Nagesh (Kukunoor) is very fond of some words. For example he loves the word khuda (God), and there are so many times he gets stuck on a line in a song, and I tell Husain, 'Ali Mir, khuda daalo' (Try and insert khuda in the song), and Nagesh will pass it. There are certain words that he loves: khwaaish, khwaab, khuda. I think he's partial to the 'kh' sound.

The beauty of Urdu comes up again and again. Screenwriter and lyricist Javed Akhtar gave a historical explanation of how that beauty was nurtured and honed over the centuries:

> Why have Urdu writers been more successful? Urdu has given tremendous importance to phonetics for centuries, the sound and usage of words. Urdu poetry has stringent rules. Urdu for a very long time was an urban language, patronized by the feudal society who had the time to do that. Language is basically a vehicle for communication,

but language became an art in itself. And that is why our trained Urdu writer or Urdu poet has a tremendous sense of drama, a tremendous sense of using the right word, the phonetically, aesthetically correct word.

Linguists shy away from assigning criteria such as 'beauty' to any language, but at least for many in the film industry, the beauty of the language is its charm. Even as knowledge of the meanings of words fades, the cachet of the language remains. Singers regularly balk when confronted with typically Hindi retroflex sounds, (ड ढ, ट, ठ, ड़, ढ़) and demand that words be changed, 'rounded edges' of Persian-root words (perhaps like the curves in Mughal architecture) being preferred over the 'earthy' sounds produced when the tip of the tongue curls back to the soft palate, e.g., theek or chhodna. In 2007 writer and lyricist Jaideep Sahni expressed his preference for the very retroflex sounds many wish to avoid:

> That's one thing which I have great arguments with music directors about. I love using them, and obviously, musically they're terrible. But otherwise, it becomes form over content. I keep giving them examples (of those sounds) from old Kishore Kumar songs.

A year later, as he contrasted the retroflexes of Sanskrit-based words with 'smoother' Urdu-based sounds, he sensed his verbal rebellion becoming more measured:

> I am not hyper-militant about using 'awkward' words anymore. Now I use them occasionally, more in a need-based way, rather than like angry stones on the windowpane of the 'fake' classical structure which we have grown to mistake for the real thing the old masters used to do. I have started using 'smoother' classical words and phrases when I think they might help and might go with the characters in the film and when their 'baggage' will not get in the way… I try to use them like expensive garnish on a 'real' dish and

hope my listener will share my admiration for them. But it's not my language or my time's language.

Mastery of Urdu need not mean weakness in Hindi, as Javed Akhtar explained:

> When an Urdu writer writes Hindi, he writes beautiful Hindi. You take Shakeel. You take Sahir. You take bhajans written by Majrooh or Shakeel—when they write Hindi, they write such beautiful aesthetic Hindi.

Farhan Akhtar, while describing his own languages as English and Hindi, spoke of his emotional connection to Urdu:

> I think it stems from my respect for my father's work. His poetry *Tarkash* moves me tremendously, whether I hear it on the CD or whether I read it—now that it's translated into Hindi text, I can read it. You know, whether it be just a song or a dialogue from a film or something that I may read, there is a place somewhere inside me that Urdu can reach that no other language can. But I know that I would never be able to think those words. If I want to write something that I think is beautiful in English, and it needs to be taken to a similar level when it's translated into Hindi or Urdu, I would go to my father and ask him to do it for me because of the kind of control that he has, and he'd rework it until it made me feel the same thing that I'd wanted to feel. And it evokes a certain kind of emotion in me and moves me and touches me in a way that I feel English can't do. I feel it is beautiful-sounding, and it's something I feel that I have deprived myself of having learned—I mean, I'm sure I can learn it now. But when I had a chance to easily have picked up the language, I didn't. I feel now that I wish I had. Because I really wish I could speak it and understand it the way he does or people like him do.

The desire Farhan Akhtar speaks of is used to comic effect in the

Farhan Akhtar–Ritesh Sidhwani-produced *Honeymoon Travels Pvt. Ltd.* (2007), directed by Reema Kagti. The Shabana Azmi character tries to teach the Boman Irani character to pronounce poet Ghalib's name with the 'ghain' sound غ /ɣ/. No matter how he tugs at his throat and tries to imitate the woman he loves, the sound that comes out is only a gaf /g/. But he tries.

Zubaan? Bhaasha? Or Both?

In the film *Jodhaa Akbar* (2008), directed by Ashutosh Gowariker, Jodhaa's father (Kulbushan Kharbanda) forms a political alliance by promising his daughter (Aishwarya Rai) to Jalaluddin Mohammad (Hrithik Roshan), the Mughal emperor, later to be known as Akbar. Jodhaa's extremely formal Sanskritized Hindi provides maximum contrast with Jalaluddin's Urdu, which, thanks to the abundant use of Urdu in years of dialogue writing, seems markedly less stilted to listeners' ears.

> Jodhaa: *Ham aapka swaagat karte hain. Ham kaise aabhar vyakt karein ki aapne yahaan padhaar kar hamaari baat sunne ka kasht kiya. Hamaari do maangein hain jinke sveekaarne ke baad hi ham aapse vivaah kar paayenge.*
>
> (I would like to greet you. How can I express my gratitude that you have bestowed me with your presence and taken the pain to listen to my words? I have two demands. Only after they are granted shall I be able to marry you.)

His eyes smouldering, his jaw clenched, Akbar asks to know her requests...or demands. After hearing that she insists on continuing to practise her own religion and that she will have a temple to Krishna within her quarters, Jalaluddin, still tense, walks out to their respective entourages. He says:

> *Aaj pehli baar hamein Rajput aan-baan aur shaan ka poora ehsaas hua hai. Amer ki rajkumari ke bekhauf jazbe aur*

gustaakhi: ko ham salaam karte hain…hamaara faisla hai ki Amer ki Raajkumaari Jodhaa se ye rishta hamein manzoor hai. Unki shartein inshaallah lafz ba lafz poori hongi.

(Today is the first time that I have truly experienced the Rajput spirit, pride and grandeur. I hail the fearless passion and arrogance of the princess of Amer…my decision is that I agree to marry the princess of Amer, Jodhaa. May Allah grant that her conditions be met word for word.)

Obviously, one can, as in this scene, create linguistic difference for the sake of distinguishing characters and backgrounds. All the same the exercise is a bit laboured, as when an English composition teacher has students replace their Anglo-Saxon root words like 'get' and 'pick' with Latin root words such as 'obtain' and 'select'. But are we talking about two different languages? Shama Zaidi, who has written dialogue for both theatre and cinema, notably for many films directed by Shyam Benegal, and has also helped to set up a television channel in Urdu, said:

> People usually link Urdu with Farsi and Arabic. I'm trying to do an anthology of Urdu–Hindi and the matrix in which Urdu has come up, which [sic] is Hindi–Urdu, Awadhi, Braj and Punjabi. All these five languages have contributed to what modern Urdu is today or Hindi is today… I think there's this common meeting ground, which is film, cinema, theatre, folk songs, marriage songs, curse words, sayings, proverbs, recipes… Two languages can't have the same swear words. It has to be the same language.

Both history and literature are essential to understanding. Yet, they are also complex and contested. German scholar Kerrin Dittmer dates the term Urdu from 1752 when the poet Mir Taqi Mir used *Urdu-e-Mu'alla* to designate courtly language.[100]

---

[100] Cited by Robert D. King in 'The Poisonous Potency of Script: Hindi and Urdu,' 2001.

Hindi literature, that is, in the Hindi script, is seen as younger, usually dated to around 1800. Importantly, both Urdu and Hindi literary traditions are far younger than those found in languages such as Tamil, Telugu and Bengali.[101] Christopher R. King's *One Language, Two Scripts* describes the complex history of vacillating colonial government decisions and education policies, which, confronted with public reaction, led to increasing differentiation within this 'one language'. Throughout the nineteenth and early twentieth centuries, ideological language debates were rampant. Yet, with prime government jobs at stake, mastering one script or another became an economic choice.[102]

That was then. This is now. So today is it one language or two? Or is it more? US academic as well as lyricist and dialogue writer Ali Husain Mir gave a lecture at the South Asian Institute at The University of Texas entitled 'Romance and Revolution in Bollywood Songs'. In his introduction, he discussed the extent to which Urdu and Hindi are intimately intertwined:

> One could make the argument that Urdu is of Hindi. The oft-cited analysis of *Farhang-i-Aasifiya*, the lexicon

---

[101] Ibid.

[102] Note that Urdu, especially in its written form, has its specificities. To name a few, there is the izaafat, that little marker in Urdu that is generally transcribed in English as -e- as in *Mughal-e-Azam*, joining two nouns or a noun and pronoun. There are the sounds brought into Hindustani from Persian /f/, /z/, /q/, /x/, /ɣ/ The last two International Phonetics Alphabet sounds are generally transcribed as '*kh*' and '*gh*'. There is also some distinguishing vocabulary such as peer for Monday, rather than the Hindi somvaar, some elegant vocabulary that most moviegoers would recognize from classic films, e.g., the formal welcome tashreef laayie, and a headache-inducing four ways of writing the sound *z*, two ways the sound *s*, two the sound *t*, and two the sound *aa*. (Obviously, anyone who puts up with reading and writing in English, a much less phonetic language than Urdu, is rather ill-placed to complain about such details!) See Ruth Laila Schmidt's *Urdu, An Essential Grammar* (1999) for an excellent overview of the language.

composed by Syed Ahmed Delvi, contends that about 75 per cent of the total stock of the 55,000 words of Urdu in the dictionary are derived from Sanskrit and Prakrit. One could also argue that Hindi is of Urdu because one can also make the claim that modern Hindi was generated by excising Persian and Arabic words from Urdu and replacing them by Sanskritized ones. But in an atmosphere where the whole point is to generate difference such arguments become meaningless.

Historical linguist Robert D. King discusses this all-too-human propensity for generating difference. He writes, 'Language…can serve either as a badge of membership in a community or as a means of exclusion and exile. This is the iconic use of language: language as a symbol to achieve non-linguistic goals.'[103]

Language, because of its often iconic use, can be a matter of contention. For actor and dubbing artiste Shaktee Singh, the Urdu sounds and vocabulary from his native Lucknow have been an important part of his linguistic background. However, he stood firm against puffed-up linguistic nationalism, emphasizing instead the place of the heart in human expression. '*Bhaasha ko hamein itni tavajjo nahin dena chaahiye. Insaan ne bhaasha banaayi hai. Bhaasha ne insaan ko nahin banaaya.*' (We should not heed language so much. Humans made language. Language didn't make humans.)

One language or two? Jaideep Sahni related a family story in which his father's answer was categorical:

> My father doesn't read Devanagari. He was born and brought up in Lahore. He can read and write English and Urdu. He can't read Hindi to save his life. He never needed to. All the government work happened in English. In fact, we had this big laugh because they made him the head of some government campaign for Hindi implementation for

---

[103] King, Robert D., *Nehru and the Language Politics of India*, 1997, p. 29.

all India. And he was terrible; he would make them write the speeches in Urdu, and he would read the speeches in Urdu, saying how important Hindi was. He said, 'I don't have any idea why this is so important. See, I can't make out the difference between Hindi and Urdu. Why should anyone create a difference?' He was a most irritated Hindi proponent. He said, 'If a man can speak Urdu, then he understands Hindi. So what is the big deal about this Hindi thing?'

Shama Zaidi continued in a similar vein of irritation mixed with inclusiveness.

I read more in Hindi because it's just this question of the script. Now I'm coming around to the point of view that it's not a different language anyway. So I refuse to say that that doesn't belong to me and this belongs to me. It all belongs to me. I can use whatever I feel like, from wherever I want.

Ali Husain Mir gave a rather practical explanation of the relationship within/between this/these language(s).

It should be fairly obvious that Hindi and Urdu are a language on a continuum. At one end you know it's Hindi. At the other end there are a lot of Farsi and Arabic words and fewer Sanskrit words, and you can call that Urdu. If you read some Iqbal,[104] you can't say it's Hindi. But if you go stand in an airport and read what's on the wall, you can't say you're speaking Urdu. So there are certain registers where one can clearly say Hindi or Urdu. But the part in the middle, the limits are hard to define… There is also a difference in the sensibilities between Urdu and Hindi. The traditions that you draw upon will change, the atmosphere and the idiom will change. But even within that I would

---

[104] Muhammad Iqbal, 1877–1938, Urdu and Persian poet and philosopher, recognized as the national poet of Pakistan.

claim that the middle is muddled. And it is in that middle that most of us reside.[105]

Farhan Akhtar gave his own example of the muddled middle.

> Hindi and Urdu, yes, they are two different languages... If my father (Javed Akhtar) were to address a gathering of people where he knows [that], say, 50 per cent of them would not understand Urdu and 50 per cent of them would, he'd find a balance in between using words that he knows both of them would understand. And that's where I fit in. I'm in that 50 per cent who would understand what he's saying, as long as it doesn't get too refined for me.

For historian Dr Ziauddin Shakeb, speaking at a July 2009 Dakkhini seminar in London, the middle ground would be the mother language, *'Dakkhini meljol, milaavat aur mohabbat ki zubaan hai.'* (Dakkhini is a language of union/reconciliation, blending and love). The BBC Hindi service quoted him:

> *Koi bhi zubaan jo apne darvaaze band kar leti hai aur shuddh ya khaalis rehna chaahti hai, taraqqi nahin kar sakti, mar jaati hai...Hindi aur Urdu donon Dakkhini ki do betiyaan hain aur donon ko apni ma se sabaq lena chaahiye.*[106]

> (Any language that closes its doors and wants to remain 'pure'—shuddh or khaalis—cannot progress. It dies. Hindi and Urdu are both the daughters of Dakkhini and both should take lessons from their mother.)

Jaideep Sahni named the song that for him best represented this composite culture. He said:

---

[105]Interviewed by Dr Akbar Hyder, The University of Texas, 2008 (translated from the Urdu by the author).
[106]BBC Hindi Service, Lalit Mohan Joshi, 'Hindi-Urdu ka sangam hai Dakkhini,' 29 July 2009.

It's a qawwaali called 'Yeh Ishq Ishq Hai'[107] from the film *Barsaat ki Raat*, sung by Manna Dey, Mohammad Rafi and others, (written by Sahir Ludhianvi). If ever there was one song that could represent the last few centuries of the lovely Urdu–Hindi, Ganga–Jamuna culture/language/history/myths/state-of-mind/and who we really are, it is this song.

An online search shows that 'Yeh Ishq Ishq Hai' is loved by many. The blogger Atul, for example, says:

> …is it really a qawwali? It begins as one and ends as one, beginning and ending with the word ishq, but in between, it discusses many topics, viz, Krishna, Radha, Meera, Buddha, Maseeh, etc. So, in effect, this is a qawwali containing elements of bhajans, Krishna-Leela, and semi-classical songs as well. It is like going from Delhi to Agra in a round about way via Mumbai, Kolkata, Bangalore, Srinagar and Guwahati.[108]

A Sense of Regret

پاکیزہ

یہ نرگس ہے، نواب جان کی چوٹی بہن جسکی دل روبہ آواز اور جسکی گھنگھروں کی جھنکار نے ایک دھوم مچا رکھی ہے. کتنے دل ہیں جو اسکی ٹھوکروں میں تڑپتے رہتے ہیں. اور یہ ان پر لاپرواہی سے ناچتی رہتی ہے. ہاں، مگر یہ کون ہے جسکے آتے ہی نرگس اپنے اس ناپاک ماحول میں مرجھا کر رہ جاتی ہے. اسکی روح فریاد کرنے لگتی ہے. شہاب، مجھے یہاں سے لیجاو. اور شہاب کی آنکھوں میں تڑپتا ہوا عشق اسے یقین دلانے لگتا ہے ہاں نرگس ان بدنام محفلوں میں پگھلتی ہوئی اس شمع کو میں یہاں پگھلنے نہیں دونگا. ایک رات میں
[109] آؤنگا اور تمہیں اس دوزخ سے نکال لے جاؤنگا.

---

[107]Written by Sahir Ludhianvi.
[108]http://atulsongaday.wordpress.com/2008/09/16/ye-ishq-ishq-hai-shq-ishq/
[109]My thanks to Yahya Khan for typing the text in Urdu.

In the 1972 film *Pakeezah*, directed by Kamal Amrohi, Nargis (Meena Kumari) is a tavaaif, a courtesan, whose noble blood has not spared her a life of ignominy. Kamal Amrohi's sonorous voice-over adds to the atmosphere of poetic longing in this, the first scene of the film. It translates approximately thus:

> This is Nargis, Nawab Jan's younger sister, whose alluring voice and ankle bells have brought in marveling crowds. How many hearts are aching for her? But she goes on dancing, paying them no heed. Yes, but who is this? As he comes in, Nargis stays, fading in this unholy atmosphere. Her soul seems to plead: Shahaab, take me away from here. And the restless love in Shahaab's eyes makes her believe, 'Nargis, I will not allow you to fade away like a dying candle in this place of ill repute. One night I will come and release you from this hell.'

If the film has touched many viewers deeply in India and around the world, it is perhaps because regret and nostalgia are part of the human condition. Even America, with its short history and its tendency towards future-oriented optimism, is nevertheless rich in literature and art expressing regret over the ravages of time. Newcomers have arrived and gazed on pristine landscapes with a sense of awe, immediately followed by sadness at the realization that their beauty will one day be defiled. The final line of F. Scott Fitzgerald's 1925 novel *The Great Gatsby* is full of nostalgic, regret-filled angst, 'So we beat on, boats against the current, borne back ceaselessly into the past.' This nostalgia occurs both at an individual and a societal level. A friend recently observed—nostalgically—that with ageng and its accompanying losses, 'What remain are the remnants.' Anxiety, then, can be 'pre-nostalgia', nostalgia before the fact, nostalgia not for what has been lost but for what may soon disappear. Writer Khalid Hasan has translated many of the short stories by the Urdu writer—and Bombay screenwriter—Saadat Hassan Manto. In this quote from Manto's journal, translated by Hasan and cited by Christine Everaert, we feel his nostalgia-laden anxiety over an uncertain future.

> One question repeatedly rose in my mind. Will Pakistani literature be different? If so, then how? Who would inherit what had been written in unpartitioned India? Or will that be partitioned too? ... Will Urdu disappear on that side? What form will it take in Pakistan?[110]

A certain pain and frustration can slip into discussions about Urdu and its role in society and film. Javed Akhtar complained:

> Urdu got marginalized. And Urdu was clubbed with Muslim fundamentalism, the Muslim communal identity and Pakistan. Languages don't belong to religions. They belong to regions. So ultimately it got a stepmotherly treatment from the present powers that be in North India, from where this language came. That destroyed that perfect and very delicate balance that was there in the language.

Elahé Hiptoola expressed her dismay at reactions to Urdu in these terms.

> It was the language for the common man during the Mughals. In fact, when the Quran was first translated into Urdu, the mullahs were up in arms because it was such a pedestrian language. And now it suddenly becomes exotic. Oh! *Achchha, aap Urdu [mein] baat karti hain.* You speak Urdu. I mean, my servant speaks Urdu! And she doesn't speak English!

Actress Shabana Azmi, on the one hand, understands and

---

[110]Hasan, Khalid, *A Wet Afternoon: Stories, Sketches, Reminiscences by Sa'adat Hasan Manto*, Islamabad: Alhamra, 2001, p. 694 (quoted from Everaert, Christine, 2010, p. 59).

accepts that language must change with the passing years and the arrival of new generations. She also takes great pride in the flexibility of the multilingual, multicultural Indian society. Nevertheless, in a spirit of contradiction which she fully acknowledged, she admitted to great irritation upon hearing Urdu mispronounced:

> Everybody says khubsoorat (aspirated k), not <u>kh</u>oobsurat, and they don't say zameen; they say jameen. It really, really sounds awful to my ears. Now there is this movement to say that a language is not merely its alphabet. And so perhaps you should allow Urdu to be in the Devanagari script. Now the Urduwaalas have said that they're willing to accept this provided that Devanagari accepts the dot, accepts the <u>kh</u> and accepts the *f* and accepts the *z*, which, of course, they're not willing to do.
>
> In *Umrao Jaan* it's a very self-conscious language. It also belongs to an era. It's not spoken Urdu at all. In *Fanaa* it's like, oh my God, painful, because so much of my father's verse was used and then changed. And when I spoke to (director) Kunal Kohli, I said, 'Kunal, how can you take a poet's verse and change it around?' And he said, 'Oh well, it sounded very highfaluting, so I simplified it into Hindi.' It's appalling! And he's telling the daughter of the writer with whom he has thus behaved. So it's not any kind of authentic language. It's to give it some kind of feel.

Writer and actor Kader Khan lamented both Urdu's displacement post-Partition and also the present and future prospects for the language:

> It was given birth in Delhi, brought up in Hyderabad and Lucknow and looked after in Punjab and all of India. But at the time of Partition it was handed over to Pakistan. It's like your own daughter, your own child, you give to Pakistan... Those people who talk nicely about Urdu's future,

they're telling lies because they're well-to-do people. They're highly placed in society. They don't know where Urdu lives.

'Where Urdu lives' is central to the plot of the 2008 film *Aamir*. The middle class, English-medium educated Muslim hero (Rajeev Khandelwal) finds himself coerced into the sordid back alleyways of Mumbai in which, as we see from the Nastaliq signs, Urdu does indeed live. This too is Mumbai, but not his Mumbai, and he recoils at its foreignness.

The other side of 'where Urdu lives', of course, is in its lasting beauty. As actor Tom Alter said:

> There's been a definite shift in the last ten-twenty years to Hindicize cinema. But the beauty of the Urdu language, the Hindustani language, runs so deep that no matter how hard people try, you can't get away from it. It's just too beautiful. And it's not that Hindi is not beautiful. It's just that Urdu has been the language in India, in northern India, for the last 150 years or 175 years. It's been the language of art, culture and politics. It just runs too deep. You cannot get rid of it.

GENERATIONS: A FATHER-SON THING

Mystery writer Ruth Rendell spoke about the challenge of integrating generational changes into her writing:

> What happens is you have a tendency to write about your contemporaries or people ten years younger than yourself, and that must be resisted... Another thing is keeping up with the way people speak. Patterns change, and the words they use, and well, everything, the clothes they wear, the cars they drive, the books they read, the music they listen to. I think it's a writer's duty to keep pace with those things. When I say that I do, I make a big reservation and say I try to, but I know ultimately it's a losing battle. I won't be able to do it. I won't be able to keep pace with those changes.[111]

In the 2007 film *I Could Never Be Your Woman*, written and directed by Amy Heckerling, we see a Hollywood version of this struggle. A television series writer (Michelle Pfeiffer), aware of her own potentially passé vocabulary, uses her thirteen-year-old daughter as a word check. 'Do kids still say "Gee"?' she yells as she puts the final touches on the episode to be shot the next day. 'Yeah Mom,' the daughter shouts back from the other room, 'Like just today I said...' Normal generational changes in language are compounded by the speed of societal change in urban India. In *Slumdog Millionaire*, directed by Danny

---

[111]Speaking with Terry Gross on National Public Radio's *Fresh Air*, 12 October 2005.

Boyle and Loveleen Tandan, the two now-adult brothers Salim and Jamal meet on the upper storey of a tall building under construction and look out on the effects of gentrification. In response to rising land values, slums like theirs have been razed to make way for a neighbourhood full of luxury high-rises. This drastically altered cityscape offers an apt metaphor for the language changes Mumbaikars have experienced in recent years. Hindi-Urdu itself has evolved at breakneck speed even as English has mushroomed, crowding out swathes of language spoken a generation ago. Given their lack of formal education, Salim and Jamal's English seems unlikely, merely a concession to international film audiences. For a growing number of real-life city dwellers, however, English is the language of choice with Hinglish its halfway house.

In a time of rapid language change, generations of writers can feel particularly ambivalent towards one another. Jaideep Sahni recounted Javed Akhtar's words at the screenwriters' conference in Pune 2006. Sahni said, 'Javed Sahib was speaking first... I remember he said, "It's a mediocre industry with mediocre writers for a mediocre audience."' Sahni described the scene when it came his own turn to speak at the conference:

> I said that we don't have as many words as his generation did, but that doesn't necessarily mean that we don't know as many thoughts as his generation did. When I came from Delhi six or seven years back, after joining the film business [...] the truth is that my vocabulary has become one half, but my power of expression has gone up ten times... Then another writer spoke. And then a very strange thing happened. Javed Sahib stood up and clapped.

Certainly, language change can be felt as language loss, particularly in North India, where Urdu is concerned. I spoke with Javed Akhtar in 2007. He voiced both annoyance and understanding of the problem.

If things are happening fast, you get accustomed to that. You start taking the tempo for granted, and you shrink your attention span accordingly. When the attention span shrinks, there isn't much room for ornate language, for metaphor, for simile, for proverbs. You tend to become telegraphic. First: attitude. Language is not important because language doesn't pay. Language was some sort of a feudal luxury in their mind. As long as you can communicate that you are hungry or you want to cross the road or you want to buy that thing in the shop, that's good enough. Why do you want more vocabulary? Second: technology made it acceptable. Third: the language of North India, which had a rich literary tradition in poetry and prose, was marginalized for political reasons. Fourth: then, a lot of immigration was taking place. People ceased to be as rooted as they were before. Now when you migrate, there are things that you leave behind, including language. And when you go to a place where people speak different languages, you look for a lowest common denominator. Bombay is a very good example of that. So putting these things together, I feel that if you meet a person who is in their twenties or thirties, that person definitely will have a smaller vocabulary of his or her mother tongue than the parents. So language in society is shrinking. It has shrunk. This is reflected in films. Now people who are in their twenties or thirties who have, say, never attended a poetry recital, who have never flipped through a book of verse, they are listening to film songs. They have no connection, no tradition of poetry behind them. And people who are producing this music are also from the same society. They also have this limitation. They are not rooted people, maybe because of migration or maybe because of peer pressure. So ultimately we are living in some kind of totally rootless culture, whether it's the culture or the language. We are confused. By this I don't mean that we should close our doors to new ideas, to new words, new metaphors. No. The more you spread, the better it is, but the more you spread, the deeper the roots should be to have the balance...

Given this gloomy assessment, I wondered, was there any hope for the younger generation of dialogue writers and lyricists? Akhtar replied:

Ultimately, I suppose that aesthetics, beauty, art, music, poetry have become almost genetic needs. So I think the younger generation is feeling the loss. And they're realizing that there was something precious somewhere, and they've lost it. They've left it somewhere. Where? They don't know. They're looking for it. I can see that a fairly large percentage of young people are interested in poetry. But it really hurts me to see how little they know. And with that limited information or exposure, when they try to write, you feel sad. You feel protective towards them and at the same time, you feel depressed. Look, it's not their fault. Something wrong has happened to them. I pin my hope on their sense of loss. That's all. Since they have this sense of loss, let's hope that one day they'll be able to discover it on their own, because they are not being helped by their elders.

But how, I wondered, can you find something you've lost if you're not even sure what it is? And how can you learn on your own? Akhtar, sounding still more deflated, replied:

The problem is too large. It's the problem of almost 1 billion people. So this is reflecting in Hindi cinema also... Like, you take a picture, say, from the 1940s or '50s. See how people talk to each other. They sound much more cultured. Today anything or anybody who has dignity looks slightly dated because dignity has become almost obsolete in our culture... I guess that you shed dignity only if you have no sense of self-esteem because dignity means poise. Poise means giving a chance to another person to observe you minutely. And you don't want that to happen because you think that if you are observed minutely, they will know how ordinary you are. So things should happen at a speed, and you should act at a speed and at a volume where nobody should be able to pinpoint one thing. That is in the music, the dialogue, the tempo of the film, the personality of people, the tempo of life. There is a brashness. You think, 'If people watch this scene properly, they will not like it, so before they realize that it is so ordinary, let me go to the next scene.' So you're changing scenes very quickly because you don't think you're worth a second look.

As though in response to Javed Akhtar's description of youth speed—or as proof of the accuracy of his observations—Airtel Broadband brought out an ad in 2009 entitled 'The Impatient Ones' in which we see in a quick-cut sequence a series of cool-looking urban youth emoting hope, dreams, anxieties and a strong sense of time. In the voice-over we hear:

> They say we're impatient. They're right... We can't wait for our turn to come. The clock to tick. The sun to rise. The tide to turn. And they say we're impatient? Impatience is the new life. Live it with Airtel Broadband.[112]

I asked Javed Akhtar if there was no solution to the problems he saw in the younger generation. We can't, I ventured, go back in time or bring back an age that has gone. We can't stop time.

Javed Akhtar agreed and added, 'There are two realities. Nothing comes back. Also, nothing stays forever. What has gone by will not come back. But then, what we have today will not remain. That is also sure. It will change.'

---

[112] http://wn.com/Impatient_Ones__Airtel

I suggested, hopefully, that treasures buried could be found again. He answered somewhat cryptically:

> No, they cannot. You don't find the coins that you have buried. When you dig in the same place, you find something else, not the same thing. Mughal treasure was never found…. Maybe Mohammad Shah, the last king Bahadur Shah's great-grandfather, buried it somewhere. Today if I found it, it wouldn't be the same thing that he buried. For him it was one thing, and for me it would be something else. For these times it would be one thing. For those times it was something else. You don't take out the same treasure that you buried.

Two days later I slightly reformulated the idea Javed Akhtar had so ably expressed and asked his son Farhan Akhtar, 'When a new generation digs up a treasure from the past, it's never the same treasure. My father buried a treasure. When I dig it up, it's not going to be the same treasure as he buried. Does that make any sense to you?' Farhan Akhtar answered:

> I think, for whatever it's worth, that as time passes, a treasure gets more valuable. I think that for people in the 1950s and '60s who spoke this language as a matter of course, I don't know if they would value that language as much as someone who almost lost it and then had to get it back.

As I spoke with scriptwriter and lyricist Jaideep Sahni the following day, he took the same metaphor and moved in two directions with it:

> When you talk about a treasure, you can bury a treasure in a currency that used to operate a thousand years back. And you can dig old bronze coins out. And they would only be of use to a connoisseur or a collector who will pay you for it. What would the masses care about that? It's exactly that. The currency is not operative anymore. It was a treasure when it was buried. It comes out now, and to the man on

the street, it's just a bunch of old coins. But for someone who cares for them, he'd be willing to pay a lot of money for them, polish them and look at them all day.

From rare old coins the metaphor turned to precious stones in a different but related conversation. Jaideep Sahni noted that Javed Akhtar had a talent for making 'words that people don't use accessible by just placing them in a context or a sentence. I guess he does it automatically, but it's like setting a precious stone. He knows that if he puts it there, it will work.'

I mentioned to Jaideep Sahni that it seemed like a shame that there was not more of a dialogue across the generations of film writers. A few attempts have been made with a few workshops and conferences, such as those held in Pune in 2006 and Mumbai in 2008. Jaideep, speaking in 2007, explained:

> There can't be, beyond a point. It's a cruel business. All the films are made on one road, from Bandra to Andheri. It's a small world and very frequently can be cannibalistic among generations. And there is very little emphasis on the art or the craft. That's the only thing there can be dialogue about, really. If you have a dialogue about values, that will just degenerate into a generation gap, generation spat. The only thing which there can be dialogue about is art or craft, for which nobody has any time. So the bridge that you're talking about is very sorely needed emotionally but not needed at all practically. The business doesn't depend on it. What the business does not depend upon always takes the last seat. It's all about today and what you're going to deliver tomorrow morning.
>
> I think, also, what happens when you talk about hidden treasures or lost treasures, you feel this burden of this whole thing descending upon your shoulders to keep their flag flying high. On the other hand, when they get an award or say something, people like me are the first ones to give

them a standing ovation every single time... It's a father–son thing, I think.

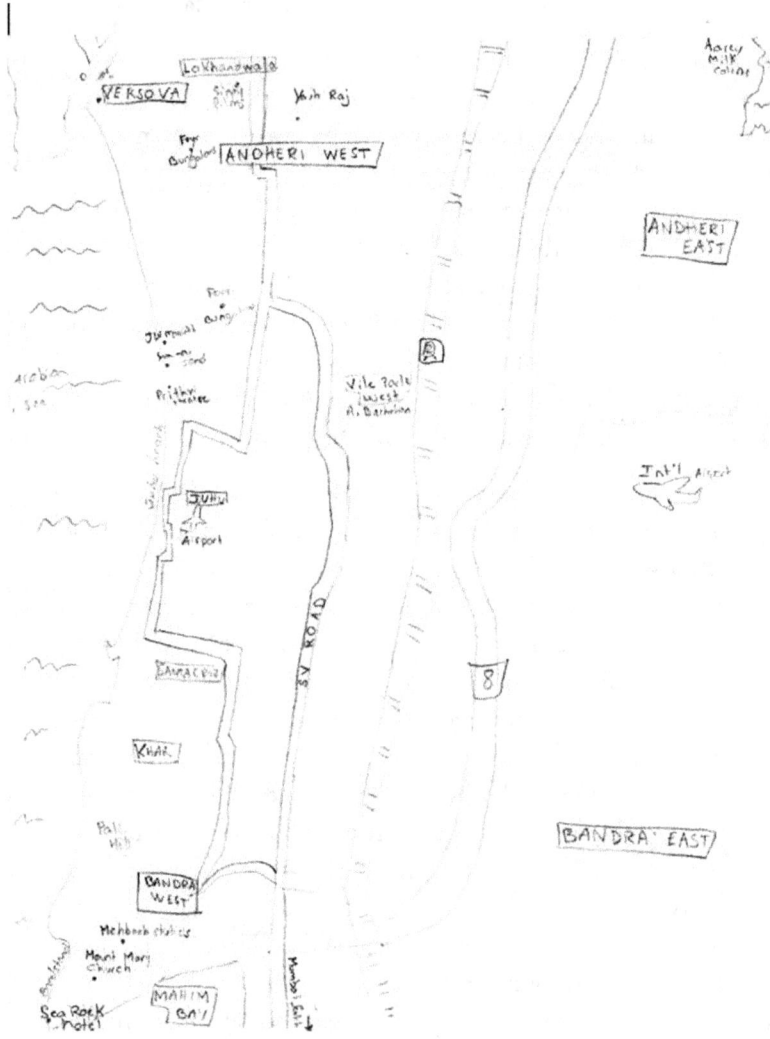

Bandra to Andheri. (Sketch by Lila Haham)

The father and the son—the generations who need each other, who are annoyed at each other, who forget each other, who respect each other...who share one another's language, fully or only partially. Any elder who observes youthful speech will note matter-of-factly or with dismay that many much-loved words of the past have disappeared; that new ones, perhaps beloved of a new generation, have taken their places but rarely having exactly the same meanings as the words left behind. Hindi cinema, with its huge audience, offers a large part of society both linguistic anchoring to the past and also the sounds of change, as the society itself speeds into the future. I asked Jaideep Sahni if he knew the expression 'naslan ba naslan'. He said he didn't know but could perhaps guess, 'To me it sounds like some way of saying generation by generation. The nasl is a generation. And ba they use in Urdu. Generation *after* generation. But I would never use it. I wouldn't even use it in my dreams.'

'But,' I protested, 'it's part of your passive vocabulary. That's sort of what I'm investigating language-wise, generation after generation, what is lost and what remains.'

'See, this is what it is,' Jaideep said. 'What remains is passive vocabulary. How would I know this expression? I've never used it. It's there from somewhere. I think you might find a lot of that treasure in my passive vocabulary. It just occurred to me.'

'Since it's there in your passive vocabulary,' I suggested, 'do you think you pull it out and rework it somehow?' Jaideep answered:

> For who? I don't know. I might, to please myself or out of curiosity, but I'm getting paid to communicate, to tell stories. Why would I depend on my and my audience's passive vocabulary to communicate something when I have a cleaner, easier way to do it? But then the line *tere talve tere tisein*,[113] on the other hand, is doing precisely this. But I didn't use it for the love of bringing out the treasure. I did

---

[113]Part of the line from the song 'Show Me Your Jalwa' from *Aaja Nachle: 'Aake dikha de mujhe tere talve tere tisein'*, which Jaideep Sahni translated loosely as 'Show me what you wouldn't show anyone else.'

it because I know it's something stored away in everyone's heads. It's a subconscious connection, just plugging my wire into the back of their heads. So I don't know. I just realized there's a duality in what I'm saying because I think I wouldn't do it, but I can find five other examples where I did use that passive language.

Perhaps the duality Jaideep Sahni mentioned, this refusing as well as embracing the previous generation's words and attitudes, is at the heart of 'naslan ba naslan'. It's an age-old story. 'From generation to generation' is about both continuity and change, ongoing connections and also renewal, pride in the past together with a lack of curiosity as to most of what happened before each of us was born. I see a small-town Texas wood-framed house and am filled with emotional memories. My Paris-reared daughter looks at the same house and sees a big wooden box with doors and windows. Inevitably, disappointment awaits the older generation as they attempt to transmit feelings, values and experiences. Well-loved music of the past, for instance, when adopted by a new generation, is appreciated in a new way, with new ears, in a new context. Farhan Akhtar spoke of having film music from the 1950s and '60s constantly with him on his iPod. And yet, the iPod itself makes the listening experience radically unlike that of someone who, in order to hear the music of *Mughal-e-Azam* in 1960, had to endure long lines and possibly resort to buying a ticket on the black market to get a seat in a movie theatre. 'You don't take out the same treasure that you buried.' In one case, at least, Hindi cinema has ritualized a generational passing of the torch. Filmi wedding scenes typically show brightly clad young women exuberantly dancing while older women sit on the side and watch, maybe tapping to the beat or at least smiling with pleasure. At some point, the young heroine may pull Granny to her feet and insist that she join in. Coyly, the older woman hesitates, then puts her hands to her hips and begins to move to the music, but only for a moment before she relinquishes the limelight to the young women so full of boundless energy and radiant sensuality. The 'Jiya Jale' song from Mani Ratnam's *Dil Se* beautifully portrays this intergenerational dynamic.

In Javed Akhtar's case, generational angst is prominent in his work. Films scripted by Salim-Javed in the 1970s showed us Vijay the rebel, as played by Amitabh Bachchan, seething with anger at society and its authority figures, and more specifically, in films like *Trishul* and *Shakti* and even *Deewaar*, at the father who has been so critically and often cruelly absent for his son. An earlier angry character of literary and cinematic history, Devdas bows to his father's wishes and forgoes marriage to the woman he loves. He turns his anger inwards, wallows in sorrow and goes moaning through his remaining life, devoid of any aspiration but to drink himself to death. Vijay, Devdas's mirror image, finds strength in his own anger. In *Trishul*, the young Vijay is raised by a single mother to grow strong enough to one day avenge his father's wrong.

> *Zindagaani ki kadi dhoop mein jalne doongi*
> *taaki tap tap ke tu faulaad bane ma ki aulaad bane*
> (I will let you burn in life's harsh sun, that you may become steel forged in heat, that you may become your mother's son.)[114]

And yet Vijay, like Devdas, cannot truly win against his father. The power of the older generation remains intact. In *Trishul* the father sacrifices himself so that his son might live, but his son follows in the father's path, constructing the Delhi of the 1970s in his father's name. In *Deewaar* and *Shakti*, Vijay will die, in the first case, at the hands of his brother in the name of duty to which the older generation subscribed. In *Shakti*, it is the father himself who will kill his wayward son.

Generational conflict is mild by comparison in the Jaideep Sahni-scripted *Khosla Ka Ghosla*. The father (Anupam Kher) has

---

[114]Lyrics by Sahir Ludhianvi.

a simple dream for himself and his family, to grow older in a bigger, more comfortable home. Little does he realize that his smart, ambitious son (Parvin Dabas) is making plans to move to America to seek his fortune. In the end, independence proves less enticing to the son than the desire to help his father achieve his dream, a dream which becomes his son's as well but not without being transformed into something new. The patriarch looks on rather helplessly as his son takes the reins of power. The son's anger at the scam to which his father has fallen victim is productive. It is channelled through brain, not brawn. Vijay, by contrast, could take on ten goons at once and walk away victorious. The young Khosla's modus operandi is to harness the energy and talent of the group—both family and friends—in the hope that right will prevail. The individual psychologies of the writers play a part in the creation of such divergent heroes, but perhaps more importantly, society in 2006 is not what it was in 1978. Jaideep Sahni explained:

> Nobody's angry. Nobody has time to be angry. Everybody wants to find a fix to whatever is ailing him and then move on. It's a different India. It's not Vijay's India. It's about smartness. Today a person would not imagine getting his bones broken just to make a point. He'd find a smarter way to do it. That's what the new middle-class India is. The values have become extremely flexible. Vijay had very rigid values, which is why he was God-like. Gods have rigid values. Today it's all grey. There was something very funny in my bad guy in *Khosla Ka Ghosla*. And there was something a little bad in my good guys.

Vijay, even as a gangster, had a simple but beautiful vocabulary, and Amitabh Bachchan's rich baritone brought further elegance to Vijay's words. The following scene from *Deewaar* is an exchange between Daavar Sahib (Iftekhar) and Vijay on the first day that Vijay has proved himself to his underworld boss. When Daavar drops a bundle of cash onto the table for Vijay, Vijay reminds Daavar in one terse line of an incident years before when Vijay, as a child, dared to challenge a customer—Daavar in fact—and demand that money be placed in his hand, not thrown to the ground for him to pick up.

The 'Phenke Hue Paise' Dialogue from *Deewaar*

डावर: गुड। विजय, आज तुम्हारे नए काम का पहला दिन है। यह लो। रख लो।
विजय: डावर साहिब, बहुत बरस पहले आप रेस खेलने जाया करते थे। और हमेशा एक जगह गाड़ी रोक कर अपने जूते पॉलिश करवाते थे।
डावर: हाँ, क्यों?
विजय: मैं आज भी फेंके हुए पैसे नहीं उठाता।

(Daavar: Good, Vijay, this is the first day on your new job. [Throwing the money on the table] Here. Keep it.
Vijay: Daavar Sahib, many years ago you used to go to the races. And you always stopped your car in the same place to have your shoes polished.
Daavar: Yes, why?
Vijay: I still don't pick up thrown-down money.)

Besides being the product of seven generations of Urdu poets, Javed Akhtar's education was largely Urdu-medium. His dialogue- and later lyric-writing show that historical wealth.

So what of the language in *Khosla Ka Ghosla*? The film is situated in Delhi, where Jaideep Sahni grew up. While the city has a long literary tradition and a current literacy, which, at 86 per cent,[115] is higher than the national average, it is also a place, as Jaideep notes, that has incorporated a great deal of brashness in recent decades. He commented,

As they say in Bombay, 'Lucknow has culture; Delhi has

---

[115]http://en.wikipedia.org/wiki/2011_census_of_India

agriculture.' So maybe I'm a product of that... You know Delhi is a little bit of a coarser culture in some way, because it's a refugee city. And everyone, including my ancestors, came as refugees after Partition. So it's got this tradition of, you know, you elbow everyone else out and just grab what is there because your system is reset to zero, and you're starting all over again. They managed to build everything again in just one or two generations, but what they have lost is civilized behaviour...

In the early 2000s Bambaiya made its presence felt. More recently, Delhi street language with its Punjabi flavour has been adding spice to film dialogue. Increasingly, films are being shot in Delhi and not simply the Delhi of the beautiful, historical backdrops—Lodi Gardens, the Red Fort and India Gate. We feel the reality of Delhi today, along with evocative accents and vocabulary in, for example, Rakeysh Omprakash Mehra's *Rang De Basanti*, Anurag Kashyap's *Dev. D*, Dibakar Banerjee's *Oye Lucky! Lucky Oye*, and Maneesh Sharma's *Band Baaja Baaraat*. Actress Anushka Sharma remarked on the language in this last film, 'Getting the lingo right was the toughest because the girls there have a tendency to talk fast, sometimes mix words and even omit words completely. The way [co-star] Ranveer and my character talk is crude but cute.'[116] Shimit Amin's *Chak De! India*, though only partly a Delhi film, has a title bursting with Punjabi energy, which the translation 'Go! India' can hardly convey. Jaideep Sahni, who wrote *Chak De! India* explained the generational nature of today's Delhi Punjabi:

> My Punjabi is different from my parents' Punjabi. It's cruder, coarser. My parents have this sweet, nice Lahore kind of Punjabi, which is all cultivated. From the Punjabi I have learned (studying with Punjabi farmers' sons in a school in

---

[116] Quoted by Shweta Mehta in 'I'm not Rajnikanth,' *Hindustan Times*, New Delhi, 26 October 2010.

Karnataka), I find my parents' Punjabi to be sickly sweet... They (the students) had a kind of reverse snobbery to city people and city Punjabi which rubbed off on me a little, for a while, for a period of my life. So it was fun. I used to find the Punjabi my parents spoke very sissy. But then I wrote a song for a band called Euphoria, and the Punjabi I chose was my parents' Punjabi. It was a romantic song about a guy telling his mother how much he misses his girlfriend who has gone away. And nobody does that in our culture. You don't tell your mother about missing your girlfriend. I just wanted to break it very softly. Instinctively, I chose my parents' Punjabi and not mine.

The father–son thing or, more broadly, the parent–child thing, i.e., the generational thing, continues through the decades, through the centuries. Whether it's words, attitudes, aesthetics, styles or simple objects, there's a mystery to what is kept, what is lost or discarded, what may or may not at some point be found, brought out and readopted or readapted, deemed worthy of museum-like treatment or simply grudgingly used for lack of a better substitute. Often the younger generation pays tribute to the past in ways that their elders would hardly recognize. 'You don't take out the same treasure that you buried,' as Javed Akhtar said. It later occurs to me that to treasure at least part of what we succeed in digging up would be quite enough.

THE PLACE OF ENGLISH IN HINDI CINEMA

Metro-Modern-Bollywood-Cool: A Language for Today?

Bollywood screenwriting is fundamentally bi- or multilingual, and English has long been part of the mix. Think of the dignified screen doctor of yesteryear, marked as an educated man by his occasional words in English. Now think: COOL! as in '*Cool cool, style ka ye usool*' (Cool is the rule for style), a refrain from a song in *Roadside Romeo* (2008). In this Disney–Yash Raj co-production, written and directed by Jugal Hansraj, Saif Ali Khan lends his voice to Romeo, the rich dog who, after being kicked out of his mansion onto the streets of Bombay, makes new proletarian friends. His confident style and his mastery of English make him a 'cool' leader, set to teach the ways of the rich to the street dogs whose English is poor, whose 'style' is lacking. *Cool* is a word, *cool* is a value. *Bindaas*, in its original meaning perhaps the nearest equivalent Hindi word, has made it to the Oxford English Dictionary, but *cool* is somehow cooler. FM radio hosts coolly whip between Hindi and English, with the advantage, at least in vocabulary, going to English, the tongue that defines upward mobility and which, accompanied by the right accent, will bring respect and a good job. Even in the film *Omkara*, noted for its use of raunchy local dialect, director-writer Vishal Bhardwaj has the Vivek Oberoi character trying to teach the obstinate character played by Kareena Kapoor to pronounce 'bottom' with an American, not an Indian, 't' sound. An American accent may be incomprehensible to a large section of the population, but it is nevertheless considered cool, as is having Snoop Dogg rap beside Akshay Kumar in Anees Bazmee's *Singh is Kinng* (2008).

Increasingly English words pop up in dialogue, much as they do in real life in metro India. With boundaries between languages fluid and quickly evolving, it is often hard to say at exactly what point a word switches status from 'English word used in Hindi' to 'Hindi word of English origin'. English or new Hindi? A few words have particularly caught my attention.

Life

English words can be heard side by side with their Hindi-Urdu-Hindustani counterparts in *Jab We Met* (2007), written and directed by Imtiaz Ali and winner of the Filmfare award for Best Dialogue. English is integrated into Hindi not randomly, rather, in ways that are both surprising and meaningful. *Sirf hansi, khel, mazaaq nahin hoti hai zindagi, Geet. Life mein serious bhi hona padta hai.* (Life is not only for laughing and having a good time; you have to be serious about life too.) This use of 'zindagi' and 'life' in one sentence may mean: I'm young, I'm modern, I'm metro, I'm on the go, but I've still got some poetry—in Hindustani—left in me. It also surely means: this is a Hindi film, so let's keep it Hindi, even if we young writers and actors are usually more comfortable in English.

One can soar in Hindi. Director Shimit Amin calls Hindi, at least the Hindi used in cinema, a bold and macho language with a different palette and different volume from English. Turning the volume down, so to speak, writer-director Nagesh Kukunoor chose the flatter '*Aadmi ko life mein practical hona chaahiye*' as the translation for his English line 'One should be practical in life' in the film *3 Deewarein* (2003). Collaborator Ali Husain Mir had offered a more creative option: '*Hosh ka palla josh ke palle se bhaari hona chaahiye*' (Conscience should weigh heavier on the scales than enthusiasm). After a much-heated debate, the line weighted towards English won.

Life is a term usually reserved for practical everyday matters; it is also ours to control. In Shyam Benegal's *Welcome to Sajjanpur* (2008), generations clash in their visions of life. First, we meet Vindhya's mother (Ila Arun) who wants to follow an astrologer's advice and marry her daughter to a dog. We then meet the motorcycle-riding, fast-talking Vindhya (Divya Dutta), who has no intention of following that plan. '*Hamaara life kauno life nahin hai ka?*' (Isn't my life a life?) she asks. She repeats her mother's words in disgust, '*Shaadi kar lo, kaam chhod do! Hmmph!*' (Get married; give up your job. Hmmph!) And she speeds off, leaving the town letter-writer (Shreyas Talpade) staring in amazement. The younger generation, with their English-influenced mindset, hold sway, for the most part, in *Welcome to Sajjanpur*. *Aamir*, written and directed by Rajkumar Gupta, shows the English-educated hero losing. He has spent years believing that life is his to shape. Calculating, determined terrorists prove they can thwart his well-laid plans, his life. The tag line significantly avoids life, reverting to qismat (luck, fate, destiny), which is obviously not in our hands: *Kaun kehta hai aadmi apni qismat khud likhta hai?* (Who says a man makes his own destiny?[117])

Time

According to the referential Platts' *Dictionary of Urdu, Classical Hindi, and English*, 'vaqt' simply means time. In film dialogue the distinction between zindagi (life) and vaqt can be blurred, at least when it includes the notion of qismat. In *Muqaddar Ka Sikandar*, directed by Prakash Mehra, with dialogues by Kader Khan, young Sikandar, the future Amitabh Bachchan character, is treated cruelly by almost everyone he meets. At one point he

---

[117]Literally: 'Who says a man writes his own destiny?'

tells a bullying adult: '*Aaj mera vaqt kharaab hai; vaqt ne mujhe maara hai. Isliye tu bhi mujhe maar le.*' (My *time* is bad. *Time* has beaten me. So you beat me too. [Emphasis mine]) And he goes on, 'But I promise on my sister's head that one day I will beat you.'

In sharp contrast, *Taxi No. 9 2 11* (2006), directed by Milan Luthria, with dialogues by Rajat Arora, uses the English term 'time', not vaqt, for that much-prized and limited commodity our watches remind us is ticking away. *Ye Bombay hai; yahaan time ka matlab hai paisa.* (This is Bombay; time means money here.) *Time* is about movement; it is not a state. Bombay, perched on the sea and facing west, no doubt inspires its people who are dashing about to make a buck, to adopt the word 'time' with its sense of modern urgency. In *Jab We Met* the nuanced distinction between time and vaqt becomes clear when the two words are used in quick succession. Aditya (Shahid Kapoor) is sitting on a train opposite a very talkative stranger played by Kareena Kapoor. The conductor asks for the young man's ticket. '*Mere paas ticket nahin hai,*' (I don't have a ticket.) he answers. The young woman takes over, hoping to help by inventing a story. '*Ticket kharidne ka time nahin mila hoga...inke saath haadsa hua hai. Bura vaqt hai.*' (He didn't have time to buy a ticket. He had a mishap. It's a bad time for him.)

'*Ye Bombay hai; yahaan time ka matlab hai paisa*':
Nana Patekar and John Abraham in Taxi No. 9 2 11.
(Sketch by Simon P. Holzman)

What Is This Thing Called Love?

Or as the beautiful song from Subhash Ghai's *Taal* (1999) goes, *'Ishq bina kya marna yaara ishq bina kya jeena?* (Without love, my love, what is death? Without love what is life?) The term 'love' in Hindi cinema is not new. True, we didn't hear it in the 1950s in classics like *Devdas* or *Pyaasa* or *Mother India*. But in *Aradhana* (1969) by Shakti Samanta, dialogue by Ramesh Pant, the Rajesh Khanna character says: 'I love you. *Tum meri ho.*' (You are mine.) And the Sharmila Tagore character answers: '*Main tumhaari hoon.*' (I am yours—significantly NOT 'you are mine'.)

Pyaar, prem, ishq, mohabbat, with such a wealth of Hindustani vocabulary, why would one add *love*? One answer could be the self-consciousness that accompanies intimate feelings. Another language, beyond the passions and reflexes associated with one's mother tongue (or 'grandmother tongue'), can offer a kind of protective curtain to hide behind, the linguistic equivalent, say, of Nargis, playing the new bride in *Mother India*, with covered head and coyly downcast eyes. Anthropological researcher Jogendro Kshetrimayum explained that in Manipur, where young people watch many Korean films,[118] they can be seen texting the Korean version of 'I love you' to one another. One of the paradoxes of Hindi cinema is that despite the focus on passion and love, one is ever aware of entering a taboo area. In the 2007 film *The Namesake*, directed by Mira Nair, based on the book by Jhumpa Lahiri, the wife (Tabu) says to her husband of many years (Irrfan Khan), 'You want me to say "I love you" like the Americans?' He timidly admits that he does. Love between parents and children can remain unspoken as well. In *Fanny*, the 1932 French classic written by Marcel Pagnol, the father

---

[118]Hindi films were banned by insurgents in Manipur in 2000. For further information see: 'Mapping Cultural Diffusion: The Case of 'Korean Wave' in North East India,' 10 April 2008, at http://mappingculturaldiffusion.blogspot.com/

(Raimu), regularly hurls invectives at his son (Pierre Fresnay); only once does he soften enough to concede, 'You know, when I tell you that you poison my life, it's not true.' And in *Shakti* it is only after the policeman father (Dilip Kumar) has fatally shot his criminal son (Amitabh Bachchan) that the father takes the dying younger man lovingly in his arms:

> Vijay: *Bahut koshish ki ki apne dil se mohabbat nikaal doon, lekin main hamesha aapse pyaar karta raha...* (I tried hard to empty my heart of love, but I've always loved you...)
>
> Father: *Main bhi tumse mohabbat karta hoon, bete.* (I love you too, son.)

This linguistic modesty can extend to the off-screen world of Bollywood. Actor Irrfan Khan, interviewed for the BBC Hindi service programme *Ek Mulaaqaat*, spoke in Hindi until asked—in English—about love. He switched into hesitant English himself, as though the concept required a different tongue.

> Sanjeev Srivastav: And your first love?
> Irrfan Khan: Love, love. I'm still understanding the interaction with the woman with whom I wanted to spend my life. Whether it's love or not, I don't know... The first woman with whom I got entangled and I got hooked on was my wife, and I'm still staying with her. *Unka naam Sutapa Sikdar...* [and he reverts to Hindi].

People in show business are regularly asked such questions. Jaideep Sahni has candidly admitted a similar confusion, 'I am not clear about the emotions of love.' That vagueness may explain the non-committal song he wrote for *Salaam Namaste* (2005): 'My dil (heart) goes hmmm...' Concerning the popularity of the song, Sahni said, 'The kids were singing it on the streets... It describes a certain feeling just right.' Perhaps then, it is the public as well as filmmakers who are perplexed by notions of love. In *Aaja Nachle* Kunal Kapoor's character may be channelling

Sahni when he asks sceptically, '*Pyaar saala kya hota hai?*' (What the hell is love?) Konkona Sen Sharma's intonation is perfect as she conveys her character's simple belief: '*Pyaar pyaar hota hai.*' (Love is what it is). It just is. And it *is*, significantly for her, in Hindi, not in English.

The imported word 'love' can offer a cover for the bashful; it can seem modern and exciting; for some, it can be culturally alienating, part of the metro India consumerist package one is urged to 'buy'. The world view that English conveys can collide with more rooted linguistic and mental patterns of thought. *Love*, as it moves more deeply into Indian languages and culture, is problematic on several levels. How does one say '*falling* in love' in Hindi...and its corollary, 'falling *out* of love'? No wonder Irrfan Khan, among others, is still wondering about the meaning of love.

Guilt

The American-returned character played by Nagesh Kukunoor in his 1998 film *Hyderabad Blues* protests to his Telugu-speaking father, 'Don't guilt-trip me, Dad.' Many English words heard in Hindi cinema add nuance or a modern flavour. Usually they have close equivalents in Hindi-Urdu. Guilt does not. I asked several people in the film industry for the Hindi translation of guilt. Most were stumped. One answer was *pachhtaava*. Yet this translates back into English better as remorse or regret. Jaideep Sahni concurred with several others that *pachhtaava* was the word for guilt. 'But,' he noted, 'nobody feels guilty.' He then added that a better translation would be *mera dil mujhe kachot raha hai.* (My heart is tight, contracting.) The dictionary definition of the English word guilt is 'a feeling of responsibility or remorse for some offense, crime, wrong, etc. whether real or imagined.' I picked up David Graeber's *Debt: The First 5,000 Years* (2011) expecting to plunge into economics with an anthropological twist. His take was surprising. Our debt to the universe—and to our parents and society—for our very existence, Graeber notes, is traditionally related to sacrifice, guilt and redemption, all terms that have both an economic and a religious dimension.[119] Perhaps then, in some form, karz (debt) would translate as 'guilt', though it would probably not find its way into film dialogue today. Jaideep Sahni concurred and pointed out that Gulzar's lyric *'Muskuraane ke karz utaarne honge'* (by smiling, the debt/burden/guilt will be taken off) from Shekhar Kapoor's 1983 film *Masoom*, no doubt carries the notion of guilt within the word for debt. 'Guilt' in the American film world brings to mind Woody Allen, who gives us a light-hearted look at the serious 'business' of guilt in his *Broadway Danny Rose* (1984):

> Danny (Woody Allen): What are you talking about? Guilt is important. It's important to feel guilty. Otherwise, you, you know, you're capable of doing terrible things. You know. It's very important to be guilty. I-I'm guilty all the time and I-I never did anything. You know? My, my, my rabbi, Rabbi Perlstein, used to say we're all guilty in the eyes of God.
> Tina (Mia Farrow): You believe in God?
> Danny: No, no. But, uh, I'm guilty over it.

Anthropologists and sociolinguists make a distinction between what they call 'shame cultures' and 'guilt cultures'. In the book *Bilingual Minds* edited by Aneta Pavlenko (2006), Alexia Panayiotou explores the workings of shame in Greek society in a chapter entitled 'Translating Guilt: An Endeavor of Shame in the Mediterranean?' Broadly, sanctions in guilt cultures are internalized. In shame cultures, societal pressures serve to keep individuals in check. In *Shakti*, Vijay (Amitabh Bachchan) is concerned what the neighbours might say if he moves in with Roma (Smita Patil) (*Log kya kehenge?*). She, on the other hand, has embraced the freedom offered by the relative anonymity of

---

[119]Graeber, 2011, pp. 59-69.

city life: *Is sheher mein itni fursat kahaan logon ko jo kuchh keh sakein?* (Who in this city has time for talk?) Guilt is not yet part of the vocabulary of 1980s films, but the Smita Patil character, at the beginning of the film, exhibits an individualism that refuses to be shackled by shaming.

Twenty-five years later, *Jab We Met* gives us an interesting mix of both *shame* (sharam) and *guilt*. Geet's (Kareena Kapoor) grandfather (Dara Singh), the patriarch of their Punjabi estate, sternly meets Aditya (Shahid Kapoor) who has accompanied Geet home. The grandfather tells Geet that he can tell in a minute what is going on between a boy and a girl. She answers, '*Daadaaji, please. Aap mujhe sharminda kar rahe ho.*' (Grandfather, please, you're embarrassing me/shaming me.) And he sternly replies, '*Sharam? Agar sharam hoti tere andar, to tu aise kapde pehenti? Aise kapde pehenkar ghar aayi hai, to Mumbai mein to nangi ghoomti hogi!*' (Embarrassed? Feeling ashamed? If you had any shame in you, then would you wear these clothes? If you have come home dressed like this, then you must be roaming naked in Mumbai!) Geet uses 'sharminda' to describe her embarrassment. The grandfather uses the same term for shame. Though she feels no guilt, she does respond to shame. By the next day she is covering her arms and using less English. The younger generation, perhaps as a result of their English-medium educations, have words to describe an internalized, individual sense of responsibility. Later in the film the Shahid Kapoor character tries to make his rival (Tarun Arora) feel bad for the callous way he has treated Geet. The rival answers, '*Mujhe guilty feel mat karaaiye.* (Don't try to make me feel guilty.) He rejects the guilt, but still, it is guilt he is rejecting, not shame.

'Sharam' was once prevalent in film dialogue. There was the common insult 'besharam' (without shame) or the related '*Sharam nahin aati?*' (Have you no shame?) More recently sharam has been used mockingly, as though it is a remembered but fading concept in some circles. In *Jaane Tu Ya Jaane Na* (2008), for example, written and directed by Abbas Tyrewala, Jai (Imran Khan) is meeting

Aditi's (Genelia D'Souza) South Bombay, rich, relaxed, modern parents. Jai thinks the meeting is to discuss a job. The parents, in fact, are broaching the subject of Jai and Aditi getting married. When the issue is clarified and the young couple balk, the parents try to apologize. The 'We're so sorry' comes out naturally, but they cannot finish the dated formula, *'Ham donon bahut sharminda hain,'* (We're both so ashamed/embarrassed), without bursting out laughing. Guilt, the serious emotion today, is, in a sense, the new sharam of film dialogue. Shame and guilt: director Shimit Amin brought the two concepts into a shared universality. As he noted, however much the two notions may diverge, both have in common the fact that they begin in the family.

In the past an actor's body language might express guilt that went by another name or even remained unnamed. In *Awaara*, directed by Raj Kapoor and written by K.A. Abbas, we see a father (Prithviraj Kapoor) obviously racked by guilt as he finally admits his own injustice in never having recognized his son (Raj Kapoor). But the father, who is a judge, refers to himself as apraadhi (a criminal, someone guilty in the eyes of the law). *Trishul* directed by Yash Chopra, written by Salim-Javed, also deals with a clash between father and son. Raj (Sanjeev Kumar) has married into wealth and power, leaving behind Shanti (Waheeda Rehman), the woman he had promised to marry. When he learns that Shanti is pregnant, Raj visits her looking contrite—and possibly guilty. In response to his vague offer of help, Shanti's voice shows pain but also fierce determination.

> *Meri madad karne aaye ho? Kitne rupaye laaye ho? Bolo. Tum jaante ho tum aaj bhi meri madad karne nahin aaye. Mujhse madad maangne aaye ho. Kahin na kahin tumhaari aatma par bojh hai. Tum mujhe bahut se rupaye dekar, shaayad ek makaan dekar, saari zindagi mere jeene ka intezaam karke, apni aatma par bojh utaarna chaahte ho, lekin main, main tumhaari ye madad lene se inkaar karti hoon.*

(Have you come to help me? How much money have you brought? Tell me. You know that even now you haven't come to help me. You've come to ask for my help. Somewhere inside there is a burden on your soul. By giving me money, maybe a house, providing for me my whole life, you want to unburden your soul. But I, I refuse to take your help.)

His soul is burdened. Is that guilt? The rest of the film is devoted to Shanti's adult son Vijay's (Amitabh Bachchan) search to avenge his mother's life of humiliation. Whatever guilt-like feelings his father may have had years earlier have been buried so deep that even when Vijay becomes a vicious business competitor and names his company after his mother, it never occurs to Raj that Vijay might be his son. Whatever the emotion, it starts with the family.

Shit

As Steven Pinker explains in *The Stuff of Thought* (2007), families and societies establish proscribed words, i.e. swearing, cursing, profanity, obscenity, oaths or epithets, rather arbitrarily. One generation's most highly charged words might be the next generation's informal but acceptable vocabulary. Still, there is a commonality to the categories of words any society is likely to deem unacceptable. Taboo words invariably relate to copulation, pudenda, orifices and effluvia, theology, death and disease, and disfavoured classes of people.[120] In the US the seven words you can't say on television refer to sexuality or excretion. One of the seven is 'shit'. Though banned from public airways in the US and the UK, the same word has become part of youthful spoken English in metro India. Reflecting the trend, even 'nice girls' like Geet in *Jab We Met* freely use the word. She does not and would not, of course, use an equivalently strong word in

---

[120]Pinker, 2007, pp. 324-339.

Hindi-Urdu, that is to say, strong by US Federal Communications Commission standards at least. And almost no one does. Some of the expletives in a scene in *Barah Aana* (2009), written and directed by Raja Menon with dialogues by Raj Kumar Gupta, are not only bleepable but bleeped; we are left to guess what offensive words are being mouthed. More recently, language once considered too vulgar for the movies has been allowed in some films, much to the consternation of a vocal part of society.

Specific taboo words can only pack their full wallop if their prohibition is learned at an early age, often painfully. I can acquire 'dirty words' from the second and third languages I speak, but they will never touch me at the same gut level as a word I was punished for saying as a child. Jaideep Sahni remembered precisely when he learned the word 'shit'. 'After class 10 all over Delhi there is this kind of Hoover effect where all the bright kids are sucked into Delhi Public School.' He heard all the other students using the word and added it to his own vocabulary. 'I don't remember thinking much about it,' he said. 'It's the age where you just pick up anything. If everyone around you considers something cool, you just assume it must be cool.' In *Sarkar*, directed by Ram Gopal Varma, written by Manish Gupta, the Amitabh Bachchan character lashes out at his grown son Vishnu (K.K. Menon) for saying 'saala haraami' (bastard) in front of a child. Vishnu doesn't say 'shit', but if he did, we are left to wonder, would the father's reaction have been so harsh? In an article on drugs, *TIME* magazine ran the quote of a Mexican rancher, 'Changing that (police corruption) will take many years and some very big cojones.'[121] The word cojones is neither in italics, nor is it translated from Spanish; it is assumed that American readers will understand the meaning. But would *TIME* magazine have printed the word 'balls'? Probably not.

---

[121] *TIME*, 4 May 2009, p. 29.

A Khichdi Language

> 'You samjao that baysharram pair,' said the eldest sister Aspinwall, 'that this sort of tamasha is simply not the cheese.'
>
> —from *The Moor's Last Sigh*, by Salman Rushdie[122]

Salman Rushdie's Hinglish is, of course, mostly English with a bit of Hindi thrown in. At the other end of the spectrum, people may speak Hindi or Urdu with a flavouring of English. Either way, the technical term—much loved by sociolinguists—for this blending of languages is 'code-switching'. 'Code' is a fancy word for 'language'. Much too precious, one might think, but the oft-quoted quip, 'A language is a dialect with an army and a navy' describes the very real difficulty of setting boundaries between varieties of language. Hence, the technical term 'code'. 'Switching' is clear, i.e. moving from one language to another, often within a single sentence. This form of communication only works, of course, if fellow speakers share two or more common languages. Further, it relies on movement between languages being socially acceptable. Bilingualism can be personal, or it can be societal. I can throw a French word into a conversation with an English-speaking friend in France. If a French word springs to mind while I'm in the US, I'm out of luck. I would fail to communicate anything other than apparent snobbishness. Most English speakers in France, however, prefer spending—or wasting—valuable communication time in the search for the proper English word even when a French term is more readily available. 'Language purist' Professor Etiemble declared war on 'franglais' in the 1960s. He was followed by lawmakers and cultural trendsetters who have strived to prevent English from 'invading' French. Heaven forbid then that English speakers should stoop to speaking 'Englench'!

---

[122] Rushdie, 1995, p. 97.

In India purists certainly exist. However, when the subject of Hinglish came up on the BBC Hindi Service radio call-in programme *India Bol*, the most adamant exponent of keeping languages rigidly separate was a caller from the UK. More often people resort to the first meaningful word, be it in Hindi or English, or in many circles, of course, any of the regional languages as well. Jaideep Sahni refers to the resulting mix as khichdi language, in reference to the dish that blends rice and lentils. Chutney is another metaphor for this most informal language blending. Rita Kothari, associate professor, Mudra Institute of Communications, Ahmedabad, has studied the phenomenon of the hybrid language in India. In January 2009 she organized a conference labelled 'Chutnefying English', also known as the Indianization of English. Journalist Chitra Unnithan quoted Kothari who said:

> Several factors like Bollywood and its permeation can be attributed to this change. Even a veteran like Gulzar, for instance, uses English lyrics for his Hindi songs these days. The advertising world has also contributed in this direction with ads like 'Hungry Kya' and 'What your bahana is?' Another factor that has led to the widespread use of Hinglish has been the increase in the migration of people within the country and in English-speaking countries. The conference is an attempt to study whether this hybrid mixture is likely to become the language of urban India.[123]

So we have khichdi. And we have chutney. Farhan Akhtar offered another food metaphor.

> For me it's a bit of scrambled eggs… Language is coming in from all directions—like Urdu from my father, Hindi from the movies, English from what I've grown up speaking. From reading books, from watching other films, from travelling,

---

[123]Unnithan, Chitra, 'Hinglish: The language of urban India?', *Business Standard*, 9 September 2008.

you pick up little expressions. So it all comes together and creates a new kind of language.

Mira Nair's 2001 film *Monsoon Wedding* was very well received in France. Interviewed for the documentary 'Planète Bollywood,' which aired on the Franco-German channel Arte in 2005, Mira Nair was, almost inevitably, asked about the use of language in her film. She clarified for French and German audiences, 'English is a bigger and bigger part of our lives...I wanted to make a realistic film about the Indian family and wedding life, and they had to speak the way we speak, genuinely, which is that we often use three languages in one sentence.'

Anupama Chopra, speaking in 2006, recommended the 1989 film *In Which Annie Gives It Those Ones*, scripted by Arundhati Roy and directed by Pradip Krishen, an early example of khichdi language being embraced. Chopra said:

> Language was like a major character in it. It was about these kids in architecture schools in the 1970s. They all spoke in this mix of Hindi, Punjabi and English. I think it was way ahead of its time. If it happened now, it would really take off. It was shown once on Doordarshan, and then it died an early death.

The complexities of language blending in daily life appear in the book *India Calling* (2011). Young Indian American reporter Anand Giridharadas, having moved back to his parents' homeland, delves into his 'new-old' country in order to move beyond childhood impressions gleaned during holiday visits. Visiting Bandra Family Court, he notes, 'The general language of the courtroom was a confident, ever-shifting admixture of English, Hindi and Marathi, and the judge had a wonderful Indian talent for knowing how to apportion the quantity of words from each language depending on who stood before him.'[124]

---

[124]Giridharadas, A., 2011, p. 188.

As Professor Kothari points out, one impetus to language mixing is population mobility. For his first script *Jungle*, directed by Ram Gopal Varma, Jaideep Sahni was inspired by his own experience as a college student years earlier.

> In *Jungle* our whole idea was that this is a gang of guys living in the jungle for twenty years. They would be from all parts of India, and they would probably have a mixture of language. It would be kind of like a boys' hostel. I used words from Rajasthani, Urdu, Hindi, all kinds of languages that I've been exposed to. It was fun because I put in a lot of words which didn't have any meaning... In earlier films the equivalent would be the dacoit. But they would be in Chambal or from UP. They would have a language that was very rooted in a certain culture. In *Jungle* they were not rooted in any culture. They were just outlaws who landed from various parts of the country. When I was in engineering college, there were some guys who had been in the hostel for ten years because they never passed out. They had created their own vocabulary. So I just took those guys as role models and created some pidgin, imaginary words, not rooted in anything.

Any number of languages can be blended. It happens throughout the world when groups of people speaking different languages are in close contact. Yet it must be noted that the Hindi verb 'karna' (to do) almost invites code-switching. 'Koshish karna' and 'faisla karna' are perfectly good expressions, yet one is as likely to hear 'try karna' and 'decide karna' in their stead. Slipping in nouns is also common. '*Dad ke saath hoon. Unke computer business mein hoon,*' the Saif Ali Khan character says to the Akshaye Khanna character in *Dil Chahta Hai* (2001). (I'm with Dad; I'm [working] in his computer business.) As writer–director Farhan Akhtar readily admitted, the characters in the film would, in fact, have spoken English to each other. The occasional English word in this Hindi film adds flavour and hints at that reality. Interjections like 'anyway' and 'actually' are frequent, even though words like 'khair' and 'darasal' are known and available. Why, then, choose to use English? Perhaps because of the prestige English carries. Knowing it well indicates a move up in society. Some who speak only a bit of English seem to enjoy practising the few words they know. Try, for instance, asking a rickshaw driver for an akhbaar stand in Mumbai. The response is likely to be, 'Oh, newspaper.'

Siddharth Anand's *Salaam Namaste* (2005) is largely situated in Australia. The young professional couple played by Saif Ali Khan and Preity Zinta fall in and out of love, often to comic effect, before they are finally capable of commitment. Lyricist Jaideep Sahni described the song 'My dil goes hmmm' as:

> Pure popcorn, but I wrote it for the characters that were in the movie. If everyone speaks Hindi and English on the street, they'll sing like they speak. There's nothing I can do about it. I have to be true to them.

In 2006 he explained the negative critical response to the Hinglish in the song, using still more food metaphors:

> There's this big flak going on, that this supposedly good writer has turned bad... A lot of critics think that today's young writers, by putting in English words, are trying to seem cooler. They thought that we thought that the audience was stupid. Or else that it's like throwing more expensive olives on the pizza so you can sell it for more. That's not what I was trying to do. I was really saying it from my heart. In fact, it just came out in a conversation with a friend, and I used it in the song.

People who regularly code-switch have the seemingly strange tendency to say something in one language and then repeat the idea in their other language. In *Kaala Patthar*, written by

Salim-Javed and directed by Yash Chopra, coal miner Vijay (Amitabh Bachchan) menacingly confronts Dhanraj Puri (Prem Chopra), accusing him of putting greed before any concern for his workers' lives. Incensed, the mine owner screams at Vijay, 'How dare you? *Tumhaari himmat kaise hui?*' Dhanraj Puri's tone and his use of English evidence his sense of self and entitlement. Linguist Shannon Finch studied this phenomenon extensively in her 2009 doctoral dissertation *Repetition as Linguistic and Social Strategy in Hindi-English Bilingual Discourse.* (Check yourself in the coming days if you're bilingual, to see if you too use this form of discourse.) Shannon Finch concludes that the reasons, generally, for bilinguals' repeating or rephrasing in a second language are many and complex. In this particular scene the repetition would seem to have practical value, that of communicating to the majority of Hindi film viewers who, particularly in 1979, were unlikely to understand English. This sort of code-switching may be conscious and even calculated. Less calculated is the code-switching that reflects the speaking habits of millions in a multilingual society. In everyday life, languages brush against each other, sometimes vying for power, sometimes harmoniously intertwining. Code-switching can be avoided, freely embraced or even seen as a solution to a sociolinguistic problem. The relatively conservative nature of Hindi means that no polite term exists to speak of sex and marital infidelity. As Anupama Chopra pointed out, having English to fall back on can mean that one need neither offend nor sound absurd. She said:

> Karan Johar's film *Kabhi Alvida Naa Kehna* is set in New York. It's about infidelity, about two people already married falling in love. But he said there were scenes where he found it very hard to say the dialogues in Hindi because in Hindi it sounded too vulgar… They had no option but to have the fighting portions in English. 'Are you sleeping with him?' How do you say that in Hindi? Even the content

is affecting what language the characters are speaking. He said they tried really hard to make it Hindi, but it just sounded terrible. So naturally, since they're in New York, they figured they [the characters] could speak in English.

The increasing presence of Hinglish on screen, I would venture, both reflects and promotes the hybrid language of today's metro India. Inserting English words in everyday situations can be an act of inclusion. English, which has largely sloughed off its status as a colonial language and been accepted as an Indian language, often serves as the mediating language, allowing those from far ends of the country to communicate. English is also a communally neutral language, neither Sanskrit-based nor Perso-Arabic-based. Hindu–Muslim identity issues, sadly present in word choice in many circles, are circumvented with words like *family*, *thank you*, *goodbye*. Nevertheless, one of the rifts in society is between those who speak English and those who do not, with those who do normally at a distinct advantage. Still, the English speakers can get their comeuppance. Take the film *Aamir*. Dressed in a suit and tie, Aamir (Rajeev Khandelwal) asks some children in a crumbling building located near a railroad track where the bathroom is. The children mockingly answer, 'Bathroom?' Aamir translates, '*Sandaas kidhar hai?*' (Where's the crapper?) '*Vahaan peechhe*,' (Out there at the back) they answer, laughing at his discomfort. These proletarian children not only do not aspire to the 'cool' English-speaking world; they thumb their noses at it.

Using English to Make Hindi Films

> The fact that I
> am writing to you
> in English
> already falsifies what I
> wanted to tell you.
> My subject:
> how to explain to you that I
> don't belong to English
> though I belong nowhere else.
> —Gustavo Perez Firmat (*Bilingual Blues: Poems,*
> 1981-1994)[125]

Some lament the preponderance of English. Shridhar Raghavan, for example, said:

> The sad part is that today, many people working in the business don't particularly read, speak or write Hindi as well as they need to. For example, if somebody worked on a script which is completely in Hindi, I think he would automatically have lost 50 per cent of his potential audience because people at the studios and production houses here couldn't read it. Executive producers have come out of these colleges with business degrees and mass communication diplomas or something. They can speak Hindi, but I would guarantee you, if you time them while reading a page in Hindi, they would take at least triple the time to read as in English, and they would give up midway. So ironically, Hindi is not, unfortunately, the language which most people are using in this business right now.

Ketan Desai, son of director-producer Manmohan Desai, has observed the film industry over the decades.

---

[125] Firmat, Gustavo Perez, *Bilingual Blues: Poems*, Bilingual Pr, 1995, p. 3.

> It's not disturbing. It's something to observe. Our titles come in English (script). We are making a Hindi film. When you go for an awards ceremony, all the people who are attending the show speak in English. 'And the award goes to X, Y, Z for the film so-and-so.' When it's on camera, everything is in Hindi. The minute you go off camera, everything is in English.

Because English-medium education has so influenced the younger generation, we tend to forget that historically, English has long been present in Hindi filmmaking. Nasreen Munni Kabir reminds us that even in what is considered the golden age for Hindi cinema, the 1950s, well-known figures like Bengali filmmaker Bimal Roy or Guru Dutt were writing scripts in English. She added:

> Even if you look back in the '40s, you have Marathis making Hindi films; you have South Indians making Hindi films. So how do all these people communicate? So this tradition of writing the actual thought or the idea of a sentence in English and then having the dialogue translated into Urdu has been there from day one, if you ask me.

Certainly the role of English in Indian society at large has expanded in recent years. Director Nagesh Kukunoor is but one of many to insist, 'Whether we like it or not, English is an Indian language now. Period.'

And English has become more dominant, more visible in the film industry. Titles in English were once the exception. Think: *An Evening in Paris*, the Shammi Kapoor-starrer from 1967. Today they are, for reasons known to producers, increasingly commonplace, e.g. *Wake Up Sid, Wanted* (2009), *Singh is Kingg, 3 Idiots, Rock On!!* (2008), *Life in a Metro* (2007), with more coming every week. So why rely on English to make Hindi films? Nagesh Kukunoor gave an example from his past that explained how notions of linguistic hierarchy are fostered and enforced.

His second film *Rockford* was almost 100 per cent in English. It dealt with the life of a boy from a boarding school. He said:

> I went to a boarding school myself. Virtually all boarding schools are completely in English. We weren't encouraged to speak any other language. If we spoke our mother tongue and the brothers caught us, then we were in trouble. So unless you were away from prying eyes, you never spoke in any language other than English.

As an American and an English teacher to boot, I am both horrified and fascinated that English enjoys such prestige in India. Many parents pay to have their children become more proficient in English than in any native Indian language. Kukunoor explained the logic:

> In the classroom the brothers were very clear that the language of choice was English. Academically, I was almost always at the top of the class, and so I spoke good English (*he said self-deprecatingly*). There was an enormous sense of pride that one could speak this language well.

Shashanka Ghosh told a story about the complications that result from the status granted to English. It had to do with an assistant director for whom he was otherwise full of praise.

> The humility and discipline that assistant directors (ADs) bring to the job is phenomenal. No studies. They've just come and spent twelve years in the business learning how to deal with the tensions and egos of fifteen different people and managing to put everything together within budget and on time for the director. It's fantastic. I was shocked when I saw how well they worked. And unsung, totally unsung! It was an amazing lesson for me. But my chief AD had a problem: his English was not very good. I mean his Hindi was superb, but he chose to communicate in a language he wasn't comfortable with while I, on the other hand, was

very comfortable with Hindi. I'm from Delhi, so it's easy! So the ironic thing was I would be talking to him in Hindi with all my gender mistakes. And he would be answering in English because for him it was like I was his director, and so he should speak to me in English.

Jaideep Sahni, in 2006, saw a downside to writers relying so heavily on English, 'The main thing is, I'm seeing more and more new writers write even the dialogue in English, as people speak English. And then they figure that someone will work the Hindi out.'

Hindi may get 'worked out' but not necessarily satisfactorily. Trisha Gupta points to the problems in her 2011 piece 'Death by Dialogue.'

> ... When the upper-middle-class, English-speaking characters in an otherwise fairly well-conceived film like *Rock On!!* or *Sorry Bhai!* attempt to have life-altering conversations in Hindi, they sound entirely unconvincing.... Navdeep Singh confesses that in his experience, characters conceptualised in English tend to be more liberal, less parochial. "As soon as you start thinking the same characters in Hindi, you suddenly become more aware of regional groupism, caste affiliations, religious affiliations," says Singh.[126]

English, Its Baggage and Its Shine

Jaideep Sahni remembers when he was young that his father would move from Hindi into English to express formality. If he had simply wanted to speak another language for emphasis, it could have been Punjabi. Instead, it was English. Sahni explained:

> For example, if I was to ask for a motorbike in my first year at college, my father would say, 'First deserve; then

---

[126] Gupta, Trisha, 1 May 2011.

demand.' He could have said the same thing in Hindi, but he wouldn't because he knows that if he says it in English, this thing's going to get stuck in my head. It's like putting it on the wall, like a poster. It's a way of underlining and making it bigger than life, which applies to all things in English.

As Trisha Gupta reminds us, English is not just any language. 'Being English-speaking,' she says, 'carries much more baggage.' Though Gupta does not elaborate on the baggage, the thought does bring scenes to mind. For example, at the beginning of Vishal Bhardwaj's 2007 film *The Blue Umbrella*, we see Nandu (Pankaj Kapoor), a village man half-napping as he listens to an audiotape. The style is motivational, the content, fortune-telling. 'You are just about to find a treasure in dollars, in pounds or in rupees! You're going to be a multimillionaire, just like Bill Gates.' A younger man who is listening along—and who understands more English—excitedly wakes the somnolent Nandu to tell him the big news. Nandu asks if that's really what the tape said, and the younger man confirms saying, *'Haan, aur vo bhi angrezi mein.'* (Yes, and that too in English!) Nandu is immediately impressed. *'Angrezi mein bhi jhooth bolta hai koi?'* (Does anyone lie in English?)

The 'baggage' takes a different form in Sanjay Leela Bhansali's *Devdas*, but the issue, fundamentally, is the power which English represents. The story is situated in the early part of the twentieth century. After many long years of studying in London, Devdas (Shah Rukh Khan) has returned to his family's rural mansion. Visiting his childhood love Paro (Aishwarya Rai), he tries to impress her with his knowledge of a grand world far beyond their borders. There's the majesty and splendour of London, he tells her. There's Trafalgar Square with its 'pigeons', which he sweetly but condescendingly translates for her: 'kabootar'. 'You are so silly,' he tells her in English. And she answers with the dated expression 'Mention not', assuming 'silly' to be a compliment. English is an important component in Dev's arsenal; it announces to all that his is a family of wealth and influence. Sensing herself to be at a disadvantage in this language exchange-cum-game of love, Paro begins to play to her strengths, quickly disarming him with her beauty, charm and emotional intelligence.

In a later scene in the same film, English serves as a weapon in a brutal attack. Dev's father (Vijay Crishna), a landowner and barrister, is distant, cruel, authoritarian, unjust and also very proud to be among the few English-speaking elite of the day. He is beholden to the British, and his own cruelty evokes the crueller side of the British Raj. After Dev's father has decreed that Dev and Paro will never marry, Paro comes in desperation to Dev's room during the night, hoping to convince Dev not to submit to his father's will. When Dev's father chances to sees the pair, he lashes out, declaring that both Paro and her mother would do well to open a brothel. Devdas erupts in rage. In response, his father slaps him and screams in English, 'Don't forget who you are, Dev!' The verbal lashing continues in Hindi. Dev is reminded just how high-born he is, just how low Paro's family are. Dev's next response evokes another aspect of the Raj's legacy in India. Empowered by English law, Dev now stands firm against his father and proclaims as a barrister would, in English: 'I object!' With English, one can announce one's superiority. But it's also with English that one can fight for justice. The Magna Carta, the document King John was forced to sign in 1215 to limit his tyranny, has served as a reference point for all subsequent demands for rights throughout the English-speaking world. The words those rebellious feudal barons spoke were different, but their essential meaning was 'I object!' Dev has integrated the spirit of 'I object' through studying English. Being Dev, however, he will soon turn his anger inward; he will slowly self-destruct rather than continue to fight for right. Still, his revolt against his father, his 'I object' moment serves to make him a more compelling anti-hero.

That was in the early twentieth century. By the late twentieth century, English had come to represent power that was only an education away and thus potentially accessible and life-changing even for the masses. In Mahesh Bhatt's *Arth*, the cleaning woman played by Rohini Hattangadi is determined to have her daughter attend a convent school. Unable even to pronounce 'convent', the mother seeks help from her employer, played by Shabana Azmi, to go to the school directors on her behalf. English has the power to assure that the daughter of a cleaning woman will not clean homes.

To speak good English—is it a laudable goal, a worthy investment in the future, or an unreasonable task? In real life, screenwriter Javed Siddiqi experienced the coercive power of English first-hand. When he came to Bombay as a young man to work as a journalist on his uncle's Urdu newspaper *Khilafat*, he learned, to his dismay, that English reigned in the city.

> English was a very difficult thing. You would be surprised that in Rampur English was started at the sixth standard. So when I came here after the tenth, my knowledge of English was only four standards. My passion was reading. I had read almost all the Urdu classics. When I came to Bombay, I realized that everybody speaks English. This is a very funny place. To survive in this city, you have to learn English... For eight years I read only English novels, saw only English films, read only English newspapers.

The confidence that goes with complete mastery of English is one further divide between the lovelorn character played by Ranvir Shorey and Dia (Madhuri Dixit) in *Aaja Nachle*. Eleven years earlier, on the day the two were to be married, Dia snuck away from the little town of Shamli before making a new life for herself in New York. Now she is back. He tries a few words of English, then timidly apologizes, '*Angrezi se zara paidal hain, magar safar lamba ho to in sab cheezon ka kya farq padta hai.*' (No translation quite does this line justice. The idea is that his English isn't very good, but in the long run, what does it matter? There is a play on words, however. He can only walk—*paidal*—in English, but if the journey—of life—is long enough, language is not the important thing.)

Because the language that opens so many possibilities can feel oppressive and tyrannical, we are ready to laugh when it is mocked. In Manmohan Desai's *Amar Akbar Anthony*, Anthony (Amitabh Bachchan) emerges from a giant Easter egg, the caricature of an English gentleman of yore, dressed in black tuxedo, top hat, white gloves, walking stick, bow tie, complete with monocle and pocket watch on a chain. Bachchan speaks the lines: 'You know the whole country of the system is juxtapositioned by the haemoglobin in the atmosphere because you are a sophisticated rhetorician intoxicated by the exuberance of your own verbosity.' The partygoers, wide-eyed and perplexed, cry in unison, 'What???' And the Anthony character begins to dance while Kishore Kumar takes over singing in playback, 'My Name is Anthony Gonzalves.' The apparent nonsensical English words are in fact an almost exact rendering of an insult that has gone down in British history. It was delivered by Benjamin Disraeli to William Gladstone in Parliament in 1878. The British Raj was at its height, yet British politicians were talking gibberish. Suspicions confirmed. Those angrez log are truly bizarre. The message is similar in Prakash Mehra's *Namak Halal* (1982): 'I can talk English, I can walk English, I can laugh English, because English is a funny language.'

A psychoanalyst trying to understand Indian society's conflicting feelings towards those proficient in English need only observe two characters in *Amar Akbar Anthony*. There is Robert (Jeevan), the villain we love to hate, with his thickly English-accented Hindi. Then, in a brief scene near the end of the film, we meet a strange character, Robert's twin brother Albert, a respected banker, we are told, who has worked overseas for ten years and has now returned to Bombay for a World Bank Conference.

He has been kidnapped so that Robert can return to London pretending to be Albert and Albert can be hanged in Robert's place. Given Albert's function, we can suppose his English to be flawless, but unlike Robert, Albert's Hindi is beautiful. He is the model of the successful cosmopolitan figure who seamlessly moves between the wider world and the country of his birth. We are left with contradictory messages, which may echo much of the public sentiment concerning this particular language issue: English is good! No, English is bad! Albert is the 'good' English-speaking Indian and Robert, his mirror image, the bad.

In the 1960s and '70s city populations ballooned as masses of people left their villages behind in a wave dubbed 'the rural exodus'. 'Rural' was the key word at the time with its emphasis on the emptying of villages more than the filling of cities. 'Metro', with its different set of images, had not yet entered the popular vocabulary. Cinema at the time often sided with the bumpkin who arrived in the city feeling lost, not speaking English, not knowing city ways. Such a fellow was gently mocked but ultimately loved in *Don*. Amitabh Bachchan had a dual role, playing both Don, a cool and cruel city sophisticate and also a paan-chewing street performer from Banaras, Vijay. When the police ask for his help, the Banaraswaala learns to impersonate his doppelganger and in the end moves smoothly between worlds and between personas, outsmarting all the bad guys in the process. Popular feelings towards the place of English in society are neatly embedded in such dual character stories. The villager can learn city ways, but at heart he remains a villager. He retains his traditional values of honesty and his sense of duty to family. It could be argued that the *Don* remake by Farhan Akhtar shows us just to what an extent times and values have changed. It is the villainous sophisticate who will win and the poor honest man who will lose. Money and slickness are in; the poor man's honesty seems passé.

English is a marker in the tension between the haves and have-nots in society. Haughtiness from the powerful can be subtle or glaring. Equally interesting is the reverse snobbery of those who find the powerful to be hopelessly helpless. Basanti, in *Sholay*, says, '*Sheher ke rehnewaale ho magar samajhdaar lagte ho.*' (Translation including the intonation: You're city folks, still, you seem smart enough.) In *Roadside Romeo*, the pampered dog Romeo, voiced by Saif Ali Khan, is at a loss when he finds himself booted out of his luxurious home and needing to fend for himself on the streets. Picking his way through the dirty streets, he suddenly sees a drop of water sparkling enticingly in the sun at the end of a street faucet. As he licks happily at the faucet, he begins to feel he can manage after all. Suddenly he hears growling and turns to see the strays who want to know who he thinks he is to try to drink without paying. Romeo's 'Well, you see…actually…' does him a disservice. One of the strays lights into him with the pent-up resentment of one who has felt society's disdain:

> Ahh the Englis medium. *Bajaaun kya kaan ke neeche? Pyaas eh? Pyaas lagi thi?* Thirst was hitting? …*Apun ke permission ke bina yahaan koi paani bhi nahin pi sakta.*
>
> (Ah, English-medium schooling. Get this straight. You're thirsty, are you? Well, no one around here drinks without my permission.)

The tone is harsh, spoken with the assurance of one not intimidated by this clueless outsider's class and education. Romeo, being the star, will of course have to win, which in this case means taking what is, to his mind, his rightful place as leader of the group. One rather wonders how those who were once derisively referred to as 'front-benchers', would react to this re-establishment of class hierarchy if they saw it.

In Rajkumar Hirani's *3 Idiots*, the 'in' group speaks Hindi. The maligned outsider is the apparent know-it-all English speaker Chatur (Omi Vaidya), 'apparent' being the operative word. Unlike Romeo, Chatur will remain the 'uncool' fellow throughout the film. His need for a dictionary to express himself in Hindi—

and the resulting Sanskritized mumble-jumble—leaves his dorm mates doubled with laughter. These are just the beginning of his language problems. Coolly reversing the long-standing convention that shows ease with English to be a status symbol, Raju Hirani's film turns the American-accented Hindi speaker into a boorish—but ultimately endearing—character in the film. This works all the better because actor Omi Vaidya is American-born, and he has worked in Hollywood. Before taking roles in Bollywood, Omi diligently studied Hindi. The klutz in this role, then, is played by an actor who is a smart fellow in real life and who can make his shortfalls in Hindi work to his advantage. As Omi said, following the release of *3 Idiots*, 'The writing and my butchering Hindi made it very funny.'[127]

English is both aspired towards and resented. The rich and powerful take an inordinate amount of space wherever decisions are being made. And yet, the poor have numbers on their side. There is a desire for upward mobility through English. There is also a disdain for the pretentions that English often symbolizes. In Madhur Bhandarkar's *Page 3* (2005) English is seen in different lights depending on the characters using the language…or enduring its presence in their lives. As their bosses' party with the rich and famous inside, the chauffeurs stand outside by their cars snidely analysing the bosses' English code.

> Bosco: *Arre, ye samajh na. Phone-vone ka ye sab setting rehta hai re. Matlab, bole to, kya hai na, suppose apun driving kar rela hai aur peechhe Sahib ko phone aaya. Sahib ne bola,* 'Hello, *haan,* yeah, yeah, yeah. I'm coming in the night. Yeah. Love you. Love you. Bye.' *Samajh jaane ka bivi ka phone hai.*
> Another driver: *Arre, baraabar bolta hai.*
> Bosco: *Abhi samajh transaction ka baat chal raha hai.*
> Another driver: *Transaction bole to?*

---

[127]See interview with Omi Vaidya: http://www.dailymotion.com/video/xbxtcz_omi-vaidya-interview-on-3-idiot_shortfilms

BOSCO: *Arre, yedu, len-den re, matlab, havaala, peti, khokha, business hai re, samajh na yaar? Abhi usse lamba baat chala na, matlab ekdam lamba vaala, matlab,* 'Ya baby, ya baby, ya baby. I love you, baby.' *Samajh jaane ka aaj vaasugiri chaalu hai. Aaj game pakka. Overtime pakka hai. In logon ko kya lagta hai, ki apun ko English nahin aata hai? Arre paagal log hain ye. Ye Bosco chhathvin fail hai, to kya hai? Bosco knows English, samjha na!*

(Bosco: Okay, get this; this is what the phone calls mean. Like, suppose I'm driving and the boss gets a call in the back. The boss answers, 'Hello. Yeah, yeah, yeah. I'm coming in the night. Yeah. Love you, love you. Bye.' You can be sure that's the wife.
Another driver: Right!
Bosco: Now let's say there's some transaction talk going on.
Another driver: Transaction?
Bosco: Havaala, lakhs, crores. Business. Got it, man? Now he's got this really long call going. You can figure there's something shady there. Overtime guaranteed. What do these people think, that we don't know English? Man, they're crazy. Bosco failed the sixth grade. So what? You can bet Bosco knows English!)

In the same film some are more humble and accepting of the fate that befalls those on the 'wrong' side of the English/non-English divide. The provincial journalists from Hindi newspapers wait patiently outside the star's trailer, then beg his secretary to let them in for an interview, '*Ham Kanpur se dubaara aaye hain, please.*' (Please, this is the second time we've come from Kanpur.) The secretary tells them not to worry, offers them tea, while instantly opening the trailer door for two young women from the English press (Konkona Sen Sharma and Tara Sharma). One man complains—mildly—to another, '*Mishraaji, angrezi akhbaar ka asar dekh liya? Aur jab ki hamaara ye Hindi akhbaar circulation mein us se dugna hai? Khair, chai pijiye.*' (Mishraaji, did you see the influence of the English press? Even when our Hindi newspaper has twice their circulation. Oh well, drink your tea.)

Jaideep Sahni, who worked in advertising before moving into films, described a somewhat similar real-life experience in which Hindi writing, at that time, took the back seat to writing in English:

> See, what happened was I joined advertising after doing IT consulting. I was trilingual. I knew Hindi, English and Punjabi, like everyone else walking in Delhi did. So I would do ads in whatever languages they gave to me to do. I would get a lot of awards for the Hindi-language work. I got half that many awards for my English work because there was much more competition. People all wanted to do English because it was supposed to be cooler. What happened is that because I didn't know that Hindi wasn't the cool thing to do, I got lumped into all the small-town ad campaigns, all the rural work, which I was very happy doing because I thought that's what advertising was. A year passed, and the awards came, and I said, 'Hey, there don't seem to be so many claps when I win the awards.' After a little while I just consciously started balancing the Hindi and English campaigns. So then I started getting some awards for my English work too. It's better now, but it can be terrible. Copywriters, the work that they do, the kids imitate. It really affects the mass culture in a very strong way... Hindi and regional-language people are being edged out of this great shining new India... If you don't know English, you don't have any buying power. The economy has no use for you.

Documentary filmmaker Paromita Vohra finds herself in contact with students when she teaches courses in scriptwriting. She criticized the attitudes she has seen prevalent among young people. 'You know, I don't believe it's a question of knowing English well or Hindi well. I believe it's a question of what your relation with language per se is.' She points to two primary culprits in the degradation of language: television, 'because people don't read' and 'the need to speak English as a way of being fashionable, successful. People feel if they can just approximate the language, it's fine. At the same time, they learn not to love their own languages'.

Journalist Mark Tully, a long-time observer of Indian society, suggests that only 2 to 5 per cent of the population is truly proficient in English. The prevailing opinion is that India has profited nicely from the elite's grasp of English. The high-tech boom is in part attributable to Indians' linguistic ease in a globalized world. Tully reminds us, however, of the obvious, that English also increases class divisions:

> The English-medium schools attract the best teachers, the resources to provide modern facilities and the brightest pupils, or I would prefer to say, the pupils with the home backgrounds which give them the best chance of making good use of their natural ability. What's more, because those with the influence to improve education do not send their children to Indian language-medium schools, they take no interest in the education provided there. The result of all this is that the vast majority of schools remain beyond the pale for all those with the means to educate their children… One of the major barriers to Hindi is that of all the major Indian languages it is, as I said before, the one which seems to attract the most scorn from the elite. It's all right to be proud of Bengali, Tamil, or Gujarati, but not, for some strange reason, Hindi. That's perhaps because Hindi is the greatest threat to the elite's beloved English. Supposing the elite were to change their attitude to Hindi, to take a pride in speaking it, what a difference that would make. Any realistic assessor must accept that English can be of

enormous value to India in its right place, but to find that place we have to accept the damage it causes at present. The present status of English in India gives enormous power to the elite, and they have yet to show they are willing to shed that power and share their knowledge with their fellow Indians.[128]

Dialogue- and lyric-writer Ali Husain Mir addressed the issue Tully raises but at a personal level, understanding the point of view of his practical, caring parents:

> My own parents spoke beautiful Urdu, and they knew Urdu literature, but they didn't teach us Urdu. Their personal anxiety was that we would grow up and need to find a job. They realized very early that English was the currency that could be traded in this marketplace. So they spoke to us in English at home. I think people who are coming of age today, their exposure to the vernacular has been very, very limited in urban India among middle classes and upper classes. For the working classes it's different. For people who come from the background I do, Urdu and the local languages come to them as affectations, as phrases. I think that's the way of the world. I don't say this [while] mourning anything. I'm not bemoaning the passing away of a time when people could speak like me. I speak very awkwardly myself, I'm embarrassed to say. But that's the name of the game today. If you don't speak good English, you won't get ahead, not in these circles.

His parents, it seems, were quite right. Several recent studies have pointed to a statistically significant improvement in wages among those with good English skills. English equals power in

---

[128]Tully, Mark, 'English: an advantage to India?' an edited version of the Oxford University Press/BBC Lecture given at the English-Speaking Union, London, and broadcast on the BBC World Service in February 1996, pp. 5, 7.

the monetary sense. One calculation:

> Does it pay to speak English? This column presents evidence from India that being fluent in English increases the hourly wages of men by 34% and of women by 22%. But the effects vary. Returns are higher for older and more educated workers and lower for less educated, younger workers, suggesting that English is becoming a complement to education.[129]

The divide between English and bhaasha[130] within the literary world can be nasty. It was palpable at the Paris Book Festival, dedicated in 2007 to India. While English-language writers garnered the spotlight, bhaasha writers found themselves assigned to smaller spaces where they were given markedly less attention. In the bhaasha–English debate, the Hindi film industry finds itself in a strange position. On the one hand, Hindi cinema has been one of the major forces for spreading and popularizing Hindi-Urdu beyond its regional home. Jawaharlal Nehru, in 1963, already recognized the linguistic power of films. 'If I may say so, all the steps that my Hon. Friend the Education Minister may take in regard to the spread of Hindi do not go as far as the influence that cinema has had on the spread of Hindi,'[131] he said. On the other hand, young actors, directors and writers tend to be more comfortable in English than in Hindi, the language upon which, in fact, their bread and butter depends, the language which connects them to huge numbers of non-English speakers who themselves may resent or envy the power of English. And yet, in spite of this, the stars, in a complex linguistic game of mirrors, regularly

---

[129] Azam, Mehtabul; Chin, Aimee; and Prakash, Nishith, 'English skills raise wages for some, not all, in India', 26 May 2010. Available at http://www.voxeu.org/index.php?q=node/509

[130] 'Bhaasha', increasingly used to indicate any Indian language other than English, has largely replaced the troubling term 'vernacular'. For reference: http://www.oxforddictionaries.com/definition/english/bhasha

[131] Quoted by King, *One Language, Two Scripts*, 1997, p. 222.

lend further prestige to English by giving interviews in flawless English while they must rely on generous doses of English to complete their interviews in Hindi. Jaideep Sahni summed up the potential problem from a film-writing perspective, 'In a very strange way, the people who are smart enough to understand what screenwriting is, and to finally break into this world, have become too smart and too English to be able to communicate to the people for whom they're making movies.'

SQUIGGLES

Learning to speak, like learning to walk, is something we humans have been doing for at least tens of thousands of years. We are born, we grow and we communicate with those around us. Writing, on the other hand, only dates back to around 3200 BC, and while it is a most convenient invention, in the stretch of human history it is very new and requires a conscious effort to learn. If spoken languages often have magical or religious dimensions, written scripts, over the centuries, have been invested with even more wonder and awe.

Javed Akhtar read out the following poem, unpublished at the time, during an interview in February 2007:

Kisi bhi jazbe, kisi khyaal aur kisi bhi shai ko
pehle pehel aavaaz mili thi
ya uski tasveer bani thi?
Soch raha hoon.
(Did an emotion, thought or object meet with sound first,
or was it that its picture was made?
I wonder.)

Koi bhi aavaaz lakeeron mein jo dhali to kaise dhali thi?
Soch raha hoon.
(How did any sound ever flow into lines?
I wonder.)

Seedhi lakeer mein alif ki jo aavaaz bhari
to kisne bhari thi?

Kyon ye sabne maan liya tha?
(Who filled the straight line of alif with sound?
Why did everyone accept this?)

Saamne meri mez pe jo ek phal rakha hai
isko seb hi kyon kehte hain?
Seb to ek aavaaz hai.
Is aavaaz ka jo is phal se anokha rishta bana hai
kaise bana tha?
(Why do they call the fruit in front of me on the table an apple?
Seb [apple] is just a sound.
How did this extraordinary relationship between sound and fruit come to be?)

Aur ye tedhi medhi lakeerein jinko harf kaha jaata hai
ye aavaazon ki tasveerein kaise bani thi?
Aavaazein tasveer bani
ya tasveerein aavaaz bani thi
soch raha hoon.
(And these crooked lines we call letters
How were pictures of these sounds made?
Were sounds made into pictures or were pictures made into sounds?
I wonder.)

Saari cheezein saare jazbe saare khayaal aur unka ta'aroof
unki khabar unke saare paighaam ko dene par fa'az saari aavaazein
in aavaazon ko apne ghar mein thahraati
apni amaan mein rakhti tedhi-medhi lakeerein
kisne ye kunba joda hai?
Soch raha hoon.
(All objects, all emotions, all thoughts and their knowledge of one another

all the sounds that are able to convey information about their messages
settling these sounds in their homes,
placing these crooked lines in their protective shelter,
who brought this family together?
I wonder.)[132]

Javed Akhtar, after reading his poem, reflected further:

> Who has put these sounds with these straight lines? And why was it accepted that one straight line will be 'aa'? Why did everybody say, 'Okay, it's fine'? And why seb [apple]? How was it decided that this particular fruit will be called this? ...Drawn lines, the object and the sound, three things which have nothing to do with each other except that they have been put together for our convenience: it is *we* who decided that these sounds are what they are. It is a totally man-made artificial relationship.

Linguists, too, grapple as they study the development of language and writing. Because no one is capable of going back to the very beginning and entering the minds of the innovators who came up with language and much later with written symbols, both the scientist and the poet are confounded. Jill Bolte Taylor is a neuroanatomist who had a rare stroke that separated the two hemispheres of her brain. In her book, *My Stroke of Insight* (2008), she describes her experience both of the stroke as it unfolded and of the subsequent healing. Her account of the process of relearning to read shows a wonder much like that of Javed Akhtar's.

> Reading was such an abstract idea that I couldn't believe anyone had ever thought of it, much less put forth the

---

[132] A special thanks to Kusum Choudhary, Dr Akbar Hyder and Peter Knapczyk for help with the translation.

effort to figure out how to do it... Together we (Jill and her mother) embarked upon the most arduous task I could imagine: teaching me to make sense of the written word. It befuddled me that she could think these squiggles were significant. I remember her showing me an 'S' and saying, 'This is an "S,"' and I would say, 'No Mama, that's a squiggle.' And she would say, 'This squiggle is an "S" and it sounds like "SSSSS".' I thought the woman had lost her mind. A squiggle was just a squiggle and it made no sound... I had to understand that every squiggle had a name, and that every squiggle an associated sound... When we string all of those combinations of sounds together, they make a single sound [word] that has a meaning attached to it![133]

French cognitive neuroscientist Stanislas Dehaene, speaking on the BBC, described the two different brain pathways we use when we read, one to recover pronunciation and another to recover meaning. With brain-imaging experiments, researchers can see that writing involves a feat of amazing complexity in which our eyes decode forms, finally allowing for a bridge between vision and a language system.[134] The scientist studies the process with amazement. The poet reacts in amazement.

Hindi, English, Urdu, Roman Hindi-Urdu

Three scripts and three or four languages, depending on how one counts Hindi-Urdu, have all been variously present whenever the spoken language needed to be pinned down in writing. After we have mastered reading and writing early in our schooling, we cease to be aware of the brainpower we are exerting to translate pixels into sound and meaning in even one script. Dealing with multiple scripts, at least when one is not fully proficient, is a

---

[133] Bolte Taylor, 2006, p. 101.
[134] BBC World Service, *The Forum*, 29 Aug 2010.

physically and mentally tiring task…and yet absolutely essential to assure one that different parts of Indian society can communicate in writing. It is perhaps surprising, then, that transcribers who can move between scripts have received so little credit over the years. Film producer Ketan Desai grew up on movie sets watching his father Manmohan Desai directing films from the 1960s to the 1980s. The job of assistant directors, as Ketan recalls, was more complex at that time. 'Back then, a director or an assistant director had to be very alert because on the set one scene was given in Urdu, the other scene in Hindi. And there were many artistes who couldn't read the Hindi script,' he said.

For actor Tom Alter, who entered Hindi cinema in the 1970s and who uses Mahatma Gandhi's term 'Hindustani' for the language, those were the days when Urdu reigned in the film world.

> If you take my generation and a little bit older than me, those who came from the north, as most did, grew up with the Urdu script. The great ones like Manoj Kumar, Sunil Dutt, Pran, anyone from that generation, they didn't even know the Devanagari script. And they're not Muslims. They're North Indian Punjabis, and their education was in the Urdu script.

This historical reality plays out in a small poignant scene from *Life in a Metro*, directed by Anurag Basu. The seventy-year-old Amol (Dharmendra) has returned to India, after forty years away, to reconnect with his first love Shivani (Nafisa Ali) before it is too late, before illness and death inevitably separate them again. In one scene the ailing Shivani is lying in bed. We watch Amol reading aloud to her from his diary, which is clearly written in Urdu. It is a warm and loving act, and yet his reading aloud is also a practical solution to a not-uncommon problem, that is, that while the two of them share a spoken language, they do not, because of their different educational backgrounds, share a common script. Even if Shivani were feeling well, she would be unable to read Amol's memories, kept as they were all these years in Urdu.

The place that the Urdu script once had on the sets is now occupied by the Roman script. Shabana Azmi noted:

> Salim-Javed were some of the rare people who used to give you a bound script way back in 1974. So their standard was that they would write all the instructions in English. And then Javed used to write the dialogue in Urdu. Then he had an assistant who would put it in Hindi. And now that process has changed so that Javed writes in Urdu, and it has to be transcribed into Roman.

Amitabh Bachchan is one of many actors who find it difficult to deal with Roman Hindi. Speaking on the BBC Hindi Service, he scolded:

> जब मुझे अपने डायलॉग रोमन लिपि में लिखे मिलते हैं, मुझे उससे बहुत परेशानी होती है। मैं मानता हूँ कि अगर आप किसी भाषा के कार्यक्रम या फ़िल्म से जुड़े है, तो उस भाषा को बोलने और लिखने में सही इस्तेमाल होना चाहिए।

> (It really bothers me when I find my dialogue is written in Roman script. I believe that if you are involved in a programme or film in any language, then you should be able to use the written and spoken language well.)

Screenplays, film titles and credits, and the brochures that have traditionally accompanied film reels as they move from theatre to theatre, could involve any combination of languages and scripts. Though rarer today, often in the past these were written in all three languages and in three different scripts, Hindi, Urdu and English. The brochure for Muzaffar Ali's *Umrao Jaan*, for example, included images from the film, the credits and a summary of the story in three versions, each on a separate page of the foldout.

Many cultures in the world are multilingual without being multi-script. India has the distinction of being both. The film *Saat Hindustani* (1969), written and directed by K.A. Abbas, calls attention to regional, linguistic and script divisions in various parts of India at the time of Goan independence from Portugal in the early 1960s. Seven characters refuse to see beyond their own grievances to the greater good of the nation. The Tamilian (played by Irshad Ali) speaks Hindi but becomes incensed at cries of 'Hindi down!' coming from his radio. In a rage he throws his book in Hindi and his nameplate in Devanagari script into a fire that has been started in the street outside his house. The camera lingers on the name. It covers over half the screen: महादेवन (Mahadevan). We can imagine the man having once proudly placed the plaque on his door. Now it is going up in flames.

In the same film Amitabh Bachchan plays an Urdu proponent who cannot read the letter written in Devanagari from his young son away studying in Mussoorie. He asks a friend for help, '*Haan, to kya likhte hain Mehmood miyaan?*' (What has Mehmood written?) When the son's letter begins with the formal Sanskrit-derived '*Pitaaji pranaam*', the Amitabh character strongly objects. He has sent his son to convent school to learn English, not shuddh Hindi!

In her book *Yaad ki Rahguzar* (2007) Shaukat Kaifi shares a letter from her husband, poet Kaifi Azmi, after he has received a letter in Devanagari from his daughter Shabana, then a child. Kaifi Azmi's reaction is not the anger that the Amitabh Bachchan character exhibits in *Saat Hindustani*. Kaifi Azmi is accepting, though we wonder if he is a bit sad.

Shaukat meri jaan…abhi abhi meri laadli beti ka khat mila hai. Vo Hindi mein hai. Isliye padh nahin saka hoon. Riyaasat ko bulvaaya hai. Unhin se padhvaaunga.
(Shaukat my love/my life…I've just received a letter from

my beloved daughter. It's in Hindi, so I haven't been able to read it. I've called for Riyaasat. I'll have him read it.)

One can imagine this sort of scene taking place hundreds of thousands of times over in a country in which different generations may not share the same script. The situation could be wrenching. Yet Kaifi Azmi speaks matter-of-factly. It's a problem for which there is a solution, in this case, Riyaasat, who knows the Devanagari script. How is it though, one might ask, that Shabana Azmi did not learn the Urdu script as a child? She explained:

> You know, I asked my parents, 'Why didn't you teach me the language?' And they said, 'There were so many pressures on you. You had to learn English; you had to learn French; you had to learn Marathi; you had to learn Hindi, and we said, one more, Urdu, you speak at home, so you understand the words and all of that. You just don't know the script.'

Since being surrounded by various scripts in daily life is so commonplace and because code-switching is the norm in many parts of society, Jaideep Sahni's idea for a new form of writing seems novel but not startling. He said:

> Sometimes I wonder about writing in a mixture of Hindi and English, each sentence, on the fly, in the language and the script that I have the thought in. But I'm not sure how taxing it would be on a reader, even if it's very comfortable when you're a listener. Also, there is the matter of converting perfectly decent Hindi or English into a kind of Indian Creole. I don't know if this would be good or bad in the overall scheme of things in the world!

Though it may be a matter of long-established convention within the Hindi film world, it is objectively strange to begin the Hindi film-viewing experience with a title in Roman Hindi, sometimes but not always followed by the Hindi and Urdu title, and then to read the rest of the credits entirely in English. Ketan Desai quoted veteran filmmaker B.R. Chopra who once complained, 'We make our films in Hindi, but our titles on screen are in English. Even when we write "The End," it's English. You're not making an English movie. Why don't you write the titles in Hindi?' The early classic *Do Bigha Zamin* (1953) followed the conventions of the time.

The Do Bigha Zamin *title in Roman script. (Sketch by Simon P. Holzman)*

An interesting exception to this mode of working is to be found in Bimal Roy's 1955 version of *Devdas*. The title and credits are in Devanagari. They open as pages of a book. The irony, of course, is that the book upon which the movie is based was in Bengali, not in Hindi. And producer-director Bimal Roy, like the author of the novel, Sharat Chandra Chattopadhyay, was Bengali, which supposes another language *and* another script.

Within films the written word is most often seen in signs, posters or graffiti on walls. It adds to the sense of place but is not essential to the plot. At times, however, a film character will read aloud something clearly written in Hindi. In Manmohan Desai's classic *Amar Akbar Anthony*, for example, we see Kishanlal (Pran) reading a letter from his wife Bharti (Nirupa Roy), whose face is superimposed over the crumpled page. Along with Kishanlal, we feel his wife's presence as we hear her voice. The audience, it is assumed, may need help with the reading, either because of literacy issues or simply because many are comfortable in a script other than Devanagari.

Devanagari, a highly phonetic script, is considered by many the most convenient in which to read both Hindi and Urdu. Actor and producer Elahé Hiptoola can quote Ghalib beautifully, but writing Nastaliq is a different matter.

> I strangely enough would prefer Devanagari because then there is no confusion of how the word should be pronounced... But communication becomes so much easier in Roman, in terms of email, in sending it out to a whole bunch of people, who either need to sift it or make copies of it.

Hiptoola learned the limits of her own written Urdu during the making of *Dor*. Pakistani singer Shafqat Amanat Ali Khan was brought in for the song 'Yeh Hausla' written by Ali Husain Mir. Hiptoola recounted:

> Husain had actually written it down in Urdu, scanned it and sent it to me. Shafqat came to sing, and then Nagesh (Kukunoor) was on the phone with Husain at 2 a.m. New York time, saying, 'Okay, I need two more lines because I'm making a sad version [of] the song.' Husain said okay and sent them (in Roman). But I didn't have those lines in the Urdu script, so I tried to do it. Shafqat ended up saying, 'You dictate; I'll write.' Terrible. It's not the handwriting. It's the little zabar there. To me it looks fine. And the word shama: it was the letter ain versus alif, right? I put sheen, meem and alif. And he was like, '*Yahaan pe ain hota hai.*'

(Here you need the letter 'ain'.) And I was like, '*Ain hota hai ya alif hota hai, kisko maaloom* hai?!' (Alif or ain, who knows the difference?!)

Bimal Roy's Devdas. *(Sketch by Simon P. Holzman)*

Columbia University's Dr Frances Pritchett continues to expand her website,[135] an immense work of love as well as an invaluable source of information for anyone curious about South Asia in general and Urdu in particular. Available at the site is an interview with Urdu writer, screenwriter and member of the Progressive Writers' Movement, Ismat Chughtai, for the publication *Mahfil* from 1972. Asked about the future of Urdu in India, Ismat Chughtai answered:

> Urdu will remain the tongue in people's mouths. People will go on speaking this language. But the Urdu script will

---

[135] http://www.columbia.edu/itc/mealac/pritchett/00fwp/

> die because our children are not learning it... My daughter refuses to study it. She says it's a rotten script. 'How can I remember the letters? All the lines are lying down with only dots around them.' The only difference is dots. I think the Hindi script is the best.[136]

Rohan Sippy would agree. He studied Urdu poetry for a time but gave it up partly because of the script. Between the Devanagari and Roman scripts he unhesitatingly chooses Devanagari. The production schedule for his *Bluffmaster!* was unexpectedly rushed, complicating the process of having the film script available in multiple formats.

> Our production schedule got advanced by about six or seven months. In April or May Abhishek (Bachchan) called me and said, 'Oh, one of my films got shifted by four months, so do you want to make your film?' So in six weeks everything had to come together. And one of the huge elements was getting that dialogue script done. Devanagari dialogue was made available to the actors who wanted it. If I remember correctly, Boman (Irani) is not comfortable reading Devanagari, so his would be in the Roman script. I'm pretty sure he reads it more freely. I myself have a pretty difficult time reading the Roman Hindi.

Experts have found that each of us tends to favour one of three sensory learning styles: visual, auditory, or kinaesthetic, known particularly among proponents of neurolinguistic programming as VAK. Some students complain that if they can't *see* it, they can't remember it, others that they must *hear* it, others still, that if they must *move* to *incorporate* the material they are trying to learn. Experienced actors, who must memorize many, many words throughout their careers, no doubt discover their

---

[136]http://www.columbia.edu/itc/mealac/pritchett/00urdu/ismat/txt_ismat_interview_mahfil1972.html, pp. 175-176.

preferred means of learning early on. For those actors who are strongly visual, script, whether Urdu, Devanagari or Roman Hindi, then, becomes a core issue that affects their ability to function at their best. Actress Shabana Azmi's answer to the VAK question was quick and categorical: she learns her lines by visualizing the written words, and those she visualizes in Devanagari.

Generally, transliterating Roman Hindi into Devanagari is a job left to a transcriber. Jaideep Sahni follows the long-established tradition in Hindi cinema of writing screen instructions in English. He types the dialogue, however, in Devanagari. It was while working on his first film, *Jungle*, that he learned the importance of using the Devanagari script, including for on-the-spot, last-minute changes. Having begun his working life as a computer programmer, Sahni naturally brought his laptop to the film sets. When he presented leading actress Urmila Matondkar her dialogues in the Roman script, she complained that she couldn't *taste* the words. Sahni quoted the actress, 'You know, I spend so much time trying to get it that I don't get it. I can figure it out, but I kind of have to see it in Hindi in my head.' Then Sahni told her, 'That's not your job. That's my job. I'll do it in Hindi.'

For Kaifi Azmi and Shaukat Kaifi, as for Javed Akhtar, the script of choice has been Urdu. For Shabana Azmi it is Devanagari. For Farhan and Zoya Akhtar it is Roman Hindi. Generation and educational background are the central factors in these differences. Politics, too, has played its role. Roman Hindi could have supplanted both Devanagari and Nastaliq long before Indian independence. The manifesto of the Progressive Writers' Association of 1935 included a list of goals, one of which was:

> To strive for the acceptance of a common language (Hindustani) and a common script (Indo-Roman) for India.
> To protect the interests of authors; to help authors who

require and deserve assistance for the publication of their works. To fight for the right of free expression of thought and opinion.[137]

With the Internet constantly gaining ground as a space for exchanging ideas, Roman Hindi–Urdu is becoming ever more common. Rules, actually multiple forms of rules, for its transcription exist within academia but are rarely followed beyond that somewhat rarified environment. Ideally, one should be able to re-transcribe a text in Roman script back into Hindi or Urdu. Only quite complex transcriptions, however, would allow for the distinctions between, say, the two 'sh' sounds: श and ष, or, in Urdu, the four ways of spelling a 'z' sound: ز, ظ, ض and ذ. Ignoring this and other details, it would be easy enough to make that most important of distinctions: अ (a) versus आ (aa). For example पार (paar) can be translated as 'the other side'. पर (par) is 'but'. Actor Tom Alter was emphatic, 'There's a very definite set of rules for Roman Hindi, which people don't follow. Like, you take the word निशान (nishaan) [it] needs double "a". It's very simple.'

Spelling Roman Hindi–Urdu with some coherence is the minimum Tom Alter would demand. However, ideally, he would like the bar set higher, 'I think the real solution is for people to learn all three scripts. I learned all three, and I don't think I'm exceptional. I can write in Hindi or English or Urdu. It requires a little bit of work. It requires a passion to learn these things, but it's no big deal.'

Passion, yes, and no doubt deep motivation. Being surrounded by multiple scripts adds piquancy to everyday life, not unlike the zest that brightly coloured fabrics give to an Indian cityscape. Were shops for 'selling' knowledge of written scripts as commonplace as fabric shops, who could resist the temptation to buy?

---

[137]Mir, Ali Husain and Mir, Raza, 2006. p. 6.

BRIDGES

In Yash Chopra's *Deewaar*, we see the young Vijay and Ravi along with their mother, victims of injustice, finding shelter under a bridge in Bombay. As adults the brothers are separated, on the opposite sides of the law, Vijay (Amitabah Bachchan) a smuggler and Ravi (Shashi Kapoor) a policeman. In a powerful scene Ravi confronts Vijay:

> यह सच्चाई नहीं बदल सकती है कि तुम भी एक मुजरिम हो, और यह सच्चाई तुम्हारे और मेरे बीच एक दीवार है, भाई, और जब तक यह दीवार है हम एक छत के नीचे नहीं रह सकते हैं। मैं यह घर छोड़कर जा रहा हूँ अभी, इसी वक़्त। चलो माँ।

> (This truth cannot change. You too are a criminal, and this truth is a wall between us, brother. And as long as this wall exists, we cannot live under one roof. I'm leaving. Now. This very minute. Let's go, Ma.)

Later, Vijay asks Ravi to meet him under the same bridge that was their childhood home.

> हम एक दूसरे से कितने भी अलग हो जाए हमारा बचपन ही एक दूसरे से कभी अलग नही हो सकता है। आज हम दोनों के बीच के सारे पुल टूट चुके हैं। तो बस यह एक पुल बचा था। यह पुल जिसके नीचे हमने अपना बचपन गुज़ारा।

> (However far apart we are now, our childhood together can never be sundered. Today, when all other bridges between us are broken, this one bridge remains. This bridge, the one we spent our childhood beneath).

The situation is dramatic, as are the words, even in their simplicity. There is a bridge that unites and a wall that separates. The wall between the two brothers finally—and tragically—proves higher than the bridge. It is a tale that resonates far beyond one family's story. We all seek bridges, connections beyond ourselves, however fleeting. 'I see what you mean.' 'I hear you.' '*Samajh gaya.*' '*Tum theek kehte ho.*' '*Haan!*' There are moments in which we feel we understand, but delving usually brings surprises and often disappointments. Conversation can bring pleasure; it can also bring misunderstandings. Language is sometimes a bridge, sometimes a wall. Attempting to negotiate the world via foreign languages can make the walls seem higher still. Among immigrant families, the children own the new language, and as its interpreters, often find themselves saddled with responsibility beyond their years. The 2004 film *Spanglish*, directed by James L. Brooks, plays this reality to comic effect; a pre-teen girl must translate her mother's rage from Spanish into English at the breakneck speed of a UN professional.

A true mastery of more than one language is surely the most effective bridge between languages. In the fall of 2010 Shabana Azmi was touring the US, appearing in the play *Broken Images*. In Austin, during an afternoon Q&A at The University of Texas, she shared a story of one of her performances. *Broken Images*, written by Girish Karnad in English, had only two characters, two sisters, both played by Shabana Azmi. One was a pre-recorded image on television, the other the live actor. In one city on the tour, an audience of 1,800 was waiting when the organizer approached her. Shabana recounted:

> He said, 'Ma'am, only 20 per cent of the audience understands English.' So I said, 'Isn't it rather late in the day to be telling me that?' And so he moves on and says, 'Could you do something in Hindi?' And I'm thinking he knows absolutely nothing about theatre. And then I actually went on stage and did the entire play in Hindi, translating

on my feet! When I think about it, I start having a heart attack! The point is about us being bilingual, actually having the audacity to do something like that. I was there on stage. The character in the television was speaking English, and I, in response to her, was speaking Hindi. Afterwards, Girish said, 'Don't do it too often.'

Would that we could all meet that high standard of fluency in more than one language, we would nevertheless eventually need help communicating with speakers in any of the other 6,000-odd languages in the world. Interpreting, that is, oral translation, probably dates back to the earliest interactions between groups of people speaking different languages. After the invention of writing, translation slowly came into its own. At times, interpreters and translators have been especially valued by societies who have encouraged their art, as for example, in Baghdad in the eighth and ninth centuries or in twelfth-century southern Spain. At other times, communication across language barriers has been at best approximate. Movies, often globalized products, required a new form of translation. The first talkie, Warner Brothers' *The Jazz Singer* (1927), opened in Paris with French subtitles in 1929. In some countries, subtitling foreign language films became the norm. In others dubbing was preferred, often originally for clearly political reasons, as in Franco's Spain, where, particularly during World War II, linguistic nationalism was furthered by decrees, which made dubbing obligatory.[138] In many cases, whether to subtitle or whether to dub was a decision distributors made as they measured their profits against the number of potential viewers. Subtitling was likely to be favoured if the numbers of speakers of a language was small and literacy rates were high.

According to Jan Ivarsson in 'A Short Technical History of

---

[138] Szarkowska, Agnieszka, 'The Power of Film Translation', http://translationjournal.net/journal/32film.htm

Subtitles in Europe,'[139] subtitling costs between a tenth and a twentieth of dubbing. Whether a movie is dubbed or subtitled, a good job is a subtle joy while clunky work can leave audiences lost, annoyed or laughing at tragedy while puzzling over comic scenes. A case in point of the latter could be found in Hindi films circulating in the 1970s and '80s in North and West Africa, parts of the Middle East and to some extent in Europe. If they were subtitled at all, the work was usually done at a centre in Cairo that churned out barely comprehensible French and Arabic subtitles, with dialogue from one language placed above the other, eating up space on the screen. Surprisingly, over thirty years later and despite time-saving technology, similarly sloppy subtitling is seen on Hindi film DVDs today. Some producers or directors care more than others and are ready to invest more time and money in good subtitling. Rohan Sippy had Rohena Gera do the subtitles for *Bluffmaster!* He said, 'She's a good writer, which is why I asked her. She did a good job in at least capturing something, unlike the kind of guys that the distributors normally use.' More unusually, writer-director Kiran Rao is credited for doing her own English subtitling for *Dhobi Ghat*, first shown internationally at festivals in Berlin and Toronto, under the name *Mumbai Diaries*.

Devoting Time and Care to Subtitling

David Sedaris, in *Me Talk Pretty One Day* (2000), has a chapter entitled 'City of Light in the Dark'. In it he recalls his Parisian moviegoing experiences. He would see six or seven American films a week, partly because his French was too limited to make French films fun and partly because Paris offered such a wonderful selection of American classics. His reaction to the subtitling though was, 'Someone might say, "Get your fat ass out of here before I do

---

[139](http://www.transedit.se/history.htm)

something I regret," and the screen will read simply, "Leave."[140]

Now David Sedaris is no doubt exaggerating for comic effect. Still, anyone who has spent time watching subtitled films has often wondered about the nuances that go missing when a long spoken sentence must be condensed into a few written words. In an article for *TIME Europe* Grant Rosenberg explained the technical constraints of the subtitling business as he observed them at LVT Laser Subtitling, located just outside Paris, where the current high-tech process for subtitling was pioneered in 1988:

> At LVT and other companies, a person watches the film scene by scene, doing what's known as spotting—marking time according to the timecode, the film's official clock—the start and end point of each spoken line of dialogue. Then the subtitler goes to work, balancing the challenge of conveying meaning accurately within the confines of space and the roughly 1.5-second-long display allotted per subtitle. The reality is that despite the reputation of subtitling over dubbing as a form of cultural purity, the eye reads slower than the ear hears, meaning that more than a third of a film's dialogue is sacrificed for what is most essential. The general rule is no more than 45 characters per line.[141]

Nasreen Munni Kabir has been subtitling films, particularly for Channel 4 in the UK, for over twenty-five years. She described the essence of her work:

> Subtitling is like translation in telegrams... I think the best subtitling is when you are kind of invisible and you allow the person direct connection with the screen and performance, because subtitling isn't performance. It is the interpretation or translation of performance.

---

[140] Sedaris, *Me Talk Pretty One Day*, p. 207.
[141] Rosenberg, Grant, 'Rethinking the Art of Subtitles,' *TIME Europe*, 15 May 2007.

She stressed the importance of maintaining cultural specificity within subtitles without confusing the audience. The trick is to be neither too literal nor too far away from the original. She gave an example from the classic *Sholay* in which the villain, Gabbar Singh (Amjad Khan), prepares to shoot three of his underlings who have angered him. One, trembling, dares to speak, '*Sardaar, main ne aapka namak khaaya hai*,' and Gabbar Singh answers, '*Ab goli kha.*' Nasreen said, 'Now in English you might find another way of expressing it, but with "Sir, I've eaten your salt" and Gabbar's "Now eat my bullet," you've got it. There is a poetic weight and balance in the sentence.'

'*Now eat my bullet*': Amjad Khan as Gabbar Singh in Sholay.
(Sketch by Simon P. Holzman)

The term 'maamu' from Rajkumar Hirani's *Munna Bhai M.B.B.S.* (2003) is another example Kabir gave of a culturally laden word that challenges the subtitler. The word is literally 'maternal uncle', but it carries various other meanings as well. Films full of Bambaiya-Mumbaiya pose particular problems. 'There is no equivalent of "maamu" in English,' she said. '*Munna Bhai* was very tough; *Rangeela* was very tough.'[142]

Taking off-colour interjections (or colourful, depending on your viewpoint) from one cultural context to another can be difficult. Kabir subtitled Rakeysh Omprakash Mehra's *Rang De Basanti* (2006) in which the Aamir Khan character reacts to any annoyance with the Punjabi expression 'pen de takke'. What to do with such an idiom? Nasreen described the give-and-take with the director that can be part of the subtitling process: 'I asked Rakeysh, and he wanted it to be "my grandfather's hairy testicles". So I said, "It's not going to work. Let's go with Grandpa's hairy balls, and it will work fine." He said, "Keep testicles," so our compromise was "Grandpa's hairy testicles."'

Most subtitlers of Hindi films go unnamed and unacknowledged. This is not the case for Kabir whose name is listed in the credits of the films she has worked on. I realized, however, at some point that my eyes were having trouble picking up 'Subtitles' in the long roll of the closing credits. Then it dawned on me: I've spent years in French movie theatres. And as David Sedaris noted enthusiastically, the Paris movie scene is chock-full of 'original version', i.e. subtitled, films. Now for Parisian movie buffs, only the subtitled version will do. What's more, a good movie buff will sit through the final shot of the final reel before rising to leave, and that is where the subtitler's name is listed, alone and in large print, which means that subtitlers' names carry weight and tend to be recognized. They are sometimes noted and praised for their skill. At other times, alas, they are open to blame, particularly when, horror of horrors, they have made even one mistake in spelling French!

---

[142]The translation for maamu, in the end, became either 'dude', when used in a cool way, or 'doofus', American slang for 'dimwit', when addressing the harsh patriarchal Boman Irani character.

The Dialogue Coach Coming into His Own

In the credits for *Rang De Basanti* I saw a job description I hadn't noticed before in Bollywood: dialogue coach. Intrigued, I wanted to interview Prakash Bharadwaj,, whose name was listed opposite the title, and learn more about what had brought him into this profession. In 2007 he met with me and was good enough to share a bit of his story. It was, he explained, while he was watching Hrishikesh Mukherjee's *Chupke Chupke* (1975) that he first noticed a credit going to 'dialogue director'. The job title struck the fancy of the young man from Gurgaon, near Delhi, who had a knack for accents and a love of cinema. His own move into dialogue coaching was not immediate, though. After leaving school, Bharadwaj studied some theatre acting in Delhi, then shifted to Mumbai where, after four hard years, he got a TV serial. In the same period he also wrote and directed a play. Soon he found his niche in the much-in-demand area of teaching language skills to actors. Bharadwaj explained that it was thanks to one of his former students that director Rakeysh Omprakash Mehra contacted him to work with the British actor who was needed for *Rang De Basanti*. In the story, young documentary filmmaker Sue McKinley finds the diary her grandfather kept, during his time as an officer of the British Raj in charge of a jail holding five freedom fighters, including Bhagat Singh. Profoundly moved by the stories in the diary, Sue scripts a film that she will shoot in India with modern-day young people playing the roles of revolutionaries from the 1920s. In preparation for the trip, Sue studies Hindi at night school. This meant that the actor who would play Sue needed to appear to speak Hindi. Alice Patten was one of two British actors called in for an audition, and Bharadwaj was given the job of preparing her to perform two or three scenes in Hindi as though she understood what she was saying. Bharadwaj, however, protested to the director:

I said, 'Mr Mehra, it's not right, because Hindi is just a foreign language for her. Just give her one scene to learn in two hours.' And he said, 'No, she needs to work hard. Please train her for two or three scenes.' So I met Alice and told her not to worry, that if she worked hard, she could do it. We worked four or five hours. Then in the evening she had an audition for the film. I saw that in one scene, while she was sitting on a chair, the mood and the flow were not right. I said, 'Alice, just get up and do your lines again as we did in the hotel room.' Then she stood up and said her lines, and she was amazing. And Mr Mehra was looking at me as though to say, 'What a job you have done!'

Getting the part was the first step for Alice Patten. The hard work continued. The young actor had a good background in theatre, but learning her lines in Hindi was a huge job. For two months before the shooting, the cast members did all-day workshops at Mehboob Studios in Bandra. Bharadwaj then worked for another four to five hours a day with Patten at her hotel, helping her with pronunciation, intonation, the meaning of the words and the emotions they conveyed. There were no grammar books, just two versions of the film script, one in English, one in Roman Hindi. The long hours paid off. Bharadwaj recounted:

> After two months Alice had learned all her lines. Then sometimes at the last moment, when there were changes in some lines, she was confused and would ask, 'Prakash, what is that?' Because when you don't know Hindi, you don't know how to react. It was amazing work.

Training a non-Hindi speaker like Patten to have a major role in a Hindi film is not an everyday sort of job. A more common challenge is to help improve the delivery of the many already in the film industry who can manage in Hindi but not necessarily well enough. It's common to hear Bollywood reporters mention in passing that such-and-such a performer is taking Hindi lessons.

The singer Shaan, who won the IIFA Best Male Playback award for 2010 for the song '*Behti Hava Sa Tha Voh*' from *3 Idiots*, admitted on BBC Hindi Service's film programme *70 MM*:

> मेरी हिंदी बहुत बुरी थी। बहुत सालों से मैं सोचता था कि मुझसे हिंदी में बोलना नहीं होगा। मैं टिपिकल वो बांद्रा का लड़का हूँ। मैं इंगलिश में बोल सकता हूँ या फिर टूटी-फूटी हिंदी, बंगाली कर लूँगा लेकिन पॉपर, स्पष्ट तरह की हिंदी मुझसे बोलना नहीं होगा।

> (My Hindi was very bad. For many years I thought I wouldn't be able to speak Hindi. I'm a typical Bandra boy. I could speak English or else broken Hindi-Bengali, but I wouldn't be able to speak clean and proper Hindi.)

Shaan finally found that there was no way around his need for the language, so he did study. We don't know how, when, where, with whom or for how long. BBC *70 MM* host Deepti Karki summed up the issue with advice directed to Shaan and to many others, '*Bhaai, agar Bollywood mein survive karna hai to Hindi bolna to seekhna padega*' (Man, if you want to survive in Bollywood, you've got to learn Hindi). Her ironical-sounding use of the Hinglish 'survive karna' may or may not have been intentional.

Prakash Bharadwaj is familiar with the problem of 'tooti-phooti Hindi'. He observed, 'A lot of people say, "We know about acting; we are just a little poor in language."' What in Bharadwaj's background best prepared him for language coaching? Having studied in Hindi-medium schools helped, but as Bharadwaj explained, he also inherited his father's gift for the spoken word. He demonstrated a Delhi Hindi accent for me, then a Haryanvi and a Bambaiya one; he spoke a bit of Punjabi, recited and explained a saying in Sanskrit and also emphasized his appreciation for Urdu literature. In Hollywood the dialogue coach would, for example, help a New Yorker convincingly play the role of a character from Louisiana. Bharadwaj has done some similar work. He helped Aamir Khan with his Punjabi accent for *Rang De Basanti*. More commonplace would be the one-off problem of clarifying the difference for an actor between the pronunciation, for instance, of the name 'Akbar' and 'akhbaar', meaning newspaper. This sort of work has always existed on movie sets, Bharadwaj believes. Typically in the past, rather than hiring and crediting a 'dialogue coach' as such, the director would simply have had an assistant director address such problems as they arose. But today, as many have remarked, the make-do approaches of the past are increasingly giving way to professionalization, particularly among the large production houses, at almost every level of Bollywood filmmaking.

The Dubbing Artiste

Rosario G. Gómez, writing for the Spanish newspaper *El País*, explains that Spain has 30,000 dubbing artists, and though the present government would like to encourage more children's programmes being aired in their original English version, the population is accustomed to hearing both films and television programmes in the Spanish voices they have come to love. No amount of cajoling from politicians can convince them to change their viewing habits. In any case, the dubbing artistes, it is felt, sometimes do an even better job than the original actors. Sylvester Stallone is given as an example of an actor who 'no sabe hablar' (doesn't know how to talk).[143] Dubbing artistes in Spain have a sort of guild to look out after their interests. The 'Asociación de Actores de Doblaje de Madrid', or ADOMA, has its own website, which is a rich source of information for professional dubbing artistes and the public alike. There we can read mini-biographies of leading dubbing artistes, many of whom have also worked in

---

[143]'Que hablen los perros—El doblaje de series animadas crece al amparo de los nuevos canales,' *El País*, 10 April 2011.

theatre, radio, film or television. Most have studied drama. More than one studied music in a conservatory.[144]

Spain is special in the recognition and appreciation it shows its dubbing artistes. In India, those who lend their voices to other actors are rarely named. Strange, I thought. I was especially curious, then, to hear Shaktee Singh (also spelled Shakti) talk about his work. Since 1982 he has dubbed six to seven hundred films. That was his voice we heard for Arvind Swamy in the Hindi versions of Mani Ratnam's films, *Bombay* (1995) and *Roja* (1992). He has also dubbed many Hollywood films, giving a Hindi voice to Pierce Brosnan, Anthony Hopkins, Mel Gibson and Daniel Craig. *Finding Nemo* (2003) was one of his favourite jobs. How does one get into the dubbing business? In Singh's case, it started in Lucknow with a passion for cinema. His farming family's budget did not include money for cinema tickets, so Singh got a job on the radio to be able to buy his own seats at the theatre. 'I used to get thirty bucks at that time, so I would earn money and then see films.' He was no doubt honing his voice in those early radio days. He also got a bit of dubbing work in Lucknow, but acting on-screen in Bombay was his dream. When he arrived in the big city, he went to a dubbing studio at the Sea Rock Hotel with a friend and found himself asked to do the voice for an incidental character in the 1983 film *Jaani Dost*. His reaction to that entry

Actor and dubbing artiste Shaktee Singh. (Photo courtesy: Shaktee Singh)

---

[144]http://www.adoma.es María del Puy.

in the profession in Bombay was, 'You can show your talent even by your voice. I felt very good.'

Since that time the dubbing business has grown and improved. Still, it remains rush-rush work.

> We don't get the scripts (usually in Roman Hindi) in advance. We have to go there and just read and perform. Everyone is in a hurry to complete the 'mission', like it's a mission. So that's the drawback, because when I've dubbed and then I see the film, I find I could have done better. But they don't allow us to do that kind of work, and they're not ready to pay.

Work, Singh explained, is contracted out or even subcontracted out. Whatever dubbing artistes might feel about their timing constraints, pay scales or the quality of the translated texts, it wouldn't do to complain. There are, after all, many waiting to take their places. It is best to do the work as well as possible, adding quality through voice and even making on-the-spot corrections to the Hindi grammar when necessary. Who does the translations the dubbing artistes receive? Who knows? The translators' work—also done in a hurry and on a shoestring budget—is not credited either.

Coming from Lucknow has given him an advantage. 'Yes, it's the language. Lucknow is a place where Hindi is very well spoken and with a pinch of Urdu.' He finds dubbing films from languages he does not understand, like Tamil, Telugu, Malayalam and Kannada, harder than dubbing an English-language film. Also, he takes pride in dubbing for Hollywood actors like Sir Anthony Hopkins 'who make their films with so much honesty and hard work'. At times, Singh has seen studio executives from Hollywood come to check the Hindi versions of their films.

> There was a person from Hollywood who was very particular about the sounds. He was very careful about the quality. But even in India there are some people who do quality dubbing, like Leela Ghosh who works on most of the big films.

There's also Ellie (Lewis) who has been doing lots of films. So they are quite familiar with the correct sounds, emotions, the language... The problem is that there's lots of cinema happening in India and lots of television, so dubbing takes a back seat... People are watching dubbed films on television and liking it, but people in India understand English also, so they prefer to see the film in English. Now the people in villages or who don't understand English, they only go to see dubbed films, but they're not intelligent enough to boost the quality of the dubbing... Dubbing gives money and a little bit of satisfaction but no name. There's one more tragedy about dubbing. You can't get it perfect. You can't go straight. You have to turn a little and then go and take your path. Real translation cannot happen, but if you keep the correct emotion and the language up to the mark at least—not perfect—I think most of the job is done. You can't achieve 100 per cent...

But sometimes the standards for a job simply fall too low. He explained, '*Kya bol raha hoon*? (What am I saying?) Then I say no, I'm answerable to myself sometimes also. "What are you doing, Shaktee? You've come here to do this kind of shit? No, not now."'

Singh came to Bombay with the dream of being an actor. Is that dream still alive? Yes. He has seen good filmmaking while working with directors like Vidhu Vinod Chopra (*Khamosh* [1985] and *1942: A Love Story* [1994]), Saeed Mirza and Aziz Mirza, and he would like more of that kind of work on screen.

In the final scene of Stanley Donen's *Singin' in the Rain* (1952) the fictional silent-era heart-throb Lina Lamont (Jean Dagen) is exposed as an imposter when the curtain is pulled open and we see that Kathy (Debbie Reynolds) is actually singing to cover Lina's shrill pitch and over-the-top Bronx vowels. The audience goes wild. A new star is born, one with a voice we want to hear. Bollywood gossip involves tales of various actors having their voices dubbed by others. One can suppose, then, that audiences now, as in the post-silent era, are curious to know who they are actually listening to. Many times we are not sure. Post-production dubbing is almost standard practice in Bollywood. Though it offers a chance for audio improvements, film director Vishal Bhardwaj, for one, objects, 'With sync sound you get much more intensity. With dubbing, actors become lazy. They know that they can correct themselves later in the studio, but when it's shot in sync they have to concentrate.'[145] And, one might add, dubbing means that the actor we see is not always the actor we hear. Cinema, by its nature, is full of tricks. A scene shot at night can be made to look like day. Sprinklers can create monsoon rain during the dry season. Is exchanging one person's voice for another's simply one more trick of the trade? Or is it deception? And if so, how many people care? It is hard to say. Actors, though, can feel strongly about being considered 'voice-worthy'. Subhash K. Jha reported on one such case in June 2011:

> Katrina Kaif is having a tough time dubbing for *Ajab Prem Ki Ghazab Kahani*, especially with director Raj Kumar Santoshi known to be very particular about his actor's diction. The actress, who has a pronounced British accent, has been practising her Hindi constantly with friends as well as in her dubbing, so much so that she almost lost her voice. For Katrina dubbing is the most difficult part of the acting process. After all, she was initially dubbed by professional artists. She finally won the right to speak on screen in her own voice.[146]

And yet we, the public, do not always know whose voice we

---

[145] Alter, Stephen, *Fantasies of a Bollywood Love Thief*, 2007, p. 17.
[146] http://www.bollywood.com/katrina-kaif-has-tough-time-dubbing-santoshis-film

are hearing. Dubbing fulfils a need, but one rather wishes the need were not quite so great, that dubbing could be reserved for foreign-language films and that this work be credited and appreciated for the value it adds to the films that we would otherwise likely miss seeing.

Innovating in Language-to-Language Communication: *Mangal Pandey: The Rising*

Mangal Pandey (Aamir Khan) in the courtroom where he is being tried for conspiracy. (Photo courtesy: Kaleidoscope Entertainment Private Limited)

Ketan Mehta's *Mangal Pandey: The Rising* (2005) is a work of passion and beauty on a wide canvas. Though rich in characters and events, the film's major focus is on the somewhat unlikely friendship between a sepoy and a British officer shortly before the uprising against the British in 1857. At the beginning of the film we see Mangal Pandey saving William Gordon's life on the battlefield. The two become inextricable friends. Mangal Pandey, as a Brahmin, ranks very high in Indian society but can never rise within the British army. William Gordon, by virtue of being British, is a captain, but his Scottish accent, his Catholic religion and his far-from-privileged schooling give him pariah status among the officers in his unit. New rifles and their cartridges, said to be greased with the fat of cows and pigs and seen as an abomination to both Hindu and Muslim sepoys, will impel Mangal Pandey to take a violent stand against the military force in which he has served. The film, scripted by London-based Farrukh Dhondy, was made not only in Hindi (or, perhaps more precisely, Hindustani) but also in an English version, with an eye to larger audiences beyond India. Within the Hindi version[147] the British speak Hindustani to the sepoys while realistically speaking English among themselves. The English scenes are neither dubbed nor subtitled for Indian audiences. Instead, a narrator (Om Puri in voiceover) creatively bridges the language divide by recounting in Hindi what has transpired in English. During the courtroom scene, for example, because Pandey has refused to defend himself against charges of conspiracy and murdering two commanding officers, Gordon is questioned in his stead and answers, 'I've known him as a brave soldier and a loyal friend, one of the finest sepoys to serve under my command.' The examiner wants only the facts, a simple yes or no. Gordon refuses to be silenced. His voice soars with rage:

> No, that will not be all! You'll hear me speak, damn it! Has this company become so blinded by arrogance and greed that it cannot see the danger that stares it in the face? We stand surrounded by our own army, 300,000 armed native sepoys, so disillusioned by our command that they are on the verge of mutiny. And what do we do to pacify them? We stoke the fire of their indignation by laughing at their concerns or suppressing them with brutality. But mark my words: if you hang this man Mangal Pandey, there will be rebellion! Bloody rebellion will sweep through this land like wildfire,

---

[147] Hindi dialogue credited to Ranjit Kapoor.

a rebellion that will lead to the end of this Company Raj!

The camera backs away from Captain Gordon. The full courtroom is in view as we hear the narrator's voice:

> *Captain Gordon ne Mangal Pandey ko bachaane ki ji-tod koshish ki. Usne chetaavani di thi ki agar Mangal Pandey ko phaansi di gayi to itni zabardast khooni kraanti hogi ki Company Raaj hamesha ke liye khatm ho jaayega, lekin Gordon ki ye aakhiri koshish bhi naakaam rahi.*

(Captain Gordon tried his best to save Mangal Pandey's life. He warned that if Mangal Pandey was hanged, there would be such a massive and bloody rebellion that the Company Raj would be finished, once and for all. But Gordon's last effort too was a failure.)

As would happen with subtitles, the long speech in English is boiled to its essence for the Hindi version. Unlike with subtitles, the narrator adds commentary. 'Gordon's last attempt,' he says, 'would fail.' *Naakaam rahi*: literally, 'a failure would continue/ would remain'. In the English translation the last word—'fail' or 'failure'—gives a finality to the sentence both phonetically and semantically. But then, English is an SVO language, that is to say, Subject-Verb-Object, while Hindi is an SOV language: Subject-Object-Verb. SVO—SOV: let's pause a moment to take a look at this very basic linguistic distinction. An example of the English Subject-Verb-Object form: The children are watching television. In contrast, SOV: *Bachche television dekh rahe hain* (literally: The children the television are watching.) The verb comes at the end. Now back to this scene from *Mangal Pandey*. The final verb, 'rahi', is intrinsically transitional: it continues; it goes on being. And then there's the sound: rahi. With no consonant to stop it, that last vowel could, theoretically, go on for as long as the speaker has breath to exhale. With the beginning of the narrator's last sentence, the camera is on Gordon as he stands winded after his harangue. As the narrator speaks, '*Lekin Gordon ki ye aakhiri koshish bhi naakaam rahi,*' Gordon's eyes move, and the camera follows to a close-up of Mangal Pandey seated in the courtroom in his red uniform, his long hair and his earring forming the principal contrast with the British soldiers in attendance. The narrator's voice descends until it comes to the word 'rahi', where it lingers ever so slightly on that last vowel. There is then a dissolve between Pandey's face and a dark stone wall and at the same time the equivalent of a dissolve between the narrator's 'rahi' and one or two bars of a wailful, haunting tune on a single wind instrument. A.R. Rahman's composition accompanies the camera as it pans along the stone wall until it comes to rest on an extreme close-up of Gordon's face, the wound on his cheek still fresh, his eyes empty as he stares listlessly down. The sound of the hooves of a horse bring him into the present. As the camera moves away, we see Gordon has been sitting alone, his back against the stone wall of the military yard, empty of all but its looming scaffold. This sophisticated integration of voice, words-and-their-meanings, camera shots and music, all used to move the story from one time-space to another, is too rapid to be pretentious, too skilled to be simply accidental and too rare not to be appreciated.

Toby Stephens as Captain William Gordon defending his friend Mangal Pandey in court. (Photo courtesy: Kaleidoscope Entertainment Private Limited)

Bridging Sensibilities

Shimit Amin had had a lot of film experience in the US, but he had only directed one film in India, *Ab Tak Chhappan* (2004), when Aditya Chopra offered him *Chak De! India*. Shimit speculated:

> He (Aditya Chopra) somehow thought I was right for the project, maybe because this script had a certain amount of nationalistic flavour that maybe needed to be toned down if I did it right. Otherwise it might have been too loud a film. It may not have worked. Or maybe that's not it, but he said, 'You'll be okay for this film.' I looked at it, and at first I thought, I don't know anything about hockey. How am I going to do this? I'm not an athletic person at all. And then Jaideep (Sahni) told me about the characters, and then I understood these were characters that I identified with because they were all outsiders. And that's what the link was: they were underdogs. And I thought, that's it, that's the movie.

If Shimit Amin's background makes him partially an outsider, writer Jaideep Sahni could be seen as the ultimate insider. By the fourth or fifth standard he had read the Indian Constitution and found in it his religion, his nationality. 'I am an Indian from *Chak De*,' he said. One of the most memorable scenes in the film has the coach (Shah Rukh Khan) of the Indian women's national hockey team attempting to turn girls who have arrived from all over India into a unified group. They line up and introduce themselves, each in turn giving her name and her region: Punjab, Bihar, Haryana, Maharashtra, etc. The coach curtly sends each one out until finally he hears the answer he has clearly been waiting for, 'Vidya Sharma, India.' *'Zor se kahein,'* (Louder!) the coach says, gesturing to the rest of the girls to pay heed. *'Thank you. Aap team mein hain.'* (You're on the team.) Lined up anew, each girl gives her name and follows it with 'India'.

'Vidya Sharma, India!' Vidya Malvade and Shah Rukh Khan in Chak De! India. *(Sketch by Simon P. Holzman)*

Director Shimit Amin felt mixed emotions about the scene.

> Jaideep wrote that scene, and I always thought it was interesting. I always felt 'India' gives you a contradictory message. Always. When you try to ask questions, there are always two answers. I felt, you are Indian, but you are not Indian. Jaideep has written it very cleverly, but still... Where do you draw that line? Where you call yourself an Indian, and where you call yourself something to do with your background? ...I think even today I'm not so satisfied with it. It works because the scene has wittiness that carries it forward. But if you really dissect it, I don't know... Again, it's a different volume, a different palette... But a lot of people are okay with it. So I think it's okay. It's part of the magic of movies.

Chak De! India had a lot going for it from the start: time devoted to detailed research into the world of women's hockey, careful preparation of the young women for their energy-consuming parts, Yash Raj financing, Shah Rukh Khan in a sober and thoughtful role, diverse and memorably drawn characters and a rhythm appropriate to the style and theme of the movie. Presumably, the film was further enriched by discussions that subtly bridged the writer's and the director's sensibilities.

The Cosmopolitans: Bridging Time, Space, Language and Traditions

Imtiaz Ali's *Love Aaj Kal* takes us to London, Delhi, Calcutta and San Francisco. In each city the protagonists (Saif Ali Khan, Deepika Padukone and Rishi Kapoor) look comfortably at home. Professional success is theirs for the taking. Love is another matter. For the older generation it was society which constructed ramparts against love. For the younger generation it is Western individualism and its by-product, fear of commitment, which make finding love seem like a fool's mission. Imtiaz Ali skilfully bridges the gap between the generations by having the older man Veer (Rishi Kapoor) retell the story of his own love to the younger, modern Jai (Saif Ali Khan) who eventually becomes capable of understanding. Each speaks the language his time. '*Main ne ek pratigya ki*,' the older Veer says of the vow he made to win the love of Harleen (Giselli Monteiro). The formal Sanskrit word, like the sentiment itself, is foreign to the younger Jai. Jai's and Meera's is a fusional generation. Just as these young people gambol from continent to continent, they hop between languages and linguistic traditions until all seem as one. The Arabic-root word 'aam' (ordinary) meets the Hindi word 'aam' (mango) a;m. 'Aam janta' (ordinary people), then, becomes mango people, shortened to mango ppl, as it shines in neon to one side of the dancers in the final song, while the word 'pratigya' (vow), is written partly in Devanagari and partly in Roman letters vertically on the other side: प्रtigya. Two linguistic traditions meet sweetly in the mango people pun. Two different scripts meet in one word, a symbol of the younger generation meeting the older generation half-way as the young people at least partially make their elders' words—and concepts—their own.

IN THE LEARNING ZONE

> Instead of us helping anybody improve their language, I think they're improving our language when it comes to writing dialogues.
>
> —Rajat Arora, screenwriter

IF RAJAT Arora looks to the public for inspiration, the public also looks to cinema for part of their vocabulary. One could stop almost anyone from the Indian diaspora in New York, in London or Nairobi and hear stories of language-learning via Bollywood films. Grannies or parents usually get the language ball rolling, and then the movies play their part, offering up new words, adding dreams as hooks to hang the words on and giving a reason to make the language of one's family's past into the language of one's own present. Saumya Verma, a student from The University of Texas, described the linguistic looping between her family and the movies this way, 'My parents, I would say, created a base of words. From hearing them speak Hindi from infancy, I could initially understand Hindi films.' But she gives a lot of credit to Bollywood. 'When I speak Hindi,' she said, 'it is very filmi, and I have seen many, many, many films.' Another University of Texas student, Sonali Brahmbhatt, who grew up speaking Gujarati with her parents, relied even more on the movies for her Hindi, 'I'm going to be honest here and say that 80 per cent of my Hindi knowledge has come from Hindi movies. I learned the words 'mehfil' and 'tanhaai' from songs. I know that I learned words like 'deevaana', 'pyaar', 'ishq', 'mohabbat' and others along those lines from Hindi movies because I definitely can't give a one-word English definition for those.' For Sarayu Adeni Hindi films were a means of keeping in step with her generation. 'I like being able to throw around colloquial words and phrases from Hindi films with friends and family back in India,' she said. What to do if you don't understand specific words from films? Subtitles might help, but the family can also be a resource, as in Saumya Verma's case, either because you ask the meaning directly or because you've heard a word in a movie, used it incorrectly in front of your parents and *then* been given the definition.[148]

What these young Indian Americans are describing sounds familiar. Throughout the world the 'Hollywood effect' is not uncommon among students of English, though the language fundamentals of English generally come from school rather than from parents. Let's say you're a thirteen-year-old in France and manage to sneak around to watch American sitcoms online while your parents think you're studying. Sure, you risk getting in trouble at home, but your love of the TV shows is powerful. As a bonus, you can later impress your English teacher with your pumped-up vocabulary that no textbook could (or would) provide. Hollywood films, of course, are a mainstream experience for people across the globe, so family-language-culture is not generally part of the attraction of the medium. A bigger distinction, however, is that *some* students latch onto Hollywood as a learning resource whereas Bollywood is a near-universal fountain of words and phrases for Hindi-Urdu learners. And Bollywood, contrary to most cinemas in the world, seems almost to beg to be understood through language. A French video rental store is likely to have a movie lover behind the counter but no matter how well the shopkeeper can analyse and recommend movies, it is unlikely he or she will speak much English. My Bangladeshi Hindi video

---

[148]Saumya Verma, Sonali Brahmbhatt and Sarayu Adeni spoke with me in 2009 in Austin, Texas.

supplier, on the other hand, learned all of her Hindi because of and through the movies.

Interestingly, the family-plus-film method of language learning described by The University of Texas students works even within India, including for filmmakers. Farhan Akhtar studied Hindi as a second language at school 'but only enough to pass the exams'. Growing up, it was English at school and mostly English at home, except with his grandmother. 'She spoke only in Hindi,' he said, 'which is surprising, considering she was Parsee. Most Parsees speak a kind of a Parsee Gujarati. But probably because she and my aunt were child stars, she spoke Hindi on the sets all the time, interacting with the director, the producer and actors. And at that point, the language that everyone really spoke on set was either Urdu or Hindi.'

For Akhtar, as for many young directors, at one level, 'everything is in English' on the sets today. At another level, speaking excellent Hindi has become essential because, as he noted, 'A lot of actors from different parts of India are really more comfortable with Hindi than with English.' Directing films has meant learning to discuss an actor's role as clearly in Hindi as in English and to explain, 'emotionally what I require from him, what I'm trying to do with the scene, where this scene needs to take the film and why it is that he's saying what he's saying. Otherwise,' he said, 'they just pick up words, but the image is really not formed in their heads.'

Translating his *Dil Chahta Hai* script from English to Hindi was a watershed moment for Akhtar. 'Thoughts,' he said, 'that I used to have only in English, now started happening to me in another language.' His language learning is ongoing. 'Songs from the past are always with me on my iPod. For me it's music from the Guru Dutt films, the Kishore Kumar songs, the Mohammed Rafi songs. I feel I want to be able to express myself like that.' Perhaps not coincidentally, it was after the birth of his daughter back in the early 2000s that Akhtar was moved to follow in the footsteps of generations past—and, more directly, of his father Javed Akhtar. He related, 'One day I had this thought which came to me for some strange reason in Urdu. And I said to myself, I'm going to write this, obviously not in the text, but still, I wrote my first poem in Urdu.'

Another member of the younger generation who had trouble with Hindi before entering films was Abhishek Bachchan. In a BBC Radio 5 interview Jaya Bachchan shared her reaction to her son's announcement that he wanted to become an actor, 'I said, "My God, this guy wants to be an actor, and he doesn't speak two straight lines in Hindi!"'

Abhishek, who was present for the interview, added by way of explanation that he was sent away to boarding school in Switzerland when he was eight or nine. 'That's just when we were learning Hindi as kids in school... I started learning French. For ten years of our life we lost touch and were not taught officially the language of Hindi. So obviously we were not very good at it.'

Abhishek's father, Amitabh Bachchan, was less concerned. Hindi, after all, was spoken in the family, and as Jaya quoted her husband having said, 'By the time Abhishek makes it, I don't think there's going to be any language barrier.'[149]

And language isn't a barrier when Abhishek is on screen. During interviews in Hindi, however, Abhishek, like more than a few younger English-educated actors, generally replies in English. This is apparently assumed to work for the Hindi film fans listening, though sticklers for form cannot but find it disconcerting to hear people conversing in two different languages.

Director-producer Rohan Sippy also went abroad to study, first to Switzerland and then on to university in the US, but only after he had finished the tenth standard in Bombay. Unlike Abhishek Bachchan, he studied Hindi throughout his primary

---

[149] BBC Asian Network, *Love Bollywood*, 14 March 2010.

and secondary school. All too typically, Sippy remembers the lessons as a necessity, not a joy.

> It was obviously a government curriculum because we were studying for the board exams. So there were some short stories by Premchand, some poetry and then there were some, you might say, socialist novels like *Ek aur Ek Gyaarah*,[150] which was about a colony of people from all over India who come together with messages about unity and diversity. I don't remember that as being a particularly great example of literature.

A shame, one might think. But what he missed at school—the passion and excitement of learning the language—came later when Sippy returned to Bombay from New York to work with his father in 1994.

> Starting out with Dad (director-producer Ramesh Sippy), we worked on a couple of television projects, one of which involved Manohar Shyam Joshi for the show *Buniyaad*. He's very fluent in English but also a very acclaimed novelist in Hindi... It was great to listen to someone who is in such command of the language... A lot of my Dad's technicians and crew were still around, so I spent time with them. There was a wonderful gentleman, Khalish Lucknavi, the dialogue supervisor on set... He was painstakingly accurate and spoke fluent Hindustani-Urdu. He wrote in Urdu as well and kept track of everything... And then there was a gentleman called Aziz Bhai, my father's construction manager, who started out in the early 1940s. So with them I would speak exclusively in Hindi.

Educational psychologists would probably qualify Sippy's language-learning on the sets as 'intrinsically' motivated. A deep

---

[150] By Gopesh Sharan Sharma 'Aatur', 1970.

desire to know is accompanied by feelings of pleasure in acquiring knowledge. Learning is its own reward. In contrast with *intrinsic* motivation, *extrinsic* motivation typically comes from parents, teachers and the system: 'You have to pass your exams!' 'You must be good in math.' 'Don't bring home a failing grade!' Extrinsic or outside motivation can be more or less gratifying. At best, you get the carrot, at worst, the stick. But no one has asked you if you wanted the carrot. Perhaps you'd really rather have chocolate cake. Most teachers have a curriculum to stick to, and chocolate cake is not usually on it. But the best teachers make the carrot really inviting, and they teach you how to go out and get the cake—or whatever your pleasure might be—by giving you the tools to continue to learn. Cinema and theatre actor Tom Alter, looking back at his school years, had great praise for one of his Hindi teachers. He related:

> Hindi is looked upon as a bore and a chore. But it can be made exciting through drama, music, films. I remember when I was learning Hindi in school and we, being from this sort of Westernized background, thought Hindi cinema was a big joke. Our Hindi teacher, though, took us to a film called *Kabuliwala* (1961) with Balraj Sahni, based on a novel (by Rabindranath Tagore). She took us to see that one film, and it changed my life.

Shridhar Raghavan, too, associates learning Hindi with going to the movies. At home he picked up spoken Tamil. At school he studied a very formal 'bookish' Hindi. He remembers 'getting traumatized' in the process.

> You learn all about dative and accusative clauses, but that doesn't really make you articulate beyond a point... We grew up in the time of Mr Bachchan, so that language is what we really picked up on. See, you go to school and you learn something for half an hour, 45 minutes a day, but you go for a movie, and you listen to Hindi for three hours. You are

seeing a lifetime... If I'm dying, if I am feeling emotional, if I fall in love, this is what I am supposed to say. When we came out of an angry Bachchan film when we were kids, we came out with a swagger... [Today] when you come out of *Munna Bhai*, you still see people talking like that. You become that character for a while. You shift into that lingo.

Cinema can teach swagger and lingo. It can also be pressed into service to encourage people to improve their reading skills. Ahmedabad-based academic and social entrepreneur Brij Kothari, understanding the attraction of cinema, has used the technology of 'same language subtitling' (SLS) with film songs on television as part of a project called Planet Read. The results have been indisputable among millions of early literates (those who can tease out the letters but are not comfortable reading), even if they have only a few minutes of viewing time a week.[151] What people love is what will motivate them to learn.

The film *Mughal-e-Azam* would probably never have been made without that kind of love. Deepesh Salgia[152] relates in the preface to *The Immortal Dialogue of K. Asif's Mughal-e-Azam* (2006), the dedication of the film's financier, construction baron Shapoorji Pallonji Mistry. For nine long years he persevered in funding the project until *Mughal-e-Azam* was finally released in 1960. Salgia wrote, 'Shapoorji, who could hardly speak good Hindi or Urdu, became so fond of the dialogue that even years after the release of the film, he would recite the lines repeatedly. The words so excited him and the fine nuances of the language never escaped him.'[153]

Documentary filmmaker and writer Nasreen Munni Kabir, responsible for bringing the *Mughal-e-Azam* book into being,

---

[151] Pisharoty, Sangeeta Barooah, 'Same to Same,' *The Hindu*, 6 April 2011.
[152] Project director for the Sterling Investment Corporation's colour version (2004) of the 1960 film *Mughal-e-Azam*.
[153] *The Immortal Dialogue of K. Asif's Mughal-e-Azam*, 2007, p. viii.

is another who largely learned the language because of and through cinema. After leaving Hyderabad for the UK at the age of two, English was the language spoken at home for her. However, her parents used the well-worn trick of switching to their private language, in this case Hindustani, when they didn't want the kids to understand. The trick seldom works for long. Knowing that they are missing out on secrets will make children prick up their ears and pick up a language in no time. Armed thus with some basic Hindustani, Kabir began watching Indian movies. In those days you had to go to the theatre to see a film, but Indian film music had already penetrated the home. Kabir explained:

> I would say we had four or five hours a day of film songs. My sister Priya used to be fanatical. She had a collection of thousands of 78s and 45s. So the language was seeping in unconsciously while we were doing other work—hoovering or cleaning or washing or living... Of course, sometimes you think you understand the words, but you really don't... Anees, my sister who lived in New York, used to come and go from London. She spoke very good Urdu, and sometimes I used to ask her words, and she would explain. One day I asked her, 'Can you show me how to read the alphabet in Urdu?' and she taught me how to read in four hours.

Indian film music travels far and to some unlikely places. Mention Hindi cinema to a cab driver in Rome, to street kids in Indonesia, to Latinos in South Texas and you may hear a burst of song. I was looking for a movie theatre in Marrakesh, asked my way of a young man, and the next thing I knew he was singing 'Yeh Dosti' from *Sholay*. He was an Arabic speaker, but he had the words down pat. Tom Alter observed the allure of film songs while on a film shoot in the Andaman Islands:

> There, the most common language is Hindi, a very simple Hindi, which basically was picked up from Hindi films.

Now they don't go into grammar too much. It's very simple, whether you're male or female, one person or two: *ham jaata hai. Tum jaata hai.* (We go. You go.) But when they sing the Hindi songs from the films, it's absolutely correct. Every bit of punctuation, every nuance is there. And these are young kids singing ancient Hindi film songs from my days.

Language-learning through films and film songs has its limits, of course. Foreign-language teachers who allow students to rank their preferred means of learning from the list of reading, writing, listening or speaking will find 'speaking' usually comes out on top. For autonomous learners, i.e. those who study on their own, listening usually ranks high, particularly if the autonomous learner is a film buff. Either way, you save having to hit the books and you still learn a lot of language. Speaking fast, you can glide over problem words. Then you can further distract from your mistakes with some prowess in pronunciation and intonation. Add some catchy colloquial phrases, and you will sound much more knowledgeable than you actually are. And yet depth of understanding of a language/culture, precision in grammar and breadth of vocabulary can almost never be achieved without tedious hours spent reading and writing, dictionary at the ready. Nagesh Kukunoor, himself trilingual, is very language-aware. He is constantly amazed, then, to see foreign-born aspiring actors approach him for a role in a film. 'The frightening thing,' he said, 'is that the whole second generation of Indians born and raised outside of India speaks this bad Hindi.' He gave the example of a girl raised in Australia who wanted to become a Bollywood actress, 'She said, "I can speak fluent Hindi. I learned it all from watching Hindi films." I mean, she said it so matter-of-factly that I was really caught off guard.'

Mastering a new language is difficult but not impossible after childhood. Psycholinguists consider that adolescence, when our identities become defined by group belonging, is the cut-off point for most of us spontaneously and flawlessly to pick up new accents. Fortunately, adolescence has an upside. We enter what developmental psychologists call 'the formal operational stage of cognitive development', an easy-to-forget term that even the specialists must find hard to love.[154] The gist is that the child's trial-and-error means of problem-solving gives way to abstract thought and deductive reasoning. Something is lost and something is gained. On the one hand, our ears are less open to fine distinctions. After childhood, for example, an English speaker, unlike a Hindi–Urdu speaker, won't realize—or care—that it takes more air to say the 'p' sound in 'pot' than the 'p' sound in 'spot'. On the other hand, the fact that 'could have, would have', and 'should have' are variations on one grammatical structure is easily apparent: I could have gone, I should have gone, and I would have gone if only I hadn't turned off the alarm and gone back to sleep, but I didn't go. We get better at connecting the dots after puberty.

Language acquisition and multilingual acting are practical questions for the many Indian actors who work in more than one linguistic region in the course of their careers. Exposure to several languages may be a given and actors do tend to have more flexibility of voice than the average person. Aishwarya Rai, who speaks both Hindi and Tamil, was on a double shift during the making of Mani Ratnam's *Raavan (Raavanan)* (2010), a film shot simultaneously in the two languages with slightly different casts in each version. If Aishwarya Rai had at least a passing knowledge of Tamil before working in Tamil cinema, the Telugu and Tamil-speaking actor Rekha reportedly only began to learn Hindi at the age of thirteen, normally a bit late to acquire a perfect accent in a new language. To compound her problems, when she entered Hindi cinema as a teenager in the early 1970s, her voice was strained, badly pitched, sometimes just screechy.

---

[154]Jean Piaget (d. 1980), who coined the term, was French-Swiss. *Le stade des opérations formelles* no doubt works a bit better than its English translation.

IN THE LEARNING ZONE 287

Rekha in Muzaffar Ali's Umrao Jaan *(1981).*
(Sketch by Simon P. Holzman)

Even her looks received harsh criticism, 'dusky' and 'plump' being the usual dismissive adjectives used to describe her. Yet, by the 1980s Rekha had succeeded in radically transforming herself. Her voice became an instrument of great beauty, comparable to her new and stunning physical appearance. She became one of the actors who rendered the language more charming simply because she was speaking it. Listening to Rekha in, say, *Silsila* or *Umrao Jaan* can be a disheartening experience for a language learner frustrated by the effort required not only to communicate but actually to sound good in a foreign language. She has clearly placed the bar of excellence exceptionally high. 'She could do it. Why can't I?' you sulk. Change the intonation, though, and that demoralizing thought becomes an uplifting stimulant, 'She could do it. Why can't I?' Yes! Why not indeed! It's all about learning, which means yoking desire to determination and hard work. All true, but then again, to attain such an exquisite use of voice in a language she was not born into probably also supposes that Rekha was, quite simply, exceptionally gifted. Would that we all could be!

A LANGUAGE LOOKING FOR ITS WAY

IN MANEESH Sharma's *Band Baaja Baaraat*, written by Habib Faisal, the highly motivated and organized Shruti (Anushka Sharma) has thoroughly researched her dream of becoming a wedding planner. The rudderless Bittu (Ranveer Singh) convinces her to let him join in as she gets her business 'Shaadi Mubarak' up and running. From the start, Shruti has had a rule, never to mix business and romance. After a particularly successful wedding, however, for which they have been rewarded with a cheque that virtually screams 'You're in the big time now!' the entire Shaadi Mubarak crew keeps on partying till the wee hours. Finally, only Shruti and Bittu remain, alone, exhausted, and dancing slowly, champagne in hand…until they stop and walk upstairs together. They awake the next morning. *'Chaai piyoge tum?'* (Will you have tea?) asks Shruti, her face resplendent with love. Bittu's reaction is immediate: shock, even terror at the mere thought of commitment. After months of working together, their relationship has always been tu–tu, i.e. the relaxed, post-college, informal, nothing-but-friends way of talking, at least in Delhi-speak. And tea-making has always been his job. With tea and 'tum', Shruti is repositioning herself. Bittu knows it. 'Tum?' he mutters in horror and disbelief before calling out *'Tu rehne de,'* insisting heavily on the 'tu'. The day before, she was a career woman who shunned any suggestion of marriage. Now she instinctively falls into patterns of language she has learned in her family. 'Tu' was fine for a friend. More respect is required for the man she loves. Bittu meets an old buddy on the street that same morning. The story comes out. '*Aaj se mujhe "tum" bolti hai. Subaah chaai banaayi mere liye. Gandi chaai.*' (Today she started saying 'tum' to me. And she made me morning tea. Terrible tea.) The friend gets it at once, 'My God! She's in love with you!' Later, at the office Shruti senses Bittu's discomfort and offers him a way out: their night together was a 'mistake', so they can go back to calling each other 'tu'. Shruti puts on a brave face as she makes this concession, but she's devastated. Bittu, meanwhile, is as heartily relieved as he is totally oblivious to the waves of pain emanating from Shruti.

These language signals work in Delhi, but they don't work everywhere. Jaideep Sahni was initially baffled by filmi language. For young people to address each other as 'tum' seemed artificial, okay for Lucknow and Kanpur, but, as he explained, 'in Delhi we used to think of that as a very nawaabi[155] kind of thing.'

A linguistic note: many or most European languages have their formal and informal 'you'. English once had, but has largely lost the thou–you distinction. Spanish still has it with tu–usted, French with tu-vous, German with du–sie and Italian with tu–Lei, to name but a few. Understanding the logic of the familiar versus formal distinction in one language doesn't mean you won't bumble and embarrass yourself in another language. For that matter, if you step beyond your region, your class, perhaps even your family, the rules may change. I am reminded of the young Venezuelan cousins who addressed each other with the formal 'Usted', contrary to anything I had heard in the Spanish-speaking world before. But that worked in Venezuela or, perhaps, in their part of Venezuela. In English today we can mess up by addressing someone by first name when a title and last name would be more appropriate. ('That's *Ms Haham* to you! I'm old enough to be your grandmother,' I find myself thinking—but not saying—when a seventeen-year-old I've never met calls me Connie. Ah,

---

[155] nawaabi: a reference to Muslim princely states and their culture.

American informality…) While you can avoid calling someone by name, you cannot converse without using 'you'. And Hindi–Urdu complicates matters—or offers greater nuance—by having a third version of you. There's tu; there's tum and there's aap. In France meeting someone new in a social setting often involves a little verbal dance before it is settled whether the two of you will have a 'tu' or a 'vous' relationship. Coming from the English-speaking world this was hard to master, but at least it was always 'tu–tu' or 'vous–vous', implying equality, at least grammatically. In Hindi-Urdu it is possible—even common—to have 'aap–tum' or 'tum–tu' relationships, that is, a fundamentally unequal use of the various ways of saying 'you'. Children may say 'aap' to their parents while parents say 'tum' or 'tu' to their children, or to their servants or to anybody on a lower rung in society. (I think the French Revolution rather did away with this particular means of 'putting someone in their place'.[156]) Oversimplification, however, is a danger when talking about as important and intimate a form as the second person singular. Whereas someone might address a friend as 'tu', they might opt for the 'tum' form with household help in order to maintain employer–employee distance. The possibilities for subtle or less-subtle distinctions are many. The loving 'tu' a mother can use with her baby is most endearing. Expressing respect for elders by addressing them as 'aap' carries weight. On the other hand, there's the (for me) extremely annoying unequal 'aap–tum' that often shows up among married couples in Hindi films—no doubt mirroring real-life speaking habits. That is to say, a woman will address her husband using the formal 'aap', while the husband will use the informal 'tum' to his wife. None

---

[156] Eighteenth-century French philosopher Étienne Bonnot de Condillac said the 'vous' form represented the language of the slave before the master. Laws were even passed during the Revolution that *only* the 'tu' form could be used. Wolff, 1990, p. 90.

of my business, you might well say.[157] Still, I can't help cringing at this overt show of male superiority, especially when we see a tum–tum relationship move to aap–tum after marriage. Jaideep Sahni gave his take on the last part of this linguistic and cultural phenomenon:

> Yeah, I've seen it happen to couples. I think when you're chasing the girl, the equation is a bit heavier on the girl's side. It isn't like that for a lot of my friends, but traditionally that's the way it has been. I think it's a worldwide thing, but it just shows more here. Once the whole chase bit is over, you get on with the serious business of life and marriage. Then it's like you fall into your job profile. It kind of lubricates the social relationships, not just with the boy but with the boy's father and mother. It's sort of a sweet way of achieving a very ugly thing, making sure the girl is off on a bad foot after she gets married. It's just brutality covered by culture.

Writer-director-actor Shashanka Ghosh, also from Delhi, worked in advertising before moving to youth and music television[158] in the 1990s, and then on to filmmaking. He described his feelings of freedom at leaving 'aap' behind:

> One of the things that came out of those twenty–twenty-five years of state-run television was the ideal language as our elders saw it. It was all 'aap'… The first few new channels that came in followed that approach. But one of the first things we did was create what we called intimate television.

---

[157]Male–female inequality isn't specific to India, of course. In the US women make, on an average, 20 per cent less than men in the workplace. And American linguists have pointed out how often young American women finish their sentences with a rising intonation that seems to say, 'Maybe what I'm saying is true?'
[158]MTV India and Channel V.

It was talking one-on-one. We threw 'aap' out of the window and stuck with 'tum' and 'tu'. My whole reasoning was that if I'm doing youth television I'm talking to youth. At best it's 'tum', but the tone, the manner, is always 'tu'.

Shashanka Ghosh told a story of what happened when he tried to transfer this insouciant manner to filmmaking:

> My chief AD—assistant director—is looking for a team for my first film.[159] A very intense young guy comes in. A lot of directors here like to hire each assistant in every department. My approach is, I want one guy to talk to, the head of the department. [So the chief assistant hires the new second assistant.] Then this new fellow is reading the script, and suddenly I hear a commotion, peek out and I see my Buddha of a chief assistant yelling. He's angry at the second AD, the one he's hired. My chief AD says, 'Sir, he's fired.' So I say, 'No, I don't believe in that. What is the problem?' Finally it comes out that the new man started reading the script and said, 'What is this crap?! What kind of language is this?!' See, my language is street language, and he can't accept that in a film. Cinema isn't supposed to be ordinary; it's supposed to be extraordinary. It should at least have 'aap'...

After some discussion the second AD did, in fact, stay on and work on the film. Later, seeing the finished film, he admitted to a vindicated Shashanka Ghosh, 'Now I totally understand what you meant.'

Back in 2000 writer-director Abbas Tyrewala was a young dialogue writer chafing at being criticized for his stilted language. In a Sulekha blog entitled 'So Who Speaks Hindi?' he vented his frustrations. The following are a few lines from his piece. The entire blog is well worth a careful read.

---

[159] *Waisa Bhi Hota Hai Part II*, 2003.

> Which Hindi film sounds like anyone talking? I understand that Hindi films necessarily speak to an entire nation. Therefore it has to transcend idioms and usage that may alienate the different regions and communities of such a vast country. But isn't talking to no one too high a price to pay for talking to everyone? Will flavour and colour and authenticity always be sacrificed at the altar of universality? [...] Where does that leave me...he of no colour save the gray squalors of Bombay? Hey, maybe I'll just write films in English. Maybe I'll talk the way people in Bombay talk, without worrying too much about the language. Maybe I'll just do storylines and scene breakdowns and let a man with a past do the dialogue. I don't know.[160]

In retrospect, it's surprising to see that writing 'the way people talk in Bombay' was but one of his options, the winning one, it turns out, since we have since come to associate Abbas Tyrewala with the dialogue writing for the *Munna Bhai* films,[161] full of the street language as expressed by the rough but endearing Munna Bhai character, played by Sanjay Dutt. '*Bole to*' (say what?), and '*tension mat le*' (cool it!) and other Marathi-influenced Bambaiya quickly came to symbolize a filmi linguistic version of the city. How Murli (aka Munna Bhai) came to have speech patterns so at odds with those of his father in the film, played by Sunil Dutt, real-life father of actor Sanjay Dutt, is never made clear. Yet showing the dignified Urdu-educated Sunil Dutt opposite Sanjay Dutt with his exaggerated but enjoyable Bambaiya is indicative of the language disconnects one can find across generations in an India on the move. 'He doesn't really speak that way,' director-

---

[160] http://abbas-tyrewala.sulekha.com/blog/post/2000/01/so-who-speaks-hindi.htm

[161] *Munna Bhai M.B.B.S.* (2003) and *Lage Raho Munna Bhai* (2006), both directed by Rajkumar Hirani and produced by Vidhu Vinod Chopra, with dialogue by Abbas Tyrewala.

producer Rohan Sippy said of Sanjay Dutt, 'but he could. He has the ear for that language. That's why he delivers it so well.'

In the first *Munna Bhai* film, Murli, with the help of his sidekick Circuit (Arshad Warsi), has forced his way into medical school where he is 'studying' to be a doctor. If he is weak in the sciences, he is strong in empathy and good at reading people. In the following scene, Murli is a patient himself. Still, he doesn't hesitate to intervene with his special brand of care which, in this case, means straightening out a suicidal young man through tough love. Suman (Gracy Singh), young, beautiful and already a doctor, tries in vain to calm Munna down.

The 'Suicidal Boy' Scene from *Munna Bhai M.B.B.S.*

आंटी: अब कैसे हो?
मुरली: अपुन ठीक है, आंटी। हीरो कैसा है?
आंटी: कुछ समझ में नहीं आता क्या करूँ। दूसरी बार खुदकुशी करने की कोशिश की। कुछ बताता भी नहीं है।
मुरली: आंटी, टेंशन नहीं लेने का। कहाँ है हीरो?
मुरली: ऐ, तेरी माँ तेरे सामने रो रही है। तेरे को शर्म नहीं आती?
आंटी: उसे कुछ मत बोलो।
मुरली: अरे कायको नहीं बोलो? मरने का है, ना? तो एक बार मर। खत्म कर। इस नींद की गोली से कुछ नहीं होता। सब नाटक है। एक चाकू ले। अपनी गर्दन पर लगा और फिरा डाल। और तब तक अपने आप पे तरस नहीं खाने का, समझा?
हीरो: मैं अपने आप पे तरस नहीं खा रहा हूँ।
सुमन: मुरली, लेट जाओ।
मुरली: एक मिनट, सुमनजी, यह आज कल के छोकरे है ना, एक पैसा का जिगर नहीं है। तुम्ही ने खराब करके रखैला है, एक आंसू नहीं टपका कि पल्लू से पोंछने चले। थोड़ा टफ होने देने का ना।
हीरो: प्लीज़, प्लीज़ चुप हो जाइए आप। आपको पता नहीं मेरे साथ क्या हुआ है।
मुरली: क्या हुआ है? एक्ज़ाम में फ़ेल हुआ है? लड़की छोड़कर गई, क्या? पैसे के वांदे है? लड़की। लड़की छोड़कर गई, हाँ? ऐ सरकैट, यह देख। ऐसे रोंदलु से कौन शादी करेगा? छ: महीने के

प्यार में मरने चला था साला। ऐ तेरी माँ तेरे को बचपन से प्यार करती है ना? उसके लिए जी नहीं सकता है तू?
हीरो: शटअप। तुमको क्या मालूम प्यार क्या होता है?
मुरली: हूँ, तू सच बोलता है। अपुन जैसे टपोरी को क्या मालूम?

(Auntie: How are you now?
Murli: I'm fine, Auntie? How is your boy, 'Hero'?
Auntie: I don't know what to do. He tried to kill himself again. He won't even talk.
Murli: Auntie, don't get worked up. Where is Hero? [To Hero] Hey, your mother is crying over you. Aren't you ashamed of yourself?
Auntie: Don't scold him.
Murli: Why shouldn't I? [To Hero] You wanna die? So die. Get it over with. Those sleeping pills won't do the job. That's just for show. Put a knife to your throat and slit it. And until then, stop feeling sorry for yourself.
Hero: I'm not feeling sorry for myself.
Suman: Murli, lie down.
Murli: Just a minute, Miss Suman. Today's kids don't have a bit of guts. And you spoiled him, Auntie. All he needs is one teardrop in his eye, and you're there wiping it off with your sari. You've gotta let him toughen up.
Hero: Please stop right there. You don't know what I've been through.
Murli: Yeah? What? You failed your exams? A girl left you? You've got money problems? [Seeing the young man's reaction] A girl. A girl left you, right? Hey Circuit, look at this guy. Who would marry a crybaby like this? Six months in love and he's ready to die. Hey, your mother's loved you since you were little, right? Couldn't you live for her?
Hero: Shut up! What do you know about love?
Murli: Yeah, you're right. What would a bum like me know?)

Munna Bhai M.B.B.S. is not the first example of Bambaiya in film dialogue. Journalist Anjana Vaswani dates it to 1963 with K.A. Abbas's *Shehar Aur Sapna*.[162] Afterwards, of course, there was the very memorable Bambaiya-speaking Anthony character in Manmohan Desai's *Amar Akbar Anthony*. The *Munna Bhai* films took one aspect of the Anthony character, his way of speaking, and made it a defining part, perhaps even *the* defining part of Munna's character. Bombay-born Rohan Sippy said of Bambaiya, 'I think it's a great, lovely entity, creation, organic kind of thing. It's our Ebonics[163] or whatever. It's very expressive. It comes out of the environment that we experience—using all kinds of languages to create something that's Hindi or Bambaiya or whatever it is. It's something I enjoy more and more.'

The Macho Pull of the East: *Dabangg*

In 2007 Jaideep Sahni said, 'Unfortunately, UP and Bihar are not much of markets now. It's gone to the multiplexes. The middle class is going to be the market which has the money.' In a few short years that analysis was spectacularly turned on its head when *Dabangg* (2010), directed by Abhinav Kashyap and written by Dilip Shukla, became one of the highest-grossing films ever. The comfortable urban audiences didn't snub the film, but its real numbers had to come from smaller-town audiences. The title, officially translated as 'Fearless', shows up in the dictionary less flatteringly as 'bully' or 'rude'. 'Lout' would be my own choice. Salman Khan, playing corrupt and violence-prone policeman Chulbul 'Robin Hood' Pandey, is made to look larger than life and invincible through a succession of low-angle camera shots.

---

[162] Vaswani, Anjana, '*Bambaiya Hindi ne language ki vaat lagaa daali*', *Mid-Day*, 2 February 2009.

[163] Ebonics was originally coined to refer to the language of the African Diaspora. Since the mid-1990s, it has been used colloquially to refer to a distinctive variety of English spoken by African Americans.

The film is clearly set in Uttar Pradesh, and with its male–female imbalance, exaggeratedly reflects the demographics of northern India today. Strutting, overbearing, Chulbul flaunts his macho power in every frame. Chulbul does not ask Rajjo's (Sonakshi Sinha) father's permission to marry Rajjo. Instead, he announces, '*Tumhaari beti hamein pasand hai aur ham usse shaadi karna chaahte hain. Padhe-likhe hain, jaat se Brahman hain, police ki naukri, rob-daab, paise, sab hai.*' (I like your daughter and want to marry her. I'm educated, a Brahmin by caste. I have a police job, influence, money, everything.) After Chulbul and Rajjo have circled the fire in a hasty wedding, the priest tells Chulbul to seek blessings from family elders. When his stepfather refuses, Chulbul, without a second's pause, puts his own hand on his head and blesses himself and Rajjo, '*Khush rahein ham aur sada suhaagan rahe ye.*' (May I remain happy and may she be an eternally blissful bride.) When the two are alone after the wedding, his new wife asks his name, '*Aapka naam kya hai?*' He answers, '*Hamaara naam hamaari personality ko shobha deta hai, Robin Hood Pandey, Chulbul Pandey.*' (My name fits my personality, i.e. gives it lustre, Robin Hood Pandey, Chulbul Pandey.) Now, through all these exchanges and others Chulbul uses the third person plural for himself. He doesn't say 'I' but rather 'we'. He addresses others—including his future father-in-law—in the 'tum' form, and he is addressed by his wife, who, it must be noted, rarely has a chance to speak, with the formal, respectful 'aap' form.

When talking to political thug Chhedi Singh (Sonu Sood) who is even more corrupt than Chulbul, Chulbul explains that he is the elephant and Chhedi the dog. Chulbul demands a pay-off in the form of bags of money, '*Varna Chhedi Singh ham tum mein itne chhed karenge ki confuj ho jaaoge ki saans kahaan se lein aur paadein kahaan se.*' (Otherwise, Cheddi Singh, I'll make so many holes[164] in you that you'll be confused—won't know—which ones

---

[164]Holes = chhed, a play on Chhedi's name.

to breathe from and which ones to fart from.) Considering the amount of uncensored violence in the film, even if a good bit is stylized, it's interesting to see that the text of this dialogue, when quoted online, uses asterisks in the place of 'paadein', thus visually bleeping the word 'fart'.

Given the vulgarity and the violence in both the images and the dialogue, it is confounding to see that the National Film Awards named *Dabangg* 'Best Popular Film Providing Wholesome Entertainment' for 2010.

And So?

In a society marked by rapid change, trying to guess winning combinations of story, character, setting and style of language to please the greatest numbers of filmgoers two to five years down the line, when the film will actually be released, is a migraine-inducing challenge for producers. Versions of 'Delhi-speak' or 'Mumbai talk' are common enough. 'Aap–tum–tu' are in flux in cinema, as in real life. And small-town UP macho vulgarity is not a one-film phenomenon. There are also some nostalgia-based films or 'Indian-Abroad' stories which continue to appeal, especially to the NRI market. A few movies are trying to give more authentic voice to various dialects from the countryside. More and more budding stars from abroad are arriving, learning Hindi, trying their luck in Bollywood and through their presence, giving Bollywood a different sort of international reach. Popular films in a very local sort of English are also an option. Then too, there are hints of a resurgence of language from the past. Farhan Akhtar saluted the use of the word paathshaala (school) in Prasoon Joshi's song from *Rang De Basanti*. 'Nobody says paathshaala among the people that I speak to,' Farhan noted.

Rohan Sippy, in flawless English, expressed his hopes for a future in which Hindi—presumably both the language and the culture it transmits—remains very central in filmmaking:

> As far as language goes, I hope, at least in the films we're making, that they remain very much Hindi films... I think a well-written line of Hindi will connect much better across the board... Part of the appeal of our cinema is that it gives you the sense that you're part of this illusion of India... There's just a certain groundedness that comes with it.

American journalist Lawrence Wright in his book, *In the New World: Growing Up with America 1960-1984* (1987), describes years of bickering with his father over politics and the Vietnam War. Things came to a head the night before Wright was to graduate from Tulane University in New Orleans. He and his parents went out to eat at the expensive restaurant Galatoire's. He recommended the pompano.

> What was it about the suggestion that set my father off? Perhaps it was the galling thought that I had been here before, educating my tastes with his money—pompano! ... It was true I had more expensive tastes than my father, who had a begrudging attitude towards restaurants anyway—but then he was the son of a broken farmer and I was the son of a successful banker, and we were bound to have different values. In some way he couldn't prevent, he had made me into his opposite. He had wanted my life to be better than his, and easier, and it had been. But look at the consequences! ... How dare I order pompano and attack capitalism?[165]

This story would appear unconnected with Indian life: another time, another place, different issues. Yet in the late 1960s, Lawrence Wright and perhaps millions of other American baby boomers were living in a world radically unlike the one their parents had known. In India, ever-higher literacy rates along with the huge numbers of people moving about, often beyond their language states and even to distant parts of the globe, cannot

---

[165] Wright, Lawrence, *In the New World*, p. 181.

but affect how generations communicate. Robert D. King, in *Nehru and the Language Politics of India* (1997), describes a basic principle of linguistics, the tendency for bilingualism to give way to monolingualism from one generation to the next.[166] He points out that the language which survives will be the one that offers the greatest opportunities. Considering the strength of the forces that favour multilingualism in India, such as custom and governmental policies, it can be assumed that many people will continue to communicate at least minimally in more than one language. But most of those will no doubt have their strong language along with one or two weak languages. When a parent's strong language is the child's weak language, how well can the generations ultimately communicate? Perhaps they can't. Or perhaps they manage, but they can't read each other's letters. One reaction to potentially profound gaps in language and culture across the generations is to lament the loss. Another is to embrace the change, to look out and marvel. Relying on metaphor, Javed Akhtar linked change and movement in space and time to life itself:

> *Zindagi badi interesting hai aur is mein nayi-nayi baatein hoti rehti hain. Nayi-nayi cheezein hoti hain. Ye soch lena ki ham ne jaan liya, sab dekh liya… ye to aisa hai ki zindagi thehri hui thodi hai. Aise hi hai train ki tarah chali ja rahi hai. Ab aap khidki band kar dein. Arre baahar to hamne dekh liya. Baahar aapne zaroor dekha tha, lekin ab baahar kuchh aur hai. Ab vo train vahaan nahin hai jahaan aapne dekha tha. Ab baahar manzar badal gaya hai. Ye kisi aur jagah se guzar rahi hai, ye train. To ye pal-pal, chhin-chhin nayi hoti hai zindagi. Aur usko har pal aap hairat se dekhiye. Yehi zaroori hai, varna to aap miss kar jaayenge cheezon ko.*[167]

---

[166]King, Robert D., p. 40.
[167]Speaking on the BBC Hindi Service during the week of his sixty-seventh birthday, 23 January 2012.

(Life is really interesting. There is always something new, new stories, new things. To think that we've learned everything, seen everything... Life isn't fixed or stagnant. Life is like a train going along. So now you close the window. Yes, you've looked outside, but now there's something else outside. Now the train isn't where it was when you looked. Now the view outside has changed. The train is travelling through a different space. So every moment, every instant, life is new. And look at it every second in amazement. You must. Otherwise, you'll miss something.)

INTERVIEW DATES

All interviews took place in Mumbai unless otherwise stated.

Anupama Chopra—April 2006
Ketan Desai—April 2006
Paromita Vohra—April 2006
Shama Zaidi—April 2006
Javed Siddiqi– April 2006
Aziz Mirza—April 2006
Jaideep Sahni—April 2006, February 2007
Farhan Akhtar—February 2007
Javed Akhtar—February 2007
Tom Alter—February 2007
Rajat Arora—February 2007
Shabana Azmi—February 2007
Prakash Bharadwaj—February 2007
Nasreen Munni Kabir—February 2007
Rohan Sippy—February 2007
Kader Khan—February 2007 (Pune)
Jahnavi Phalkey—February 2007 (Madison, Wisconsin)
Shimit Amin—March 2008
Madhur Bhandarkar—March 2008
Shashanka Ghosh—March 2008
Elahé Hiptoola—March 2008
Nagesh Kukunoor—March 2008
Piyush Mishra—March 2008
Shridhar Raghavan—March 2008
Harish Bhimani—February 2009
Shaktee Singh—February 2009

BIBLIOGRAPHY

Akhtar, Javed, *Talking Songs: Javed Akhtar in Conversation with Nasreen Munni Kabir*, New Delhi: Oxford University Press, 2005.

———, *Quiver*, (bilingual Hindi-English, translated by David Matthews), New Delhi: Harper Collins, 2001.

Alter, Stephen, *Fantasies of a Bollywood Love Thief*, Orlando: Harcourt Inc., 2007.

Asif, K., *The Immortal Dialogue Of K. Asif's Mughal-E-Azam*, translated by Nasreen Kabir and Suhail Akhtar, Delhi: Oxford University Press, 2007.

Aviv, Nurith, *Misafa Lesafa, D'une langue à l'autre*, Swan Productions, ZDF/Arte, 2004.

Azam, Mehtabul; Chin, Aimee; and Prakash, Nishith, 'English skills raise wages for some, not all, in India,' 26 May 2010. Available at: http://www.voxeu.org/index (retrieved January, 2011).

Banaji, Shakuntala, *Reading 'Bollywood': The Young Audience and Hindi Films*, New York: Palgrave, Macmillan, 2006.

Bolte Taylor, Jill, *My Stroke of Insight, A Brain Scientist's Personal Journey*, New York: Viking Press, 2006.

Cardullo, Bert (ed.), *Satyajit Ray Interviews*, Jackson: University of Mississippi Press, 2007.

Chefitz, Mitchell, *The Curse of Blessings*, Philadelphia: Running Press, 2006.

Chion, Michel, *Audio-Vision: Sound on Screen* (*L'Audio-Vision*, Editions Nathan, 1990), translated by Claudia Gorbman, New York: Columbia University Press, 1994.

———, *The Voice in Cinema* (*La Voix au Cinéma*, Editions de l'Etoile, 1982), translated by Claudia Gorbman, New York: Columbia University Press, 1999.

Chopra, Anupama, *King of Bollywood: Shah Rukh Khan and the Seductive World of Indian Cinema*, New York: Warner Books, 2007.

———, *Sholay: The Making of a Classic*, New Delhi: Penguin Books India, 2000.

Clingingsmith, David, 'Industrialization and Bilingualism in India' (working paper), July 2011. Available at: http://faculty.weatherhead.case.edu/clingingsmith/default.html.

Derrida, Jacques, *Le Monolinguisme de l'Autre*, Galilée, Paris, 1996.

Dreifus, Claudia, 'The Bilingual Advantage', *The New York Times*, 30 May 2011.

Easwaran, Kenny, 'The Politics of Name Changes in India,' June 2001. Available at: http://www.ocf.berkeley.edu/~easwaran/papers/india.html (retrieved 3 February 2010).

Everaert, Christine, *Tracing the Boundaries between Hindi and Urdu: Lost and Added in Translation between 20th Century Short Stories*, Leiden/Boston: Brill, 2010.

Fey, Tina, *Bossypants*, New York: Little Brown and Company, 2011.

Finch, Shannon, 'Repetition as Linguistic and Social Strategy in Hindi-English Bilingual Discourse', Ph.D. dissertation, The University of Texas, 2009.

Frayn, Michael, *The Human Touch: Our Part in the Creation of a Universe*, London: Faber and Faber, 2007.

Ginsburgh, Victor and Weber, Shlomo, *How Many Languages Do We Need? The Economics of Linguistic Diversity*, Princeton: Princeton University Press, 2011.

Giridharadas, Anand, *India Calling*, New York: Times Books, Henry Holt and Company, 2011.

Graeber, David, *Debt: The First 5,000 Years*, Brooklyn, NY: Melville House, 2011.

Gupta, Trisha, 'Death by Dialogue,' *Caravan Magazine*, 1 May 2011.

Jain, Giyan Cand, *Ek Bhaashaa, do likaavaT, do adab*, Delhi: Ejūkeshnal Pablishing Hāūs, 2005.

Haham, Connie, *Enchantment of the Mind: Manmohan Desai's Films*, New Delhi: Roli Books, 2006.

Hohenthal, Annika, 'English In India: Loyalty and Attitudes,' *Language In India*, Volume 3, 5 May 2003. Available at: http://www.languageinindia.com/may2003/annika.html

'Ismat Chughtai: A talk with one of Urdu's most outspoken woman writers,' *Mahfil* 8, 2-3 (Summer-Fall 1972), pp. 169–188. Available at: http://www.columbia.edu/itc/mealac/pritchett/00urdu/ismat/txt_ismat_interview_mahfil1972.html (retrieved August 2010)

Kabir, Nasreen Munni, *Talking Films: Conversations on Hindi Cinema with Javed Akhtar*, New Delhi: Oxford University Press, 1999.

———, *Lata Mangeshkar. . .in her own voice*, New Delhi: Niyogi Books, 2009.

Kesavan, Mukul, *The Ugliness of the Indian Male*, New Delhi: Black Kite Press, 2008.

Kachru, Braj B., *The Alchemy of English: The Spread, Functions and Models of Non-native Englishes*, Illini Books ed. / Urbana / 1990.

Kaifi, Shaukat, *Yaad ki Rahguzar*, New Delhi: Rajkamal Prakashan, 2007.

Kaku, Michio, *Hyperspace*, Oxford: Oxford University Press, 1995.

Kellman, Stephen G., *The Translingual Imagination*, Lincoln: University of Nebraska Press, 2000.

King, Christopher R., *One Language, Two Scripts*, Bombay: Oxford University Press, 1994.

King, Robert D., 'The Poisonous Potency of Script: Hindi and Urdu,' *International Journal of the Sociology of Language*, CL, 2001, pp. 43-60.

——, *Nehru and the Language Politics of India*, Oxford: Oxford University Press, 1997.

Kipen, David, *The Schreiber Theory: A Radical Rewrite of American Film History*, New Jersey: Melville House Publishing, 2006.

Krashen, Stephen D., *The Case for Narrow Listening System*, Vol. 24,1, 1996, pp. 97-100.

Lelyveld, David, '*Zuban-e Urdu-e Mu 'alla* and the Idol of Linguistic Origins,' *Annual of Urdu Studies*, Issue 9, Madison: University of Wisconsin, 1994.

'Mapping Cultural Diffusion: The Case of 'Korean Wave' in North East India,' 10 April 2008. Available at: http://mappingculturaldiffusion.blogspot.com/ (retrieved October 2011).

McGinn, Colin, *The Power of Movies: How Screen and Mind Intersect*, New York: Vintage Books, 2005.

Mehta, Shweta, 'I'm not Rajnikanth,' New Delhi: *Hindustan Times*, 26 October 2010.

Micciollo, Henri, *Satyajit Ray*, Lausanne: Éditions l'Age de l'Homme, 1981.

Mir, Raza, 'Hindi Songs? You Mean Urdu Songs.' Available at: http://www.viewsunplugged.com/ VU/20021226/arts_music_urduSongs2.shtml (retrieved 13 February 2005).

Mir, Ali Husain and Mir, Raza, *Anthems of Resistance: A Celebration of Progressive Urdu Poetry*, New Delhi: Roli Books—India Ink, 2006.

Pavlenko, Aneta, ed., *Bilingual Minds: Emotional Experience, Expression, and Representation*, Clevedon: Multilingual Matters, 2006.

Pérez Firmat, Gustavo, *Bilingual Blues*, Tempe, Arizona: Bilingual Press/ Editorial Bilingüe, 1995.

Pinker, Steven, *The Language Instinct: How the Mind Creates Language*, New York: W. Morrow, 1994.

——, *How the Mind Works*, New York: W. W. Norton, 1999.

——, *The Stuff of Thought*, New York: Viking Press, 2007.

Pisharoty, Sangeeta Barooah, 'Same to Same,' *The Hindu*, 6 April 2011.
Platts, John T., *A Dictionary of Urdu, Classical Hindi and English*, Oxford: Oxford University Press, 1974.
'Que hablen los perros — El doblaje de series animadas crece al amparo de los nuevos canales,' *El País*, 10 April 2011.
Ramanathan, Vaidehi, *The English-Vernacular Divide: Postcolonial Language Politics and Practice*, Bristol: Multilingual Matters, 2005.
Rane, Ashok (concept and edited by), *Views and Thoughts on Scriptwriting*, Indian Film Academy, 2005.
Rich, Katherine Russell, *Dreaming in Hindi: Coming Awake in Another Language*, New York: Houghton, Mifflin Harcourt, 2009.
Rosenberg, Grant, 'Rethinking the Art of Subtitles,' *TIME Europe*, 15 May 2007.
Rushdie, Salman, *The Moor's Last Sigh*, London: Jonathan Cape, 1995.
Santiago, Bill, *Pardon My Spanglish: ¡Porqué Because?* Philadelphia: Quirk Books, 2008.
Schmidt, Ruth Laila, *Urdu, An Essential Grammar*, London: Routledge, 2004.
Sedaris, David, *Me Speak Pretty One Day*, New York: Little, Brown and Company, 2000.
Sen, Amartya, *The Argumentative Indian*, New Delhi: Penguin Books, 2005.
Singh, Santosh, 'Bihar teachers learn to speak English,' *Indian Express*, 20 November 2011.
Szarkowska, Agnieszka, 'The Power of Film Translation,' published online by proz.com, document 345, 10 June 2005.
Tannen, Deborah, 'Metaphors: We Are What We Speak,' *The Argument Culture: Stopping America's War of Words*, New York: Ballantine, 1998.
Tandon, Prakash, *The Punjabi Century 1857-1947*, Berkeley:

University of California Press, 1968.

Trivedi, Harish, 'All Kinds of Hindi: The Evolving Language of Hindi Cinema,' *Fingerprinting Popular Culture: The Mythic and the Iconic in Indian Cinema*, edited by Vinay Lal and Ashis Nandy, New Delhi: Oxford University Press, 2006.

Tully, Mark, *No Full Stops in India*, London: Viking, 1991.

———, 'English: an advantage to India?' an edited version of the Oxford University Press/BBC Lecture given at the English-Speaking Union, London, and broadcast on the BBC World Service in February 1996, pp. 5, 7.

Tyrewala, Altaf, *No God in Sight*, San Francisco: MacAdam/Cage, 2006.

Unnithan, Chitra, 'Hinglish: The language of urban India?' *Business Standard*, 9 September 2008.

Walters, Keith, 'Is Using Minority Languages In The Workplace A Civil Right? A Human Right? Neither?' Draft paper, 24 September 2003.

Walters, Keith and Brody, Michael, ed., *What's Language Got to Do With It?* New York: W.W. Norton & Company, 2005.

Wolff, Philippe, 'Le tu révolutionnaire,' *Annales historiques de la Révolution française*, Vol. 279, 1990, pp. 89–94.

Wright, Lawrence, *In The New World: Growing Up with America 1960-1984*, New York: Alfred A. Knopf, 1988.

ACKNOWLEDGEMENTS

I am grateful to Dipa Chaudhury for her excellent work in editing my first book and her early encouragement that I pursue this present study, to Nasreen Munni Kabir for facilitating my stays in Bombay and opening many doors for me, to Anupama Chopra, Jaideep Sahni and Shabana Azmi, and Raj of Cine Dreams for putting me in touch with several interviewees.

Many thanks to all who were good enough to grant me time for interviews: Javed Siddiqi, Shama Zaidi, Jaideep Sahni, Ketan Desai, Anupama Chopra, Paromita Vohra, Shabana Azmi, Farhan Akhtar, Javed Akhtar, Rohan Sippy, Kader Khan, Tom Alter, Aziz Mirza, Prayag Raaj, Shashanka Ghosh, Shimit Amin, Shridhar Raghavan, Shaktee Singh, Piyush Mishra, Nagesh Kukunoor, Elahé Hiptoola, Madhur Bhandarkar, Harish Bhimani, Suromita Roy, Mujtaba Hussain, Jahnavi Phalkey, Nasreen Munni Kabir, Rajat Arora, Prakash Bharadwaj and Hindi novelist K. Vaid. Thanks, too, to Hemant Jeswani for his additional insights. And to Sudarshan Rattan for his help in procuring permission for an illustration.

I want to thank Sonali Brahmbhatt, Saumya Verma and Sarayu Adeni for providing me with their personal insights into the linguistic matrix of film-family-study among young Indian-Americans. My thanks go to Ramu Kharel for sharing some of his work and language experiences with me.

Many thanks as well to those who helped me in my language studies: Dr Akbar Hyder, Shanaz Hassan and especially Shilpa Parnami, who got me talking. Also, to those who helped in verifying or correcting certain Hindi-Urdu lines: Shilpa Parnami,

Kusum Choudhary, Zaheer Iqbal, Peter Knapczyk and Yahya Khan.

I very much appreciate Simon P. Holzman's wonderful work as an illustrator and his curiosity about the characters and contexts in each of the scenes he sketched. Thanks, too, to Lila Haham for her rendering of the 'Bandra-Andheri' map.

A special thanks to Alipta Shah and her mother Padma Shah, whose thoughtfulness and gracious generosity enormously facilitated my visits to Bombay.

I am grateful to Dr Elaine Horwitz who made it possible for me to continue studying at The University of Texas at Austin after completing my master's in foreign language education; to Dr Keith Walters, whose excellence as a teacher and whose research into sociolinguistics sparked my curiosity; and to Dr Robert D. King for his encouragement and insights into historical linguistics. And a special thanks to the university's wonderful Help Desk techies.

I would like to thank my friend Elisabeth Mattatia, who wisely reminded me of suggestions I first gave her and then promptly forgot, about staying on track in writing; Helene Meyers for her friendship and perspicacious questions about my writing; Mayanne Wright, Shilpa Parnami and Patricia Jobe for writing suggestions; Laura Stahnke, Lea Isgur, Kathleen Schmitz, Roger Chenu, Jogendro Kshetrimayum, Johnana Clark, Char Dison, Liz Murphy and Paul Converse for their interest, thoughtful encouragement and for helpful bits of information; Jahnavi Phalkey who gave me valuable insights into growing up in India and who made me feel in a few hours that we had known each other forever; Jonathan Bibliowicz and Samia Belabbes for stimulating conversations about living multiculturally; Rebeca Romero, for lightening the load of daily life in Paris; my students of English and in particular Maëlys Etamé, who have regularly taught me ever more about the value and the process of learning; my children Lila and Lemuel and granddaughters Somaya and

Kalina, who have reminded me again and again of the breadth and range of perceptions of life and approaches to it; my husband Jean whose dedication to the violin has offered continual proof that persistent effort pays off; and all those who I am surely forgetting but whose help directly or indirectly made this book possible.

Finally, I must express my appreciation to the many rickshaw-wallas of greater Mumbai who made getting around the suburbs possible and who, like so many in the bustling, mushrooming metropolis, amazed me with their ability to work patiently for long, long hours.

www.ingramcontent.com/pod-product-compliance
Lightning Source LLC
Chambersburg PA
CBHW071956220426
43662CB00009B/1146